D1223321

the new

Collie

collie club of america
fourth edition

HOWELL
BOOK
HOUSE

Howell Book House
A Simon & Schuster Macmillan Company
1633 Broadway
New York, NY 10019

MACMILLAN is a registered trademark of Macmillan, Inc.

Library of Congress Cataloging-in-Publication Data

The New Collie/Collie Club of America.— 4th ed.
    p. cm.
ISBN 0-87605-127-1
1. Collie   2. Smooth collie   I. Collie Club of America.
SF429.C6N48   1996   96–6819
636.7'37—dc20   CIP

Manufactured in the United States of America
10 9 8 7 6 5 4 3 2 1

Blueprint
of the Collie

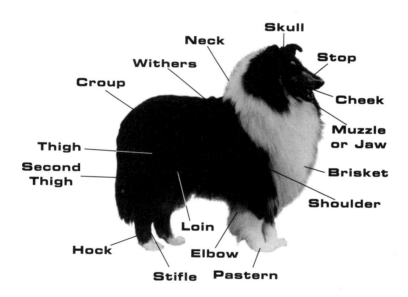

Skull

Neck

Stop

Withers

Croup

Cheek

Thigh

Muzzle
or Jaw

Second
Thigh

Brisket

Shoulder

Loin

Hock

Elbow

Stifle Pastern

Contents

Ch. Starr's Blue Jeans (1979), by Ch. Karavel Sudden Wyndfall ex Hi Vu Silver Mystery, owned by Louis and Pamela Durazzano, was the first bitch to win the Collie Club of America Specialty in twenty-two years and the first blue merle bitch to ever win the event. *Krook*

Introduction

On behalf of the Collie Club of America, I want to thank Howell Book House for the opportunity to update *The New Collie* with additional information on the most recent years of our history, as well as some added historical material from the archives of CCA. The editor is grateful to John Buddie and Gayle Kaye for their participation in this project, and to all those who contributed new articles as well as material which was written for the 1962 edition of *The Complete Collie* and the 1983 revision entitled *The New Collie*. We also thank the owners who loaned precious photographs of their winners, obedient Collies, herders and beloved companions.

We have tried to be consistent in style, listing all dogs with the name by which they were known in this country, and in the case of titles, "Ch." alone means a title granted by the country of origin; other titles include the country where these honors were awarded.

We appreciate being granted use of material which has appeared in part or in whole in the *CCA Bulletin* and *CCA Year Book* or *Collie Expressions*. Special thanks go to all the authors who wrote material for the first edition that is included here in whole or in part. Claudia Schroder Allen, Sue Barlow, the late Mr. and Mrs. Benjamin F. Butler, Jo Campbell, Theresa Hamilton, Inga Holm, Doris Werdermann and particularly Karen Phelps Pacenza, who edited the 1983 edition. We hope that you will enjoy the material we have gathered for you here, and find it useful.

This book is dedicated to the memory of Barbara and Win Kellogg, who will be missed by all who knew them. The Debhill hospitality was renowned, and they were never too busy to advise, comfort and just talk, about Collies or the state of the world. Barbara as a breeder led the way to face Collie health problems and do something about them, and she was the mentor supreme for generations of new fanciers. As chairperson of the CCA Education Committee, she worked tirelessly to prepare and disseminate informational material for novice and breeder. She left a legacy of dedication that we can all aspire to deserve.

—*Sara B. Futh, Editor*

THE CUR DOG
By Bewick

THE SHEPHERD'S DOG
By Bewick

THE SHEPHERD'S DOG (Curr)
By Howitt

THE BANDOG
By Bewick

Illustrations from James Watson's *The Dog Book* (1905).

Old Cockie (1868) and Eng. Ch. Charlemagne (1879).

Chapter 1

History of the Collie

Guarding, herding and driving livestock is one of man's oldest occupations. From the time primitive man abandoned the life of the nomadic hunter for that of a settled farmer, dogs played an important role in his ability to control large numbers of animals essential to his livelihood and continued sustenance.

In every culture and country where livestock raising developed as an essential activity, dogs came into being with special adaptations to suit local conditions, climate and customs. Today such widely varying breeds as the Briard from France, the Puli from Hungary, both Welsh Corgis and our own Collie from Scotland all share their integrity as breeds through the stockman's requirement for a dependable dog to help in working with flocks and herds under the local conditions in which they must work.

The exact heredity of the Collie is lost in the mists of time and clouded by centuries of debate and conjecture. There can be little doubt, however, that the breed was molded by the dictates of a harsh livelihood in an unyielding environment. In the Scotland that gave the Collie birth, a pretty dog was not enough. The Collie needed to be courageous, resourceful and in every way a contributing member of a working partnership. The farmer could not afford to keep anything else. This chapter explores the Collie's early history as a stock dog and the steps taken on the road which led to the universal esteem in which he is now held as show dog, working dog and companion to young and old, great and small, the world over.

The Collie is believed to have evolved in the hilly border counties of Scotland and northern England, where a hardy, quick-witted dog was needed to handle sheep. Some enthusiasts claim that the Collie's ancestors were brought to the British Isles by Roman conquerors in the middle of the first century A.D. But Britain's earliest invaders, the Stone Age nomads who settled in what is now southern England, brought dogs with them, too.

Excavations at Neolithic sites in Wiltshire, ca. 3000 B.C., uncovered the remarkably well-preserved skeleton of a large, rangy dog combining the slightly tucked-up abdomen, deep chest and long, thin tail typical of the Greyhound family with the shorter muzzle and full stop suggestive of the Mastiff. The people of the Windmill Hill settlement, where this dog's remains were found, kept many cattle, sheep, goats and pigs. Naturalists speculate that this dog may have been kept primarily for herding duties, although he was undoubtedly used also for hunting.

Herding and hunting dogs figured prominently in the pre-Roman British economy. Among exports to the continent early in the first century A.D., were "cattle, iron, hides, slaves and dogs." These British dogs, acclaimed for great courage and high intelligence, despite an unprepossessing appearance, were probably ancestral terriers. English dogs were still highly prized in Italy in the eleventh century. Growth of the wool industry in the Middle Ages was abetted by bandogs and curs, fifteenth and sixteenth century English guard and herding dogs, respectively.

Not until the agricultural revolution of the mid-eighteenth century did scientific breeding of domestic animals begin. The enclosure movement did away with the old feudal system of planting and pasture rights on strips of open field. Common land was replaced by individually walled or fenced fields and pastures in which the tenant could do as he liked. The only way to improve farm stock, including dogs, was to prevent animals from wandering together as they had always done, ensuring "the haphazard union of nobody's son with everybody's daughter."

ORIGIN OF THE COLLIE

The Collie's origin has been a subject of misinformation for many years. The unfortunate truth is that little is known about the beginnings of the breed. That little information has been embellished by ignorance, error, and fancy, so that most of us think we really do know from whence the Collie came. We do know something, of course; the rub is that what we know is largely inaccurate. In this chapter we shall set forth only those facts which seem established and conjectures supported by the weight of evidence.

The name, "Collie," is as uncertain of origin as the breed it denotes. Etymologists are not sure whether the word is of Gaelic or English derivation. We do know that it was at one time pronounced "coally." It was only so spelled, however, by writers from the South of England and the Midlands, in an attempt to render Northern pronunciation—a device familiar to readers of American dialect stories.

The modern Collie is actually a breed of diverse ancestry. Assorted Scottish and Northern English stock dogs went into its making, as well as certain hunting breeds. We have no idea of all the elements that went into the crucible, but we can isolate a few.

The principal or at least most famous ingredient was the sheepdog common to the eastern Lowlands of Scotland and that fertile enclave of the Highlands known as "golden Moray." This sheepdog was generally black-and-white, smallish (weighing twenty-five to thirty pounds), relatively short-legged and long-bodied. In most cases, forelegs were bowed and rear legs cow hocked, since the shepherd-breeders regarded these as desirable working characteristics. Shepherds also tended to keep these "runts" and destroy most other pups, believing that runts were more intelligent.

This breed was marked by a broad, domed skull; slight, pinched muzzle; pronounced stop; overshot bite; round, yellowish eyes; and low, hanging ears. Its handsomest feature was a very dense double coat, the outer coat being remarkably harsh to the touch. Ordinarily, the coat was not especially long, although some kept as pets by the landlords, as opposed to those actually working, possessed frills of almost excessive length. Some selection based entirely on appearance may have been applied to these gifts from shepherd to master. This is of some importance, since it was the laird's or yeoman's pets, rather than the actual workers, who were purchased by the first "professional" breeders.

The sheepdogs of the Scottish border counties, particularly Dumfries, Roxburgh and Selkirk, also contributed a good share of their inheritance to the modern Collie. These types were largely taller, and proportionately shorter in body, than the Dundee and Moray dogs. They also tended to be slightly stronger in muzzle, less domed in skull and shorter coated than their northern cousins, but were otherwise similar. The border dogs were also peculiarly unsound by modern standards. Here, too, black-and-white was the common color, but all-blacks, black-and-whites with tan markings and even "reds" occurred. In this area, poaching farmers, compelled by poverty to make one dog perform the work of two, first tried Irish Setter and Labrador Retriever crosses—the only alien admixtures for which we have positive evidence.

The Irish Setter cross (which is also the reputed source of the Gordon Setter) was of great importance to the Collie. It changed the dominant color of the breed, even though it took some time before the modified shade we call sable became roughly standardized. In the early nineteenth century, James Hogg, the "Ettrick shepherd" of literary fame, was writing of "red" Collies, and as late as 1910, the framers of the English Standard decided to retain a clause asserting undesirability of "red Setter color." The auburn shade characterized a great stud of even more recent date.

Students of genetics tell us that only by such a cross as that with the Irish Setter, could the Collie color pattern have been so abruptly changed; the dominant color of one breed in such a cross establishing ascendancy over the other's dominant color. Our modern sable color also suggests that this dominance is incomplete.

This Setter cross helped to make the Collie taller, heavier and straighter in leg. It also filled the Collie's muzzle, blunting it at the end, but making it frequently flat-sided, and introducing a tendency to lippiness. All writers of the early nineteenth century remark on these characteristics in the "red" Collies. We know that Old Cockie, credited with establishing dominance of sable in the modern breed, was stronger in muzzle and more acceptable in skull than his Scottish-born contemporaries—Trefoil and Tricolour, for example—but was inferior to them in coat, his outer coat being softer and undercoat less dense.

The English writer Idstone has cited authenticated cases of the Labrador admixture, but whether or not this cross entered the mainstream of modern show Collies, we cannot be sure. The physical effects, in any event, would have been similar to those produced by the Setter cross.

One of the most significant contributions to our modern breed was made by the so-called "bandog." This was a smooth-coated dog of obscure origin, fairly tall and rangy, reasonably straight and firm in quarters, and bearing a striking resemblance to contemporary Collies in head properties. It would be safe to say that, apart from the coat in Roughs, current Collies resemble the bandog more than any other ancestors. Scottish stockmen going to the great Birmingham market "discovered" these dogs and used them liberally as a cross on their own sheepdogs. Resulting litters contained coats of all lengths, and short-coated ones were bred back to the bandogs to create the Smooth Collie. Reinfusion of Smooth bloodlines in the 1880s is probably responsible for the move to the modern type.

The bandog introduced one unfortunate characteristic: Some specimens were bob-tailed and are the probable source of a fault that has appeared off and on ever since, though rare today.

HISTORY OF THE SHOW COLLIE

The fancying of Collies began in the English midlands city of Birmingham in the 1860s. Birmingham was then the greatest livestock center in Great Britain and the world. Stockmen from all over the British Isles made the trek to market and brought their dogs with them. Some of these dogs caught the public eye, and for the first time serious breeders took hold of them. They had various elements to work with: sheepdogs from eastern Scotland, often crossbred herders of the border country, smooth-coated drover's dogs from Cumberland and Northumberland, and bandogs, already loosely called "Smooth Collies." The eastern Scottish dog, first to be called a "Collie," had taken the fancy of Queen Victoria, and became the dominant factor in breeding, finally giving its name to the combined product.

"Collies" were first exhibited at Birmingham in 1860, a motley crew collected under the catchall title of "Scotch Sheep-dogs." Whether or not the winners at that show played any part in the development of the breed, we do not know. We do know that the Collie Fancy developed rapidly during the next thirty-odd years.

According to James Watson, breeder, judge and a founder of the Collie Club of America, the Rough Collie was virtually unknown in London as late as 1860; the bob-tailed smooth sheepdog was more common to that area. The Rough Collie came down from Scotland and the border counties to farmers' markets at Birmingham, following development of the railroad.

The railroad changed travel habits of the English and made dog shows possible. Birmingham was the third formal dog show at which conformation of individual animals was judged, and the first all-breed show ever held (two earlier events were limited to Sporting breeds). That event had 267 entries, representing twenty-five breeds.

None of the sheepdogs could boast of any great popularity during this first decade of exhibition. The few Collies shown were generally working dogs without pedigree, picked up from farmers and dealers at local cattle markets. They were small, weighing from twenty-five to forty-five pounds. (The lighter dogs were said to be in "working condition.") They were relatively short-legged and long-backed; necks were short and thrust forward; feet and legs tended to be unsightly. Many were cow hocked, fiddle-fronted and over-angulated, faults found in working sheepdogs to this day. Tailless Collies were not uncommon and tailless, half-tailed and full-tailed dogs sometimes occurred in the same litter. Heads were proportionately heavier; skull circumference and length of head were similar to that of today's dogs, but muzzles were shorter and narrower. Eyes were lighter, too dark an eye being considered foreign and terrier-like in appearance. Coat length ranged from near-smooth to the extremely long mane and frill noted in one black-and-white Scottish strain. In color these dogs were usually black-and-white or black-and-tan, but sometimes gray, dull brown and mixed brindle sables were also seen.

The Collie's popularity began with Queen Victoria (1837–1901), who fell in love with the breed on visits to her Scottish retreat, Balmoral. When it became known that Collies were in the Queen's kennels, the lowly working dog was suddenly elevated to canine aristocracy. It became fashionable to own a Collie and show entries rose. Of more importance for the breed's future, canny men took the Collie in hand and concentrated on improving conformation.

With a few notable exceptions, the most enthusiastic fanciers were concentrated in the Birmingham district. The Birmingham show, which had been the first to offer classes for sheepdogs, was to play an even more important part in Collie history. There in 1870 a dog named Old Cockie was placed second in a class of fourteen.

Old Cockie (1868)

Early historians were extravagant in their praise of Old Cockie and made exaggerated claims for him. In his time the most common colors were black, tan-and-white, black-and-white and blue merle. All show Collies trace to Old Cockie through his sable-and-white grandson, Charlemagne, whose known pedigree shows only two sables: Maude, his dam, and her sire, Cockie.

Aside from establishing the sable color, Cockie's impact on the breed has been equaled by few dogs. He was two years old when first shown by Mr. W. White of Sherwood Rise, who refused to make his origin known; the mystery has never been solved. Cockie's head was balanced and smooth, with correct finish of foreface ahead of his time. His ears were tipped naturally, although not so high as today's Standard dictates. His expression was thought to be of surpassing sweetness; he had a harsh, dense outer coat, profuse undercoat, heavy mane and frill.

Not surprisingly, Cockie was highly successful in the showring, where he won more than forty prizes. He was sold at six years, and had two other owners within the next two years before being sold to James Bissell, another of the ardent Birmingham fanciers. Cockie's show career was long over, but Bissell looked to the whelping box for the next big winner at his Great Barr Kennels. He obtained Meg, tricolor daughter of Old Mec, as the mate for Old Cockie. Meg had inherited her sire's good outline and coat, but not his head properties. Bred to Old Cockie in 1875, Meg produced Maude, a short-legged sable with the harsh double coat of her sire, nice expression, and a head said to be rather short but of desired type.

Cockie lived to be fourteen years old, cherished and pampered as befits age and royalty, an honor to the memory of James Bissell.

Old Mec (1870)

Old Mec was born in the year of Cockie's ring debut, bred by Peter Gerrard. Mec's pedigree is also obscure. Although he defeated Cockie twice, the consensus was that Cockie was the better dog. Both shared important virtues, being well built, shapely and sound. Writers were especially impressed by their legs and feet, at a time when much improvement was needed there. Both carried good coats, but Mec's inclined to waviness.

Mec was black-and-tan with white chest and thin blaze. His head was long and nicely molded, but did not have the virtues of Cockie. Mec's expression did not please contemporaries, due to his ears being a bit slack in carriage, and his eyes were considered too dark and foreign.

Twig

While the Fancy was being started in Birmingham, S. E. Shirley, M.P., was busy as chairman of the new Kennel Club he founded in 1872; the first organization to exercise national control over the sport of exhibiting dogs. On his estate in northern Ireland, Mr. Shirley kept Collies and other livestock. In 1873 he brought out a handsomely marked tricolor called Shamrock. Shirley liked Shamrock enough to breed his dam, Bess, to her own great grandson, a dog named Twig, by Old Twig. We wish there was more information about Old Twig and his son; they are at the top of the sire line of every show Collie now living.

Trefoil (1873)

Bess whelped her litter by Twig, including Trefoil, just five years after Old Cockie. He was far more successful at shows than Shamrock. Trefoil was a "shapely, gay, attractive looking dog with a long coat," black-and-tan with white on breast and frill. His coat was not dense, but he was known to sire dogs with frills that nearly touched the ground. Today we would probably call him flashy. We are told that Trefoil had a good eye and used his ears well. Although he was slightly cow hocked, Hugh Dalziel described him as "the champion of his time in good looks and genuine Collie qualities."

Encouraged by Trefoil's brilliant show career, Shirley repeated the breeding in 1875. The litter contained two males: Tricolour, who was tan-and-white, and Tartan, who was black-and-tan. If Trefoil got faint praise from critics, his brothers got none at all.

Nevertheless, James Bissell sent Maude, daughter of Old Cockie, to Tartan. From this mating he got two prize-winning bitches: the tricolor, Watch, which went to M. C. Ashwin's kennel, and the sable and white, Lorna, kept by Bissell. Bred back to her grandsire, Old Cockie, Lorna produced Wolf, which had a respectable show career and sired the greatly acclaimed Rutland.

The canny Bissell was sufficiently impressed with Trefoil, and with Maude's litter by his brother, to send Maude to him also. In 1879 six puppies were whelped. "Remarkable," says Wheeler, "for their dissimilitude one to the other." This litter, however, produced several dogs that would make important contributions to the breed's history.

Trevor, a sable and white, was, unfortunately, very gay of tail, so much so that his handler carried a stick into the ring for the purpose of correcting this fault. He was to sire Ch. Flurry and The Lily, the first white Collie to appear in foundation pedigrees. Two bitches in this litter were also notable: the red sable, Effie, which easily won her championship when exported to the United States, and Flirt, dam of Ch. Eclipse. The most outstanding puppy in the litter was Charlemagne, which was to create a stir in the Fancy as no Collie had done since Old Cockie.

Eng. Ch. Charlemagne (1879)

Old Cockie was eleven when his famous grandson arrived. Charlemagne's show career began inauspiciously enough. As a puppy at the Birmingham show he won a VHC (Very Highly Commended, an award given for entries of merit which did not place in the class) while first prize went to Old Cockie's son, Wolf. It was five years before any Collie was to place over Charlemagne at

Birmingham again, and this honor went to Wolf's son, Ch. Rutland. From 1880 until 1885, however, Charlemagne was unbeatable.

To Charlemagne goes the credit for establishing the dominance of the Trefoil sire line. He is the first Collie described as possessing grandeur. A brightly colored sable with showy white markings, his coat was profuse and close-fitting, with good texture. His beautiful color is remarked upon in every account; he must have presented quite a contrast to the blacks, black and tans, and smutty sables being shown. It is probably to Charlemagne, rather than Old Cockie, that we owe the preeminence of the sable color.

Charlemagne was said to have good bone and an excellent front, but he was cow hocked, which worsened with age. Rawdon Lee grudgingly acknowledges that he was handsomer than Cockie, but describes him as "more the drawing-room dog," with an expression docile and intelligent but "a little lacking fire." Charlemagne's ears broke very high and were criticized for being too erect. When he was eleven years old, Charlemagne came out of retirement to compete at the Collie Club show in 1890. He went from the Veterans class to Best in Show, a proper finale for a popular old champion.

Ruby III

While fortune was kind to James Bissell, another Birmingham enthusiast, Rev. Hans F. Hamilton, was acquiring the nucleus of his Woodmansterne Kennels. In 1878 he purchased two males, Captain and Tricolour II, and two bitches, Eva and Ruby III, daughters of Tricolour II. Eva and Ruby became to the female line what Trefoil and Cockie were to the male line, producing bitches which consistently begot top quality sires.

Ruby III was sent to Ch. Marcus, a black-and-white dog of unknown ancestry, his only claim to fame being the litter which resulted. Whelped in the same year as Charlemagne, this litter was amazingly consistent in type, containing three show winners: Donald, Zulu Princess and Madge. Zulu Princess was exported to the United States where she joined Charlemagne's sister, Effie, at Hempstead Farm and won her American championship. She was black-and-white, said to be pricked-eared except when in the ring.

Madge (1879)

Madge was a lovely bitch which had no trouble gaining her English championship. Correct in head, expression and ears, she was matchless in full coat. She is credited with introducing higher, more attractive ear carriage.

Three of Madge's offspring by different sires made significant contributions to Collie history. Peggie II, sired by Ruthven, traces to Twig three times and to Old Cockie once, and represented an advance in type, excelling in head, expression, character and coat. Bred to Ch. Metchley Wonder, she was to become the dam of Ch. Christopher.

Eng. Ch. Christopher (1887) represented a major advance in type, especially in head. His two sons, pictured below, were to stand at the head of their own sire lines.

Eng. Ch. Stracathro Ralph (pronounced Rafe) (1888) stands at the head of the sire line that produced Eng. Ch. Magnet twelve generations later.

Edgbaston Marvel (1888) is the head of a line that produced Eng. Ch. Laund Limit eight generations later. Limit was a key sire in creating the foundation American families.

The second of Madge's famous children was Ch. Rutland, a black-and-tan dog sired by Cockie's son, Wolf. The third was Sefton (1884), sired by Ch. Charlemagne. The bitches in the litter containing Sefton inherited their dam's superior head qualities. Sefton, unfortunately, did not, and the entire litter was afflicted with rickets, which marred their legs and feet. Sefton's place in Collie history is secure, however, because he sired Ch. Metchley Wonder.

The fame of Ruby III does not rest only on the Marcus litter. Bred to Cockie's son Wolf, Ruby III whelped Lady Clare, in turn the dam of Grove Daisy, by Ch. Eclipse. Grove Daisy, bred to Ch. Metchley Wonder, produced Apple Blossom, Grove Peggie and Bridesmaid. Apple Blossom was Heather Ralph's dam and Bridesmaid was the dam of Wishaw Rose, granddam of Ch. Wishaw Clinker. Any discussion of the dogs behind the modern Collie is certainly incomplete without mention of Ruby III and her extraordinary family.

Eng. Ch. Metchley Wonder (1886)

Metchley Wonder was sired by Sefton out of Minnie, owned by Charles Wheeler. She was described as a small, high-quality bitch, particularly nice in head and expression, but prick-eared and short on coat. Wonder was a handsome, well-marked sable-and-white dog, exceptionally good in body, legs and feet. Wheeler credits him with correcting the weak pasterns and cow hocks plaguing the breed. His coat and frill, like Charlemagne's, were beautiful; his head and ears were described as "typical." Although Rawdon Lee preferred a broader skull, he concurred that Wonder was the best show Collie so far produced.

The increasing size of Collies is evidenced in the description of Wonder as a medium-sized dog. He measured twenty-four inches at the shoulder and weighed fifty-six pounds, while large dogs of only a few years earlier averaged less than fifty pounds.

Eng. Ch. Christopher (1887)

A. H. Megson, who was already successful in several other breeds, began to exhibit Collies in 1882. His kennel soon housed the foremost dogs in the country. It was not long before Metchley Wonder joined them, for the price of £530. The prices Megson was willing to pay for famous champions astounded the Fancy and undoubtedly spurred breeding top quality Collies, for only the best could hope to command such sums.

Madge's daughter, Peggie II, was sent to her nephew, Wonder, when he was just eleven months old. The influential fruit of this union, Christopher was whelped on April 16, 1887. After his first show he was sold to Thomas H. Stretch of Ormskirk fame. His new owner campaigned Christopher to his title and started him on his illustrious stud career.

Christopher showed his ability as a sire quickly; in his second year he produced four prize winners from four dams. No one could have foreseen his final dominance of the sire line. Every show Collie in the world today traces directly to Trefoil through his great-great grandson, Christopher. He represented a major advance in type, especially in head. His longer, arched neck was a marked change, his expression was superb, his coat excellent and color beautiful.

At the Collie Club show in February, 1890, Christopher defeated his sire and attracted the attention of Mitchell Harrison of the Chestnut Hill Kennels in Philadelphia. He was exported to the United States, but unfortunately never won his American championship, although he was Winners Dog at the first Collie Club of America Specialty in 1894. He was in this country from the time he was three until his death at fourteen, but left no worthy descendants here. Watson attributes this failure to the dearth of good bitches in the early days of the American Fancy. Wealthy fanciers found it easier to buy big winners abroad and import them to show than to breed winners at home.

Christopher's sons that would carry on his influence remained in England: Eng. Ch. Stracathro Ralph and Edgbaston Marvel, whelped the same day, September 1, 1888, out of different dams.

Stracathro Ralph (1888)

Stracathro Ralph was sired by Christopher out of Stracathro Fancy, tracing back to Trefoil through her grandsire, Smuggler. Ralph was said to have a head similar to his sire's, but the only likeness we have is a painting showing a longer, leaner head, more refined in both muzzle and backskull. His son, Heather Ralph, provided the next link in the sire line by producing Ch. Ormskirk Emerald. Ralph was no mean prize winner in his own right, and hardly deserves the shadow into which his son's greater brilliance cast him.

Eng. Ch. Ormskirk Emerald (1894)

Aughton Bessie, the dam of Ormskirk Emerald, was owned by M. P. Barnes, brother-in-law to Hugh Ainscough. He followed Ainscough's advice in sending Bessie to Heather Ralph, and sold the entire litter with Ainscough's blessing to Mr. Stretch for £25.

Emerald was not a heavy-coated puppy and did no winning until he was thirteen months old. Charles Wheeler had tried to buy him at the 1895 Liverpool show, where he was shown in poor coat and did nothing. Mr. Stretch had learned his lesson with Marvel and replied emphatically, "Not for sale." The height of Emerald's career came at the 1896 Birmingham show where he easily defeated Portington Bar None, Wellesbourne Conqueror and Southport Perfection, the best of their era. Stretch had a different answer for Mr. Megson, and Emerald changed hands for the equivalent of £1,300.

Heralded as the epitome of Collie perfection, Emerald is said to have inherited the beautiful head of his dam with the unsurpassed body, legs, feet and coat of his sire. Wheeler describes his head as "exquisitely shaped—the merest trifle Roman toward the end of the nose" (no doubt what we would call drop-off today). He admired Emerald's eye placement, expression and ears. The photograph we have of Emerald is disappointing; balance and sound body are there, but eye and expression are hardly pleasant. We are not surprised to read in the reminiscences of Ada Bishop, daughter of W. W. Stansfield of Laund fame, that he was a difficult dog to handle.

Ormskirk Galopin (1896) and Am. Ch. Heacham Galopin (1897)

Galopin's dam, Ormskirk Memoir, was said to be the best bitch of her time, a granddaughter of Christopher. Galopin is described as a big, handsome, well-balanced dog with large but well-carried ears and a long head, marred by excessive depth through the cheeks. He was imported to the United States by J. Pierpont Morgan, the world-renowned financier and art collector, whose interest in Collies began in the late 1880s.

Galopin's son, Heacham Galopin, followed his sire to America, to the Ravenwood Kennels in Illinois. He did considerable winning, finishing his championship, although he never carried much coat and his eyes were somewhat light colored. Wisely, his good head, correct ears and sound body were valued above his faults.

Eng. & Am. Ch. Wishaw Clinker (1898)

Robert Tait of the Wishaw Kennels in Scotland was sufficiently impressed with the quality of Heacham Galopin to send a bitch to him. Last Rose was a granddaughter of Ormskirk Agreement, another winning son of Christopher, which was exported to Australia at the height of his career.

Clinker grew famous as a winner and sire before he was imported to America by J. P. Morgan in 1904, where he continued to win. Clinker's description as symmetrical, sound in limb and profuse in coat is borne out by his photographs. His eyes were well-placed, ears correctly carried and head well-shaped but too strong. The most striking thing to notice is his resemblance to Christopher. He appears higher on the leg, better in ear carriage and less refined in head, but could almost be the reincarnation of his ancestor, a telling argument for Christopher's indelible imprint on the breed. Clinker was the grandsire of Eng. & Am. Ch. Squire of Tytton (1904), generally considered to be the best and most potent sire in the Ralph line until the appearance of Magnet in 1912.

The Edgbaston Marvel Sire Line

Edgbaston Marvel (1888) was sired by Christopher out of Sweet Marie, a Smuggler daughter. His head showed the continuing improvement in balance between muzzle and backskull for which Christopher did so much. Marvel's show chances were ruined by low ears, inherited from Smuggler, along with his short neck. At his first show, Marvel showed signs of distemper, so rather than risk his entire kennel by taking the sick puppy back, Stretch sold him for a fraction of his value. Charles Wheeler was impressed with his quality and bought him from his new owner for £30, and after proving his siring ability with Champions Portington Bar None and Southport Pilot, resold him to Mr. Megson.

Ch. Southport Perfection (1892)

Bred by Hugh Ainscough, Perfection carried the banner for the Marvel line. He was well balanced and sound, with good ears and a well-shaped head. However, his eyes were not sufficiently oblique to please connoisseurs. His measurements reveal another gain for the breed: He was twenty-five inches at the shoulder and weighed sixty-eight pounds.

Ainscough sold Perfection for £450 at seven months to W. E. Mason of Southport Kennels, who later sold him to A. H. Megson for £1,000, when the dog was three years old. Perfection's sensational show career, during which he won the Collie Club's celebrated Challenge Trophy five times (the record of six wins was held by his great-grandsire Ch. Metchley Wonder), was somewhat eclipsed by the advent of Ormskirk Emerald.

Perfection failed as a sire of top-quality dogs, despite considerable opportunity. The son that continued his line was Wellesbourne Councillor (1894), which did not have much of a show career, but sired the beautiful Ch. Wellesbourne Conqueror (1895). Conqueror was bred by William H. Charles. The Charles brothers had been actively interested in Collies since the days of Old Cockie and had won publicity for the white Collie by presenting specimens to Queen Victoria and her son, the Prince of Wales. Conqueror's dam, Wellesbourne Beauty, was by Edgbaston Marvel, so he traced four times to Christopher in four generations. He is described as a well-built dog with a cleanly cut head, nice eye and neat ears.

When Conqueror was seven years old, he was imported to the United States by J. I. Behling of Bon Ami Collies in Milwaukee, Wisconsin. Mr. Behling was the leading importer of Collies in the Midwest, bringing over many of the Parbold, Wellesbourne and Barwell dogs for his kennels. Conqueror continued his winning in America, despite his age. Obviously he had something many of his antecedents had lacked: He held his quality and did not coarsen with age.

Ch. Parbold Piccolo (1899), the leading son of Conqueror, was bred by Hugh Ainscough. His dam, Parbold Pinafore, was by Balgreggie Hope, a tail-male descendant of Eng. Ch. Metchley Wonder.

Piccolo's success as a show dog and sire equaled that of Eng. & Am. Ch. Wishaw Clinker. Piccolo had good bone, body and coat, but his outline suffered from a short neck and tail. His ears were well-carried and always showing, according to Wheeler, who also noted that Piccolo's muzzle was too deep and needed refinement. In his photograph, Piccolo's head is heavy-looking, and he lacks the elegance which was emerging in dogs such as Ch. Wishaw Clinker. Piccolo was big, measuring twenty-seven inches at the shoulder and weighing about eighty-five pounds. Piccolo was imported by Mr. Behling for a reported $5,000, but shortly after his arrival the dog disappeared and was never seen again. Piccolo was undoubtedly a great loss to Mr. Behling, but his famous sons, Ch. Ormskirk Olympian and the beautiful but controversial Ch. Anfield Model, both came to America. Fanciers here continued to find it easier to import winners than to breed them.

Combining the two great sire lines descending from Christopher became the orthodox formula for producing champions at the turn of the century. With Stracathro Ralph in the tail-male position, this practice was ultimately to produce Magnet, to whom all American show Collies trace. There were, of course, many more Collies and people involved in the creation of the breed than can be discussed in one book. Ted Kattell of Borco fame once wrote that a complete pedigree of his Ch. Black Douglas of Alstead (1939), tracing twenty-six generations back to Trefoil, would include over sixty-seven million names. Then it would have taken an ace typist three years full time to produce such a pedigree; today with computers we could do it in minutes,

Shown here are (from left) H. Ainscough, C. H. Wheeler, W. E. Mason and H. E. Packwood, four pioneer fanciers who championed the Collie when the breed was making its first appearance on the English show bench.

but how long would it take to read it? It would be even more interesting to see how many individual dogs were in the pedigree, because the key individuals were used heavily. The dogs mentioned above would account for a high percentage of those millions.

CONTINUED DEVELOPMENT OF THE COLLIE

The breed was still in a stage of development—by the end of the first decade of this century the best Collies had reached a good level of quality in body, legs and feet by our standards, although they had lighter bone. Heads had not advanced as far as bodies toward what is generally considered the modern Collie.

The Edgbaston Marvel line descends four generations to Eng. Ch. Parbold Piccolo (1899). Within three years in England Piccolo had sired several sons who started sire lines of their own: Ch. Anfield Model, Ch. Ormskirk Olympian and Parbold Pierrot. What Piccolo's influence might have been had he not disappeared, no one can say.

Model's grandson, Ch. Parbold Picador (1910) was imported by Dr. Bennett. Picador was instrumental in this country as a sire, being behind both Magnet and Limit. The Magnet/Limit cross was the most influential and enduring and is responsible for our sire lines today. Picador sired Laund Limit as well as Magnet's dam.

In the Stracathro Ralph line the chief source was Eng. & Am. Ch. Squire of Tytton (1904), imported by Samuel Untermeyer. Squire's line descends through his son, Seedley Squire (1905), four generations to Magnet. Another Squire line went through another son, Grimsby Squire, to Ch. Southport Sample.

Ch. Southport Sample

Ch. Southport Sample sired eight American champions, an unheard-of feat at the time. Despite this achievement, Sample did not set off a sire line of enduring consequence, although his name is found in significant pedigrees. Laund Limit's dam, Laund Lily, was by his English son, Laund Leader. From Sample's sons and daughters earning their titles here, the only champion descendants continuing were through his son, Ch. Southport Sceptre.

Ch. Southport Sceptre

Through Sceptre and Limit, the Sample line found its place in American Collie pedigrees. Sceptre was in a litter which contained a second champion, a trait of great stud dogs. Again and again in the creation of the American Collie, producing ability has passed through dogs in litters where such a concentration of quality existed. Sceptre sired the famous Ch. Ardshiel Wendy and through his son, Alstead Adonis, is the grandsire of Ch. Alstead Aeroplane.

Ch. Parbold Picador (1910) was one of the breed's most influential sires in America during the early part of the twentieth century.

Eng. Ch. Magnet (1912), bred by John Morley and imported by Eileen Moretta, sired Ch. Poplar Perfection and Eng. Ch. Laund Legislator.

Eng. Ch. Laund Limit (1912) possessed tremendous siring ability in his own right and the versatility to "nick" with bitches from other producing families.

During this decade, R. H. Lord (Seedley), W. W. Stansfield (Laund), and Fred Robson (Eden) shared the limelight by the stunning success of their exports to America. They followed T. H. Stretch (Ormskirk) and Hugh Ainscough (Parbold). A broadside of exports to the United States was made by E. Mason of the Southport Kennels, which was to include Mr. Mason himself. The decade which began in 1910 set the stage for the 1920s when the flood tide of imports reached its crest, subsiding as the American Collie emerged. Without question the two most important events of the decade were the births of Limit and Magnet, both in 1912.

Ch. Laund Limit (1912)

Ch. Laund Limit was a sable-and-white dog bred by W. W. Stansfield in England. His son, Eng. & Am. Ch. Bellhaven Laund Logic (1917), imported by Mrs. F. B. Ilch early in the 1920s, sired Laund Lucas before coming to America. Through Laund Lucas the famed Lucason line derived at Bellhaven in the 1930s. Limit also sired Eng. Ch. Alstead Laund Luminous (1914), imported by Mrs. Lunt. He proved himself for her by producing Ch. Starbat Strongheart, first of the great American-bred sires, and a second litter containing two champions. Limit had enormous siring ability, successfully establishing his own sire line, but also nicking so well with the Magnet line that the American sire line dominant today is based on the Magnet-Limit cross.

Ch. Magnet was also sable-and-white. He came to the United States as an older dog, but left sons in England through which his line continued on our shores. To judge by pictures, Limit had style, balance and physical soundness with a beautifully arched neck. Magnet possessed a more desirable head and expression than Limit. Both dogs, however, were elegant and carried excellent coats.

MAGNET: SIRE SUPREME

by Gayle Kaye

The title "Sire Supreme" applies to only a few stud dogs in any breed. In Collies, Ch. Magnet truly deserved this accolade. Almost every Collie in America traces in tail-male to Ch. Magnet. He also played an important role in the distaff side of Collie bloodlines as a sire of great bitches. He is without a doubt the most influential Collie sire of all time, but also one of the least appreciated. Many dogs have sired more champions, but none made as great an impact. He came along at a time when certain attributes were desperately needed, attributes he possessed. He sired several dogs which collectively brought about the turning point in the development of the modern Collie.

Magnet was whelped in England on December 29, 1912, bred by John R. Morley, but owned and campaigned by Mr. T. Laidlaw. He was very different in type from most of his contemporaries. Most Collie heads of the period were "common," leaning toward a pie shape. Magnet was anything but common; his head was very refined but balanced. He was known for his sweet expression, readily apparent in his pictures. He had lasting head qualities, sorely needed when many dogs did not age gracefully. He was also noted for his sweet disposition, which he passed on to most of his puppies. Collie temperament at the time had become overly aggressive due to the popularity of certain sires. In spite of his many attributes, not everyone was a Magnet fan. Some felt that he was too refined to the point of lacking masculinity; others considered him to be tall, slab-sided or rangy, lacking in substance . . . not a very flattering description.

In spite of whatever flaws he had, Magnet won his championship easily, finishing on May 5, 1915. The judge that day, Mr. J. Landers, critiqued him as follows: "Ch. Magnet was shown in good bloom. His head retains its quality and balance, while his perfect-fitting coat and stylish contour of body help to make as near an ideal Collie as one can expect to come across." Mr. R. Tait of the famed Wishaw Collies made this prophetic statement after judging at Crufts that year: "Ch. Magnet is a Collie all over and is hard to fault. His head is ideal in length, shape, eye and expression, but his ears are not quite what is wanted. In size and shape he is near perfection and should leave his mark on the breed."

Magnet was not imported to this country until he was seven years old, when he had already done his best siring. American breeders were still importing dogs regularly from England, believing that we could not yet produce quality dogs of our own. Mrs. Lunt of the Alstead Collies in New Jersey, imported him; she often acted as a clearing house to distribute dogs she brought over, and she sold him to Miss Eileen Moretta of the Glenrose Kennels in New York. Why she imported him at that advanced age, with several of his outstanding sons already making their mark in this country, is not clear. He was shown several times, winning four points shortly after his arrival, but not campaigned to his championship. He was shown several times for Specials only, for exhibition. When Magnet was ten, Dr. O. P. Bennett of Tazewell commented that he had never seen a higher quality dog for his age, and several others said that he put the younger dogs to shame.

Magnet was used successfully in this country, but his greatest siring had been done before he came to America. The English champions, Poplar Perfection, Laund Legislator, and (Alstead) Seedley Supremacy, were his outstanding sons which established major sire lines in this country as well as in England. (Alstead) Spotland Supremacy, Seedley Shrew, and Pinewood Papyrus were other champions by Magnet. Laund Legislator and his son Laund Luke were behind the tail-male line going down to the leading sire Lodestone Landmark; this family, as well as Hertzville, appear mainly in bitch lines today. Ch. Alstead Seedley Supremacy sired three champions out of three different bitches as well as the remarkable Alstead Aviator, sire of Ch. Halbury Jean (of Arken).

Most prolific of the three was Perfection, whose sire line is dominant today. His son, Ch. (Alstead) Eden Emerald was imported by Mrs. Lunt, but owned by Dr. Bennett. His son El Capitaine of Arken sired Ch. El Troubador of Arken, sire of foundation sire, Ch. ToKalon the King's Choice and, even more important, Ch. Future of Arken. Future's sons, Ch. Honeybrook Big Parade and Ch. Sterling Stardust, are major influences in Collies today. To Stardust trace the Brandwyne and other Sterling-descended lines, and Big Parade's son, Ch. Silver Ho Shining Arrow, most importantly sired Ch. Silver Ho Parader. Emerald also sired ToKalon Black Wrestler, foundation of the ToKalon tricolor line to which Brandwyne traces through Ch. ToKalon Storm Cloud and Ch. Gaylord's Mr. Scalawag.

Because Magnet had many qualities needed in the breed in his day and was dominant for those qualities, he became known for his ability to upgrade. He became a legend in his own time and in generations to come, so we now give credit where it is due, and name him as "The Sire Supreme."

EMERGENCE OF MAJOR AMERICAN LINES

At last the stage was set for the crucial 1920s and climactic 1930s. Four new giants made their appearance: Mrs. Elisabeth Browning of ToKalon, Mrs. Florence B. Ilch of Bellhaven, Fred L. Kem of Lodestone, and Charles Wernsman of Arken. It is also important to identify in chronological order the five significant events for which these influential fanciers were responsible. First, Mrs. Ilch bought Ch. Starbat Strongheart. Second, Mrs. Lunt imported Eden Emerald. Third, Mrs. Browning sent ToKalon Wendy to Eden Emerald. Fourth, Mr. Wernsman bought Halbury Jean. Fifth, Mr. Kem obtained Lodestone Landmark.

Ch. Starbat Strongheart (1920)

Ch. Starbat Strongheart, an eye-catching sable and white with a profuse coat and proud carriage, was the first of the great American-bred sires, preceding the others by nearly a decade. He was also the biggest winner of his day. Although Strongheart was the dominant American sire of his day, he did not create a producing sire line which has survived. His two best producing sons were Ch. Bellhaven Stronghold (through whom the line extended furthest and strongest) and Ch. Bellhaven Bigheart, who sired Gaily Arrayed of Arken, dam of the famous Ch. El Troubadour of Arken. Stronghold was in one of the three-champion litters sired by Strongheart, out of Seedley Solution. Bigheart was in the other three-champion litter, that of Seedley Snowdrop, both whelped in 1924, another example of the transmission of quality through litters in which there is a concentration of quality.

Ch. (Bellhaven) Starbat Strongheart (1920), a noted winner and the sire of thirteen champions. Unfortunately, he did not create a surviving producing line.

Ch. Bellhaven Seedley Snowdrop (1924) stands behind the legendary Ch. El Troubador of Arken.

Ch. Bellhaven Seedley Solution (1919), a successful producer of champions.

Eng. Ch. Poplar Perfection (1936) was a Magnet son and the sire of Ch. (Alstead) Eden Emerald. *Baskerville*

Eng. Ch. (Alstead) Eden Emerald exerted a tremendous influence on the Collie. Over 75 percent of the Collies in England *and* America trace back to him!

Four generations of Bellhaven champions: Ch. Lucason of Ashtead O' Bellhaven (1928) by Lucas of Ashtead, ex Jean of Ashtead; his son, Ch. Bellhaven Black Lucason (1931), ex Viola of Ashtead O'Bellhaven; his son. Ch. Bellhaven Standard Bearer (1933), ex Ch. Bellhaven Lady Lector; and his son, Ch. Bellhaven Gold Standard (1935), ex Ch. Eden Edith of Bellhaven.

Eng. Ch. (Alstead) Eden Emerald (1922)

The second significant event for the Collie Fancy of the 1920s was the importation of Eden Emerald by Mrs. Lunt. Emerald was a grandson of Magnet on his sire's side, and his dam was a maternal granddaughter of Limit. So in Emerald, as in Magnet, there was a blending of the two great lines descending from Christopher. Emerald's use by Mrs. Browning and Mr. Wernsman sounded the knell for English sires in America. By sending one bitch each to him, these fanciers started sire lines that exist today, through which 90 percent of modern American Collies descend.

Eden Emerald was also to leave his influence in England. Before he was exported he sired two sons that were to have equally far-reaching effects: Ch. Backwood's Fashion and the untitled Eden Educator. Through Educator's two sons, Eden Electron, and particularly Eden Extreme, can be traced over 75 percent of the champion Collies in England today.

When one considers that the majority of top-winning and producing Collies in England and the United States can be traced directly to Eden Emerald, his ability as a sire becomes evident.

ENTER THE GIANTS

The first decade of this century was marked by an enormous growth in the still-small Collie world and the entrance of the first giants who were to fashion the American Collie.

Mrs. Clara May Lunt, Alstead

Most notable among the fanciers of the period perhaps was Mrs. Lunt, of Rahway, New Jersey, whose interest in the breed continued undiminished until her death in the 1950s. It is impossible to measure Mrs. Lunt's influence upon Collies. By 1920 she was the leading fancier in America, and her kennel was to house many key dogs in the development of the breed in America. Look at the significant pedigrees in the formative 1920s and 1930s peppered with the Alstead prefix. Mrs. Lunt may have been the most important single influence in fashioning of the American Collie, but it is ironic that she did not create any of the great sire lines from dogs she bred. It was her importation and use of Eng. Ch. (Alstead) Eden Emerald (1922) that was most influential.

Four other newcomers in this decade were also to become giants: Dr. O.P. Bennett of the Tazewell Kennels in Washington, Illinois; Chris Casselman of Hertzville in Chicago; Edwin L. Pickhardt of Sterling in the Midwest and later Connecticut; and Willard R. Van Dyck of the Honeybrook Kennels in New Jersey.

ToKalon Wendy (1923)

Wendy's paternal grandsire was Ch. Alstead Aeroplane, descended from Ch. Southport Sample. Wendy's paternal granddam, Ch. Alstead Alyssum, was a granddaughter of Magnet. Mrs. Browning's choice of Emerald for Wendy was a brilliant one. It resulted in ToKalon Black Wrestler, sire in separate litters late in 1932 of Ch. ToKalon Blue King and Ch. ToKalon Blue Eagle, the latter sire of the great Ch. ToKalon Storm Cloud (1940). Mrs. Browning thus set in motion one of the great American sire lines.

Ch. Halbury Jean (1924)

Momentous event number four in the 1920s was the purchase of a lifetime by Charles and Lillian Wernsman. Gayle Kaye tells the story of this legendary Collie.

THE ALL-AMERICAN BROOD BITCH

In her own way, Ch. Halbury Jean of Arken was as important an influence on early Collie bloodlines as was Ch. Magnet; in many ways she could be considered his female counterpart. Even though bitches do not have the potential for the unlimited influence of a male, they are every bit as important. On a smaller scale their influence can be just as far-reaching. Many old-time Collie breeders considered bitches to be a more important resource than males. To quote Edwin L. Pickhardt, "A great dog is a gift to the breed, at large for stud, all may use him, but a great bitch can make a breeder of her owner, make a kennel, produce a great dog, and she is the possession of the owner, her puppies are his to select from. Consequently, I never envy another's possession of a great sire, but I confess in bitches it is another story." Halbury Jean was one of those great bitches everyone envied or wished to own.

Jean could easily be considered America's foundation bitch, a turning point in development of the modern Collie. She was that rare combination every breeder dreams of owning, a top show bitch and successful brood bitch. She came along when importing dogs from England was starting to level off; Americans were finally beginning to breed their own quality dogs. As luck would have it, Jean was several generations American-bred.

Jean was whelped on April 8, 1924 at the Halbury Kennels in Connecticut. She was purchased for $250 at the age of nine months, the buy of a lifetime for Charles and Lillian Wernsman of Arken and a purchase which would forever alter the course of Collie history. Jean's sire was the unshown American-bred Alstead Aviator, grandson of Magnet, son of imported Ch. Alstead Seedley Queen, a Limit granddaughter, from the trusty Magnet/Limit cross. Her dam, Halbury Expression, was also American-bred. Jean is described as a beautiful mahogany sable, with full white ruff and tiny blaze on her forehead. Her head qualities were superb, structure very sound, and temperament sweet and steady. She was considered by many early breeders to be one of the finest Collies of all time.

Her show record was phenomenal; she finished her championship in 1926 and was retired for breeding. At the age of seven she came out of retirement after four litters to go Winners at the 1931 CCA National Specialty under judge Pickhardt. (In those days it was common practice to show finished champions in the open classes.) She repeated the win in 1932, going Best of Winners at the national under Dr. O. P. Bennett, who commented "She is one of the best Collie females that I have ever seen. Sound, good coated, grand head, eye, ears and expression, chock-full of Collie character." Winners Dog at the same show was her grandson, Ch. Cock Robin of Arken. At the age of eight she took many Best of Breed wins and was finally retired from the showring at ten with another five-point Specialty breed win.

Her producing record was even more phenomenal. She produced five litters with a total of six champions and held the breed record as top producing dam for several years. In addition to the champions, she was the dam of a very important dog that was never shown, but helped to alter Collie history.

In 1926 Jean was bred to Magnet grandson Ch. Alstead Eden Emerald. In the litter were two very beautiful bitches, Ch. Glorious Morning of Arken and Ch. Peeping Stard of Arken. The litter also contained a male, El Capitan of Arken, never to be shown due to a puppyhood injury to his nose. He in turn sired Ch. El Troubador of Arken. Mr. Wernsman bred Gaily Arrayed of Arken, a daughter of Ch. Bellhaven Bigheart to El Capitan, intensifying the Limit cross. Mrs. Lunt had made this mating in 1928 without significant results but for Mr. Wernsman's faith in what he was doing, in 1930 he got the celebrated Ch. El Troubadour of Arken and the lesser known Ch. El Gael of Arken.

Jean's next litter, in 1927, was by Ch. Alstead Adjutant, producing the dog Ch. Town Talk of Arken and the bitch Ch. Spirit of Arken. Bred again to Adjutant in 1929, she produced Ch. Nymph of Arken, a top winner and producer like her dam. Jean's final litter was by her grandson, El Troubador, and produced one living puppy, Ch. Monsieur the Count of Arken. She almost single-handedly founded the Arken line, a major factor in the American Collie's development. Nymph, a CCA winner like her dam, was bred to her nephew, El Troubador, to produce a pivotal dog in breed history, Ch. Future of Arken. He was as important to the breed in the pedigree of every living American Collie as Ch. Magnet had been in earlier years.

Future was a sensational show winner himself, and sired eleven champions. Two sons were very important in the scheme of things: Ch. Honeybrook

Big Parade was grandsire of Ch. Silver Ho Parader. Ch. Sterling Stardust was the double grandsire of Ch. Sterling Starmist, paramount in formation of the Gaylord-Brandwyne family and also important to the Parader line.

El Troubador was also instrumental in the development of the ToKalon and Poplar families, as he sired Ch. ToKalon the King's Choice. Another grandson, Future's brother Ch. Cock Robin of Arken, owned by Dr. Bennett, was an important factor on the distaff side. His granddaughter, Ch. Cainbrooke Clear Call, with seven champions, supplanted Jean as breed record holder for many years. Jean's influence is still with us today in all major American bloodlines.

Much of the credit for Jean's success must go to the Wernsmans, who recognized her quality and potential. With Mrs. Lunt's help, they bred her wisely; without their planning, Collies would not have progressed as quickly as they did and would not exist as we know them today. Arken was one of the most important kennels in the development of the American Collie.

It is fitting to end a tribute to Jean with a quote from Edwin L. Pickhardt: "Ch. Halbury Jean is one of the greatest bitches of all time, exquisite in head, having marvelous refinement in skull with great strength of foreface and excellence in balance, beautiful dark eyes of correct size and placement, perfectly carried ears and delightful Collie expression. A large, heavy coated, and good bodied bitch, with good bone, excellent legs, feet and gait. She has made an all time record on the bench and is the dam and granddam of numerous champions." She definitely has our vote for all time top Collie brood bitch.

Lodestone Landmark (1929)

Meanwhile out in Indiana, Mr. Kem was working with an American-bred bitch named Kentucky Egyptian Princess (1924). Her sire was a grandson of Limit, and Magnet appears three times in her pedigree. Mr. Kem sent Princess to Alsmot Aristocratic, a son of American-bred Ch. All Sett Sande. Sande was a great-great-grandson of Magnet on the sire's side and a grandson of Limit through his dam. Aristocratic's dam, Ch. Alstead Bergamot Buttercup, was by Alstead Aviator, in the two-champion litter he sired. The litter whelped in 1929 contained the appropriately named Lodestone Landmark, and Ch. Lodestone Lute, a bitch who came east to the Noranda Kennels of Mrs. William H. Long, Jr. Once again, the Magnet/Limit cross, and a concentration of quality in one litter was the result.

Before looking at the great Collie families in the 1930s, remember these were the financial depression years, and so the following record is all the more impressive. Only 1,526 Collies were registered in 1930, fewer than in either 1910 or 1920, and less than in an average month today. Yet, if you owned a bitch in the 1930s, there were three great American-bred studs in the East to choose from: Ch. Bellhaven Black Lucason, Ch. El Troubadour of Arken and Ch. Honeybrook Big Parade, each of whom sired 15 or more champions. In

Ch. Halbury Jean (1924) was one of the breed's most influential matrons.

Ch. El Troubador of Arken (1930) sired fifteen champions and had a widespread, beneficial effect on the modern Collie.

Ch. Future of Arken (1931) sired five champions including Ch. Sterling Stardust and Ch. Honeybrook Big Parade.

the Midwest, there were Lodestone Landmark, a fountainhead for the breed, and his son, Ch. Hertzville Headstone, sire of ten champions.

Ch. El Troubadour of Arken (1930)

Ch. El Troubador of Arken was an influential stud dog, and his pedigree is worth studying. He was sired by El Capitan of Arken, littermate of two champions. El Capitan's sire, Eden Emerald, produced nine champions in the United States, including two multiple-champion litters. El Capitan's dam, Ch. Halbury Jean, produced six champions, including two litters with multiple champions. El Troubadour's dam, Gaily Arrayed of Arken, was by Ch. Bellhaven Bigheart, from one of Ch. Starbat Strongheart's three-champion litters. Bigheart's dam, the imported Ch. Bellhaven Seedley Snow-drop, also produced six champions. Gaily Arrayed's dam, Ch. Alstead Aida, was by Emerald out of a Logic daughter, Eng. Ch. Alstead Seedley Queen. Queen, bred to imported Ch. Spotland Sterling, produced Ch. Alstead Adjutant, sire of four champions, two in one litter. Bred to Eng. Ch. Alstead Seedley Supremacy, Queen produced Alstead Aviator. Mr. Wernsman was working with families where the concentration of quality and producing ability ran high.

Bred to his aunt, Jean's daughter Ch. Nymph of Arken, El Troubadour sired his most famous litter, containing Ch. Future of Arken, who stayed in the East, Ch. Cock Robin of Arken, who went to Dr. Bennett's Tazewell Kennels in Illinois to become an influential sire, and the bitch Ch. A'Glow of Arken. The litter was whelped when El Troubadour was only fifteen months old, a propitious start for a brilliant stud career. El Troubadour also produced Ch. ToKalon The King's Choice (1934), setting in motion Mrs. Browning's second famous line as well as siring the dam of Ch. ToKalon Storm Cloud.

Ch. Future of Arken (1931)

Future was El Troubadour's most famous son, and justly so. All five champions Future sired were whelped in 1934. Three of the four males started their own lines. Once more we see the three-champion litter in action. Out of Token's Flush of Arken were Ch. Sterling Stardust, Ch. Future's Flash Again of Arken and Ch. The Duchess of Arken. Out of Honeybrook Helen there was but one champion, Ch. Honeybrook Big Parade. Stardust headed the famous line running through his grandson, Ch. Sterling Starmist, which has proliferated very successfully.

The great contribution of Bill Van Dyck to Collies was breeding Honeybrook Helen to Ch. Future of Arken. Helen was a daughter of Ch. Aalveen Anchor (Bellhaven) and Gene of Arken, a half-sister to El Troubador. Ch. Honeybrook Big Parade (1934) was the result. His most significant mating, which was to exert his influence widely, was to Silhouette of Silver Ho, producing Ch. Silver Ho Shining Arrow (1939), in turn sire of Ch. Silver Ho Parader.

With a blaze of enduring glory, the first great American Collie families burst upon the scene from only a small group of progenitors. The 1930s were not only the years in which the American Collie became an established, independent force; they were also in many ways a golden age in the history of the breed.

Chapter 2

Our Collie Legacy

by Mr. and Mrs. Benjamin F. Butler

The 1940s marked another turning point in American Collie breeding. Until the 1930s, imports from England dominated the winners' circle, but the second World War brought an abrupt halt to importation of breeding stock. This source of new blood was no longer available; nor did Collie imports return as a factor after the war. America was on its own. Breeding stock from the golden age of Collies was our endowment. How well American breeders took advantage of that heritage is the story of Collies from the 1940s into the present.

This period also saw the demise of the traditional, professional kennel managers, many brought over from Europe because of their knowledge of dogs. These early kennel managers were craftsmen, highly skilled in selecting, breeding, kenneling and showing dogs. They possessed superior knowledge of the breeds they worked with and placed particular emphasis on overall quality of their dogs. In the Collie Fancy they exerted great influence on several large kennels which led to the development of the foundation stock available by 1940.

The last of these masters was Mike Kennedy. He served his apprenticeship in the Greystone Kennels of millionaire Samuel Untermeyer, in Thomas P. Hunter's Knocklayde Kennels and at Mrs. Clara Lunt's Alstead establishment. Subsequently, he became manager and handler of Mrs. Florence B. Ilch's Bellhaven Collies in Red Bank, New Jersey—an association that spanned forty-five years (1920–66).

Another phenomenon was the change from localized activity to a nationwide interest in the Collie. Some influence outside the East had occurred previously, notably in the Midwest at Hertzville, Lodestone, Sterling and Tazewell and in California at Borco. Prior to 1940, progress had been dominated by Eastern breeders, particularly those using English imports.

In the wake of all these changes came the proliferation of small breeders. In the 1940s they were disparagingly referred to as "backyard breeders"

29

by those associated with the more affluent kennels, an unfair designation to the contributions of the smaller breeders. They were to become more the rule than the exception, and several new faces that would exert their own influence on the Collie appeared during this period.

Mrs. William H. Long, Jr. (Noranda): Located in Oyster Bay, New York, Mrs. Long began in Collies in the 1920s with three foundation bitches: Ch. Lady Lukeo of Cosalta, Ch. Lodestone Lute, litter sister of Lodestone Landmark, and Bellhaven Brightness. Her unfailing interest and successful results spanned several decades. She believed in Collies as working dogs and was founder of Dogs for Defense during World War II. Always keeping a small kennel, with many of her dogs as household companions, she was a popular judge, president of the Collie Club of America, and of the Long Island Kennel Club for many years.

Ch. Cadet of Noranda, Ch. Invader of Noranda and Ch. Ink Spot of Noranda were all Best in Show winners. Ch. Noranda Daily Double later won three all-breed BIS and Best of Breed at the Collie Club of America Specialty (1968) as well. One of Mrs. Long's noteworthy accomplishments was to have a champion in all four colors at the same time. Among her contributions to posterity was as the breeder of Silhouette of Silver Ho, the dam of Ch. Silver

Ch. ToKalon Stormy Weather (1947), by Ch. ToKalon Storm Cloud ex ToKalon Blue Heather II. *Tauskey*

Ch. ToKalon Golden Ruler (1949), by Ch. ToKalon Still A King's Choice ex ToKalon Lady Phyllis.

Ho Shining Arrow. Silhouette was sired by Master Lukeo of Noranda, the first champion Collie with a CDX Obedience degree.

Florence Cummings (Arrowhill): A tiny, soft-spoken lady, Florence Cummings was quietly breeding Collies in Oklahoma, physically outside the center of much breed activity. Here, untouched by fads and foibles, Florence Cummings made the name Arrowhill synonymous with quality for fifty years. She bred the first Collie champion in Oklahoma. One of her first champions, Ch. Arrowhill Maid Marion, was a BIS winner in 1928 and Ch. Arrowhill Oklahoma Tornado, one of her last, won a BIS in 1970.

Ch. High Man of Arrowhill was the sire of Ch. Black Hawk of Kasan, the first Smooth BIS winner and the greatest Collie producer of champions of all time. He was also the first Smooth to win Best of Breed at the Collie Club of America Specialty show. Ch. Arrowhill Miss Oklahoma and Ch. Arrowhill Personality Plus, CDX were Working Group[1] winners. Ch. Arrowhill Oklahoma Redman, sire of eleven champions, was one of sixteen

---

[1]*Prior to the establishment of the Herding Group in 1983, the Collie, like other Herding breeds recognized at the time, competed in the Working Group.*

Ch. Arrowhill Oklahoma Tornado (1964), by Ch. Cul-Mor's Conspiratour ex Promise of Arrowhill, a noted Best in Show winner.

Ch. ToKalon's Blue Banner, CD (1957), by Ch. Tokalon Ice Storm ex ToKalon Lady Jane. In 1964 his owners, Mr. and Mrs. R. L. Rickenbaugh established an annual award in his memory. Offered as a Collie Club of America challenge trophy to the top winning blue merle of either Variety, the award was intended to encourage breeding of blue merles. That the intent succeeded is evident in the greater popularity of the blue merle color phase with Collie enthusiasts today.

sired by Arrowhill Ace High. The Arrowhill kennel name has been carried on by Miss Sandra K. Tuttle, Hawk's owner, in California, as well as by Laurie Jeff Greer, granddaughter of Mrs. Cummings' long-time associate, Nina Campbell, in Oklahoma.

As judge, writer, lecturer, club worker and friend, Florence Cummings had an influence on the lives of many breeders. Louis and Leila Wachtel built on an Arrowhill foundation bitch for their Tel's Collies in Louisiana. Ada Shirley of Shirhaven, Mary Kittredge, Jane Kuska's Crag Crest, Parader, Kinmont, Wickmere, Philamour, Wee Park and scores of others were founded on or used Arrowhill dogs in their breeding programs. While Mary Kittredge never had more than a half dozen dogs at her Oak Creek Canyon home in Arizona, her influence in the Fancy extended nationwide. Her foundation bitch, Arrowhill Skysail, was the dam of the great Ch. Kittredge Adventuress, BOS to her sire Venture at the 1955 CCA Specialty and dam of four champions including Ch. Kittredge Temptress and Ch. Kittredge Sorceress. Ch. Kittredge Sorceress was the dam of five champions including the BIS winning Ch. Kittredge Jeanie and Ch. Kittredge Conjurer, whose daughter Ch. Gregshire's Little Honeycomb was dam of Ch. Jadene's Breezealong.

Dr. J. P. McCain (Cainbrooke): The 1940s saw the entrance into the Fancy of Dr. and Mrs. J. P. McCain of Pittsburgh. He was a gentle, scholarly man who taught a generation of Collie breeders racial tolerance, and earned the respect and affection of breeders throughout the country. Their judicious use of Hertzville, Lodestone and Sterling stud dogs produced an impressive list of descendants: Ch. Cainbrooke Miss Tazewell and her daughter, Ch. Cainbrooke Honey Chile, in turn her son, Ch. Cainbrooke's Mr. Bones and his son, Ch. Cainbrooke Beau Ideal. Most famous of all was Ch. Cainbrooke Clear Call, one of the greatest bitches of all time and dam of seven champions, a record few bitches have equaled or surpassed her, even to the present.

Cainbrooke Collies were impressively coated and structurally sound. It was not surprising that they won all-breed BIS awards (Ch. Cainbrooke Commandant) or sired BIS winners (Ch. Pleasant Hill Torch Song, by Black Sheik of Cainbrooke). Cainbrooke influenced Collie strains in many parts of the country.

Mr. and Mrs. James Christie (Saint Adrian): St. Adrian Kennels imported and homebred Collies were outstanding show winners during the early 1940s, housing numerous champions.

Although American-bred Collies came into their own and the use of American stud dogs was widespread in the 1940s, three English imports were the top winners of this period and won the National Specialty five times in ten years. All three were upstanding dogs of commanding presence. The imposing entry for Saint Adrian was Ch. Beulah's Golden Sultan (1938), bred by Mrs. Nadine K. George of England, BOB at the CCA Specialty in 1941, 1942 and 1944. Mr. and Mrs. Christie, from North Hanover, Massachusetts, were active in the parent club and Mrs. Christie's interest in Collies continued until her death in 1980.

Mrs. Florence B. Ilch (Bellhaven): Bellhaven entries dominated the showring during the years in which they were shown. Ch. Braegate Model of Bellhaven (1938) was a medium-sized mahogany sable with a sweeping coat and regal bearing. He won BOB at the Collie Club of America Specialty in 1943. Ch. Laund Liberation of Bellhaven (1942) was the greatest winner of his time and won at the National Specialty in 1946. However, Mike Kennedy was astute enough to know that the bitch is the foundation of any kennel, and both promoted and campaigned the Bellhaven bitches, imported and homebred alike. Among their top dams were Ch. Eden Edith of Bellhaven, dam of six champions, and Chs. Bellhaven Seedley Solution and Seedley Snowdrop, each the dam of five champions. Mrs. Ilch compiled a record of over 100 homebred and imported champions, which is unlikely to be surpassed now that the large kennels have passed from the scene. Her kennel manager, Mike Kennedy, shared in the triumphs, which were due in large part to his skill in conditioning and handling his charges, as well as his acumen in breeding. Bellhaven continues in the female lines of many kennels today.

Mary Gray (Wooley's Lane): In 1947 and 1948 two litter sisters, the tricolor Ch. Wooley's Lane Electra, and Ch. Wooley's Lane Leal, a sable, went from the classes to defeat male champions for BOB at the National Specialty. This was an outstanding feat for Long Islander Mary Gray, since no bitch again overcame male entries until 1960 when Ch. Country Lane M'Liss was BOB. This feat was duplicated in 1982 when Ch. Starr's Blue Jeans took the top spot, going BOS in 1984 and again BOB at CCA's centennial show in 1988. Ch. Pebblebrook Intrigue came down from Canada to go BOB in 1993.

Charles and Lillian Wernsman (Arken): To put into perspective the influence of American breeders on today's Collies, one must turn to Charles and Lillian Wernsman and their Connecticut-based Arken Collies.

In the early 1940s the Butlers had the pleasure of visiting Arken. There they saw Ch. Future of Arken, a magnificent dog whose extraordinary quality has seldom been matched. He possessed an enormous, harsh, sable coat and was a sound dog of excellent conformation. He was one of the few specimens to approach Collie perfection to this day. Dr. McCain said of Future,

> He was a big, upstanding sable-and-white dog with a profusion of coat I have not seen since his day. This dog was impressive in and out of the ring. To look at him was a privilege. He affected one as would a great painting done by the hand of a Master.

In writing *The Arken Story*, Theresa Hamilton said, "It is really something of an understatement to say that Arken was in the thick of developing the Collie in America—it was in the vanguard. Of course it is always easier to look back on success and see how it happened than it is to be sitting in the driver's seat, as was Mr. Wernsman. In establishing his line, he used only dogs of superior quality and type, from producing families. But he had to make those choices on which success or failure always rest and he made them astutely."

The Arken Collie family and its wide proliferation through pedigrees of other breeders in the 1940s carried those qualities the breed so desperately needed, and by which it so fortunately benefitted. Ch. Future of Arken's line descends today most strongly through two sons: Ch. Honeybrook Big Parade and Ch. Sterling Stardust.

Ch. Honeybrook Big Parade, owned by W. R. Van Dyk, was undefeated in the classes, won BOB at the Collie Club of America Specialty show three times, and sired seventeen champions. In addition to Ch. Silver Ho Shining Arrow, he sired Ch. Astolat Peerless, whose daughter was bred to Ch. Sterling Starmist to continue that family through Ch. Sterling Syndicate. Big Parade also sired Honeybrook Golden Boy, out of Lodestone Bandoliera II. Golden Boy's daughters were bred to Bandoliera's son by Shining Arrow, Ch. Silver Ho Parader, to establish the Parader line. Mr. Van Dyk served as secretary and president of the Collie Club of America and established its yearbook. He was a well-known writer and judge.

Elisabeth Browning (ToKalon): The ToKalon Kennels of Mrs. Robert Browning in West Hurley, New York, consisted entirely of homebreds during the 1940s and they enjoyed an outstanding record of show wins.

Ch. El Troubadour of Arken sired Ch. ToKalon the King's Choice, who headed the sable sire line at ToKalon and also sired the dam of Ch. ToKalon Storm Cloud. Others were descended from Eng. Ch. (Alstead) Eden Emerald, grandsire of El Troubadour; thus, ToKalon used many of the same Collies in its breeding program as did Arken. While Arken was strictly a kennel of sables, ToKalon produced outstanding sables, tricolors and blue merles. More than any other kennel in America, ToKalon was the foundation for blue merles through Ch. ToKalon Blue Eagle and his descendants. Here were two kennels, which essentially traced back to the same antecedents, yet achieved different, highly successful breeding results, both wielding a strong influence on Collies today. ToKalon Peaches Browning was the dam of five champions, and Ch. ToKalon Lone Pine Rhoda was one of the most beautiful bitches the Collie Fancy has ever seen.

Ch. ToKalon Storm Cloud (1940) was perhaps the most famous ToKalon stud dog, and his offspring made their mark at Collie Club of America Specialties. In 1953 Ch. Gaylord's Mr. Scalawag, a Storm Cloud grandson, went BOB. In 1958 and 1959 Ch. Cherrivale Darn Minute, a Scalawag son, was also BOB. Ch. Wind-Call's Night Hunter won in 1965, tracing back five generations to Storm Cloud, and in 1968 Ch. Noranda Daily Double, a great-grandson of Scalawag, won the honors. Erin's Own, Brandwyne, Bannerblu, Clarion, Royal Rock, and Starberry are a few of the families which successfully utilized ToKalon bloodlines.

Mrs. Browning's daughter, Mary, with her husband Lloyd Beresford, established the Poplar kennels which also scored many showring successes in the 1950s. Through their Storm Cloud son, Poplar By Storm, came the successful Brandwyne line founded on Mrs. Mangels' bitch, Poplar By Storm's Gem. The Poplar Collies, like the ToKalons, excelled in elegance, coat and body, counteracting the ranginess found in other lines of the time. Poplar Matinee Star was the dam of five champions.

Nancy L. Caldwell (Silver Ho): Schoolgirl Nancy Caldwell's purchase of a puppy bitch from Mrs. Long in 1939 was a significant event in modern Collie history. Registered as Silhouette of Silver Ho, she was eventually bred to Ch. Honeybrook Big Parade, by Ch. Future of Arken; there was one male in the litter: Ch. Silver Ho Shining Arrow. When the mating was repeated, it produced Ch. Arrowhill Admiral of Silver Ho. These full brothers were also destined to have a strong influence on later Collie generations.

Ch. Arrowhill Admiral of Silver Ho was bred to Ch. Arrowhill Silver Ho of Glamis, CD, by Shining Arrow ex Silver Ho Starlight, a daughter of Shining Arrow and Ch. The Duchess of Arken, by Future. A bitch from this

Ch. Silver Ho Parader (1943), by Ch. Silver Ho Shining Arrow ex Lodestone Bandoliera II. This unforgettable head of the "Parader dynasty" sired thirty-seven Rough champions.

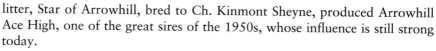

litter, Star of Arrowhill, bred to Ch. Kinmont Sheyne, produced Arrowhill Ace High, one of the great sires of the 1950s, whose influence is still strong today.

Silver Ho Tall Dark'N Handsome, a son of Ch. Silver Ho Shining Arrow was lost to the Fancy at an early age, but before he died he sired a litter for Lois Hillman's Roneill Kennels in California. His legacy was Ch. Dark Town Strutter of Roneill, grandsire of the great winner and producer, Ch. Lewellen Cali-Collaire. Dam of Cali-Collaire was a bitch from the Parader-Starmist cross. Again, we see the merging of producing families from common ancestry resulting in a potent sire. Cinderella, LuNette, Three Trees, Shadaglen, and Valley-Hi are only a few of the West Coast lines active or found in pedigrees today descending through Cali-Collaire.

Stephen J. Field (Parader): The second event of the 1940s which was to have a momentous effect upon modern Collies was Stephen Field's breeding Lodestone Bandoliera II, a great-granddaughter of Lodestone Landmark, to Ch. Silver Ho Shining Arrow, producing Ch. Silver Ho Parader. He stands at the head of the Parader family which has proliferated more than any other bloodline in this country today. Parader Collies excel in eye, expression, coat, soundness of body and temperament.

The Parader dynasty resulted from the merging of Lodestone, Arken and Noranda bloodlines, through individuals some generations remove from their Magnet/Limit English ancestry.

Ch. Silver Ho Parader (1943) was the first premier American sire, with thirty-seven champions to his credit. For many years he stood alone at the top of the sire list until his own descendants surpassed his producing record. Ch. Silver Ho Parader did more than just sire champions—he sired producers!

In the mid-1940s Ch. Silver Ho Parader was bred to Sterling Starsweet, a daughter of the great sire Ch. Sterling Starmist, to fortify further the quality of the line through Ch. Parader's Golden Image. He left a strong sire line through Image and Image's son, Ch. Parader's Bold Venture. The line continued through Venture's son, Ch. Parader's Country Squire and his sons, Ch. Parader's Reflection and Ch. Two Jay's Hanover Enterprise.

Ch. Parader's Golden Image (1945) was the result of the Parader-Starmist cross, merging two producing families descended from Ch. Future of Arken. Image produced twenty-four champions. The lineage from Image comes down through Ch. Parader's Bold Venture (out of Parader's Cinderella) and Am. & Can. Ch. Kinmont Sheyne (out of Ch. Parader's Pamela). Two of Sheyne's sisters were also influential: Ch. Cherrivale Parader's Portrait, the dam of Ch. Cherrivale Checkmate and founder of Gus and Edna Sigritz's Cherrivale Kennels; and Parader's Grand Girl, dam of the great Ch. Lewellen Cali-Collaire. Image also produced Ch. Lord of Lilac Lane to which Franluart, Crafthaven, Pleasant Hill, Patriciane and Vikingsholm trace.

Ch. Parader's Bold Venture (1950): In 1955 and again in 1957, Ch. Parader's Bold Venture went BOB at the CCA Specialty, marking the start of the dominance of the Parader line's influence at that premier show. In addition to siring twenty-four champions, Venture also won four Bests in Show. At most of the CCA Specialties held since his win, a Parader descendant has captured BOB laurels.

Another influential Venture son was Ch. LuNette's Top Sergeant, used to good advantage by the Lick Creek Collies.

Ch. Parader's Country Squire (1958): Venture's son, Country Squire, continued the Parader line by siring twenty-four champions including Ch. Parader's Reflection (sire of seventeen champions) and Ch. Two Jay's Hanover Enterprise (sire of forty-five Rough champions). The Enterprise son, Ch. Baymar's Coming Attraction, a Collie Club of America BOB winner, sired thirteen champions. Many kennels have linebred on Enterprise bloodlines including: Bandor, Chris-Mik, Hanover (his breeders), Two Jays (his owners), Tamarack, Twin Creeks, Younghaven and Azalea Hills, owners of the 1980 Collie Club of America BOB winner.

Ch. Parader's Reflection (1966): Continuing the great Parader sire line, Reflection produced seventeen champions. He is the grandsire of Ch. Sujim's Mr. Onederful, sire of eighteen Smooth and three Rough champions. Reflection sired the litter brothers Ch. Antrum Alltheway II, sire of eighteen Rough champions and two Smooth champions and Ch. Antrum All-Try of Northshield, UDT, sire of five Rough and four Smooth champions. Many California Collies come down through these two including DeaHaven, Kanebriar, Merrill, Chris-Mik, San Lori and Stoneypoint. Another Reflection son, Ch. Parader's Kingsmark, carried on the Parader lines at home and through Gerthstone and Twin Creeks.

In addition to Ch. Parader's Golden Image, Ch. Silver Ho Parader produced five other sons which contributed to the development of the American Collie:

Parader's Future Sensation sired Bellbrooke's Master Pilot, the sire of Ch. GinGeor Bellbrooke's Choice (sire of thirty champions) and Ravette's Wayside Traveler, double grandsire of Ch. Tartanside the Gladiator, leading sire of his day. Master Pilot is also the sire of Ch. Bellbrooke's Master Pilotson, maternal grandsire of the dam of Ch. Shamont Sabrina (dam of seven champions). Master Pilot's influence as a sire is no surprise; his dam is a sister to Ch. Parader's Bold Venture. Hi Vu, Tartanside, Ravette, Wickmere, Wayside and Shamont are only a few of the bloodlines descending from him.

Graham Farm's Parader was influential in the Northwest and is behind the Alandale, Sandamac, Pride, Shadaglen and Shadalon bloodlines.

Ch. Proud Chief of Floravale was the grandsire of Ch. Merrie Oaks Humdinger (sire of fifteen champions) and his descendants continue in the Midwest.

Ch. Teecumsee Temptor sired Ch. Cul-Mor's Conspiratour, sire of twenty Rough and six Smooth champions, one of the few sires influential in both varieties. The Cul-Mor and Rudh'Re kennels of Misses Virginia Holtz and Joan Graber continue today and their influence is strong through Hanover and Two Jays as well as in most contemporary Smooth lines. Temptor was also sire of the beautiful Ch. Tanair's Tender Trap, a top Specialty winner.

Ch. Vi-Lee's Parading Chieftain headed the Vi-Lee sire line, from which Debhill, Rudh'Re and Lochlomun also descend. Seven generations later Ch. Twin Creeks True Grit, despite his untimely death, sired over forty champions, and established the kennels of Joyce and Ben Houser as a dominant force in the showring for the past twenty years. Numerous winning lines including Mariah's and Westwend, Executive's, and Twin Oaks, to name but a few, stem from this family.

The widespread influence of Ch. Silver Ho Parader cannot be fully appreciated until one realizes that nine of the breed's top ten sires trace to him.

Mrs. E. F. Mansure (Merrie Oaks): Ch. Merrie Oaks Humdinger was a leading sire of the 1950s for Judy Mansure of Maryland and later La Honda, California. His grandson, Ch. Merrie Oaks Midnite Star, by the Venture grandson, Ch. Merrie Oaks Star Boarder, sired foundation stock and numerous champions for Alteza, Celestial, Wickmere and others.

George and Virginia Horn (GinGeor): The outstanding sire in this line was Ch. GinGeor Bellbrooke's Choice, sire of the BIS and CCA Specialty winner, Ch. Jadene's Breezealong, whose champion dam was of Arrowhill-Parader background. Bellbrooke's Choice was also the sire of Ch. GinGeor's Indelible Choice, sire of twelve champions, including Ch. GinGeor's Indelibly Blue, the first blue merle to win at the Collie Club of America since the 1920s. His dam was of Erin's Own background. Altogether Bellbrooke's Choice produced twenty-eight Rough and two Smooth champions.

Patricia Starkweather (Glen Hill): The Collies of Glen Hill come down through Venture's son, Ch. Parader's Typesetter, sire of Ch. Glen Hill Dreamer's Nobleman. Nobleman was out of a Lodestone dam, the same kind of breeding that produced Ch. Silver Ho Parader. He in turn produced Ch. Glen Hill Emperor Jones, who sired Ch. Glen Hill Full Dress, through whom all Glen Hill stock descends today. Full Dress is behind Ch. Tartanside The Gladiator and can be found in Hi Vu, Patriciane, Ravette, Shadowmont and Briarhill kennels, among others.

Edwin L. Pickhardt (Sterling): Ed Pickhardt began breeding Collies as a youngster in St. Louis under the tutelage of some of the old masters of the early American Collie Fancy. Like other breeders of the prewar period, he used imports, but when that source was temporarily cut off, he realized that American-bred Collies had come of age, and turned to producing his own line. Mr. Pickhardt's purchase of Ch. Sterling Stardust, by Ch. Future of Arken, was the keystone to development of the Sterling line.

Edwin L. Pickhardt relaxing with Ch. Sterling Starmist, the sire of fourteen champions, and Ch. Sterling Syndicate. In addition to his long, illustrious association with Collies, Mr. Pickhardt was one of America's most popular all-breed judges.

Dr. J. P. McCain is warmly remembered in the Fancy for the quality of his Cainbrooke Collies, his abilities as a judge and his energies on behalf of the breed. He is shown here with Ch. Starberry Mistress Mine, CD, handled by her co-breeder Sara Futh. *Shafer*

Ch. Sterling Starmist, double grandson of Stardust, was described by Stephen Field as "a beautiful Collie with a sweet expression, a balanced refined head and a full smooth muzzle." Perhaps the most important of these virtues, because it was badly needed at that time, was his well-rounded muzzle, which he passed on to his progeny.

The Starmist bloodlines, and Sterling head type, come down to us today through Brandwyne, San Lori, Royal Rock, Accalia and Starberry, to name only a few. In 1962 and 1963 Ch. Stoneykirk Reflection (1958) won Best of Breed at the Collie Club of America Specialty show, with his daughter Ch. Mayoline Welcome Reflection Best of Opposite Sex in 1962. He was a great-great grandson of Starmist and holds the all-breed Best in Show record for Collies, with nine such wins.

Dorelane's Crusader, a Starmist grandson, sired the great Ch. Wharton's Country Gal, owned by Alice Wharton of California. A Working Group winner, she produced three champions by Am. & Can. Ch. Kinmont Sheyne including Mrs. Hillman's famous Ch. Country Lane M'Liss.

As president of the Collie Club of America, Pickhardt helped to make the club a truly national organization. He was also an all-breed judge and wrote many articles and a book on the breed as well as mentoring breeders who went on to achieve prominence in the Collie Fancy in their own right.

Jane and Hazel Youngjohns (Hazel Jane's): It is the dream of all Collie breeders to win Best of Breed at the annual Collie Club of America Specialty show. Present are Collies from all over the country: the young puppy hopefuls, the choice mature dogs vying for championship points and finally the glittering array of the best in Colliedom, those seasoned campaigners: the champions. There is only one National Specialty each year and one Best of Breed award at the end of the judging. Many successful breeders spend their lifetimes in litter box and showring without attaining this coveted, elusive victory.

Thus the Cinderella story of Collies has to be that of Jane and Hazel Youngjohns, two sisters barely out of their teens, who with an elegant, mahogany male from their first litter won at the Collie Club of America not once, but four times, a record still unequaled today. Ch. Hazel Jane's Bright Future also went from the classes, over champion Collies, all the way to BIS at a large all-breed event. Bright Future is one of only a half dozen Collies to win five or more BIS awards.

The Youngjohns sisters conditioned their dogs superbly and handled them with great expertise in the showring; they also had the wisdom to heed the advice of Chris Casselman of Hertzville in their breeding program. Unfortunately, Bright Future's own career as a stud dog was cut short when he and his lovely daughter, Ch. Hazel Jane's Future Sensation, broke away from their owner and were killed by a truck. Despite Future's eight champion offspring, his line comes down through three untitled sons: Bellochanty Bright Banner, Hazel Jane's Future Reflection and Rob Roy of Scotlyn. From Bright Banner come the Cul-Mor Smooths, through Future Reflection, the Kimblewyck Smooths. Rob Roy was the most prolific and it is through him that the line descends most strongly. He is responsible for champions at Brandwyne, Glen Knolls, Valley View, Impromptu, Laurien, Clarion and for several Smooth lines.

Bright Future himself was a great-great-grandson of Lodestone Landmark and was an instrumental link in the perpetuation of Landmark's sire line. The Dorwood, Bellochanty and Caledon families, which were dominant in the Midwest in the 1950s, shared the Hertzville ancestry of the Youngjohns' Collies.

The James Mangels (Gaylord and Brandwyne): The 1950s saw the beginning of the Gaylord Collies of Dr. James H. and Mrs. Jean Mangels, and later Trudy B. Mangels' Brandwyne line. The Connecticut kennels' most famous sire was Ch. Gaylord's Mr. Scalawag, a grandson of Ch. ToKalon Storm Cloud and Ch. Sterling Syndicate. Scalawag's two most notable sons were Ch. Cherrivale Darn Minute from which the Patriciane and Shadowmont Collies descend and Ch. Erin's Own Professor, to which Royal Rock, Glen Knolls, Bobbi-Jeen's/Starberry, Clarion, Knightswood and Impromptu' Collies trace.

Trudy Mangels founded her Brandwyne line on Long Island, also by combining ToKalon and Sterling. She later used an outcross to Ch. Scotlyn's Casanova (Hertzville/Cainbrooke) to good effect. Gaylord's Major Merrymaker, brother to Scalawag's dam, sired her Brandwyne Tom Foolery, out of a Poplar By Storm daughter. Tom Foolery sired seven champions. His most notable sons were Ch. Glen Knolls Flash Lightning, white sire of seven champions; Brandwyne's New Legacy, sire of six champions including Ch. Impromptu Ricochet (sire of twelve Rough and four Smooth champions); and Ch. Brandwyne Needless To Say, sire of seven champions and grandsire of Ch. Brandwyne Destiny's Echo. Echo was the leading Brandwyne sire with twenty-three champions—twenty-two Rough and one Smooth—to his credit.

Gaylord and Brandwyne Collies scored many notable wins from 1950 through the 1970s and are behind many of today's most distinguished families. Bayberry, Clarion, Curtacy, Cyn-San, Debonair, Erin's Own, Glen Knolls, Impromptu', Honey Hill, Laurien, Mel-Bar and Wyndfall are only a handful of the kennels who utilized Brandwyne lines to their benefit.

Brian and Bridie Carabine (Erin's Own) produced a string of beautiful, elegant Collies at their Erin's Own Kennels on Long Island. Ch. Erin's Own Professor was a leading son of Ch. Gaylord's Mr. Scalawag. The beautiful Ch. Erin's Own Gold Dust was a Specialty winner and dam of Ch. Erin's Own Professor's Touch, sire in turn of the top producing Ch. Royal Rock Gamblin' Man.

Miss Leslie Canavan and Mrs. Verna Allen (Royal Rock) have produced consistent winners from their Long Island–based Kennels over several decades.

Gamblin' Man stands out as their most famous standard-bearer. Their dogs have gone Winners at the National Specialty show repeatedly over several generations and Miss Canavan handled Gamblin' Man's great-grandson, Ch. Noranda Daily Double, to BOB at the Collie Club of America, in addition to his BIS triumphs. Janet Leek has used Royal Rock with Brandwyne in her Bayberry Collies and Royal Rock is also behind many successful Smooth lines.

Wind-Call and Pleasant Hill: The vital influence of Parader, ToKalon, Sterling and Brandwyne on the modern Collie has been documented in detail. There are other bloodlines, independent of these main families, which also provide stock for the future of the breed. Glen Twiford, in Colorado, was active in Collies longer than any other breeder of today. His Wind Call Collies went directly back to Kelmar and Arken, although he also used ToKalon and other strains for infusions of outcross blood. His stock excelled in soundness and elegance.

Billy Aschenbrener also produced successful Collies in Specialty and all-breed competition for half a century from his Pleasant Hill Kennels in Oregon. He has also judged at the National Specialty on numerous occasions.

Marcia Keller (Marnus): Assisted by husband Ron, Marcia Keller has been a successful breeder for over fifty years, in the Buffalo, New York area. She is probably known best as owner-handler of the crowd-pleasing Ch. Marnus Evening Breeze, twice BOS at the National Specialty. The Kellers have consistently produced quality bitches, as well as some outstanding male winners, notably the BIS winner, Ch. Marnus Gold Medalist, BOB at the 1990 CCA show.

Bobbee, George and Shelley Roos (Wickmere): Great bitches have been the trademark of the Wickmere Kennels ever since this highly successful breeding program was established. Their successes have included BIS winner Ch. Wickmere Rapunzel, Ch. Wickmere Golden Chimes, best puppy at CCA when her sire was BOB, and her daughters, Ch. Wickmere Wedding Bell and Ch. Wickmere Anniversary Waltz, and the tricolor male, Ch. Wickmere Chimney Sweep, also a BIS winner and BOB at the 1972 CCA Specialty, one of the largest in the history of the Club. "Sweeper" was sired by Ch. Wickmere War Dance, like Ch. Wickmere Reveille. The late Barbara Roos, in addition to being a sought-after judge and speaker, was a prolific writer and led the first successful CCA judges' seminars. She was one of the great ladies of the Collie Fancy like Mrs. Long, Mrs. Browning, Mrs. Ilch and Mrs. Lunt before her.

Mr. and Mrs. William Hutchinson (Hi Vu): Established in 1962, the Hi Vu Collies have enjoyed success in the showring and have also been a positive factor for other breeders. Many other kennels, including Candray and Tartanside, have produced champions with Hi Vu heritage. The Hutchinsons' foundation bitch, Ch. Hi Vu Ravette Mist was bred to Ch. Glen Hill Full Dress to produce Ch. Glen Hill Blue Dress, dam of five champions including the dam of Ch. Berridale Macdega Mediator and the dams of Ch. Briarhill Glen Hill Sky High and Ch. Hi Vu Inspiration whose daughter founded Asgard and Champagne Collies. Bred to the Full Dress son Ch. Hi Vu Valiant, Mist produced Ch. Hi Vu Silver Siren and Hi Vu Silversmith, sire of Ch. Hi Vu Silver Myth and Silver Mystery, foundation bitch of Starr's Collies. Her daughter, Ch. Starr's Blue Jeans, produced eight champions between her CCA BOB triumphs, as well as Star's Classic Gold, dam of five champions, and Starr's Dark Crystal, dam of eight.

THE PRESENT AND FUTURE

What about tomorrow's winners? Which of today's Collies will provide their heritage for the future? Many decades will pass before this is known. From history and past experience we know that mating top specimens from producing families with common ancestry such as Trefoil-Cockie, Magnet-Limit and the Arken family crosses, for example, has produced potent sires which exerted great influence on our breed. Astute breeders have recognized outstanding brood bitches and concentrated their influence in establishing and perpetuating successful lines. Similar patterns will be productive in the future.

Today's Collie breeders are faced with the challenge of finding breeding patterns that will benefit their counterparts of the future. That is what breeding, in its finest sense, is all about.

Some Leading Kennels of the 1990s

John Buddie (Tartanside): Beginning as a teenager on Long Island, John Buddie has crafted a line known for expression and Specialty-winning type. The "Gladiator look" results from linebreeding to the top sire of champions of his day, Ch. Tartanside the Gladiator. A double grandson of Ravette's Wayside Traveler, in the Bellbrooke Master Pilotson branch of the Silver Ho Parader tail-male line, he was by Ch. Hi Vu the Invader, Winners Dog, 1968 CCA Specialty. He is one of only a handful of three-time National Specialty BOB winners, having turned the trick in 1973, 1974 and the third time from the Veterans class in 1978. On this last occasion, his granddaughter, Ch. Tamisett's Golden Dream, was BOS and his grandson, Ch. Shamont Stormalong, was Winners Dog. Tartanside dogs have fairly dominated the National Specialty with Ch. Rio Bravo's Achilles, BOB in 1979, and Glenecho Set the Style, Winners Dog—both Gladiator grandsons. A son, Ch. Azalea Hill's Top Man, won in 1980, grandson Ch. Carnwath's Evergreen in 1981, and Evergreen's litter brother Ch. Carnwath's the Great Pretender, BOS to Blue Jeans in 1982. Another grandson, Ch. Tartanside Apparently, won Best of Breed in 1985 with a younger full brother Winners Dog. Grandson Ch. Kingsbridge Lancer was BOS to Blue Jeans at the CCA Centennial show in 1986. Ch. Honeybun's Blaze of Tartanside, the 1976 Winners Dog,

Ch. Grandhill Heirloom, the 1990 BOS, Ch. Aurealis Silverscreen the 1991 BOB and Tartanside Imagination, Winners Bitch at the same Specialty, were all Gladiator descendants.

Supplanting the Gladiator as leading sire is the Heir Apparent son, Ch. Tartanside th' Critic's Choice, currently the breed's leading sire with a total of over fifty champions at the time of this writing.

James Frederiksen, James Noe (Two Jays Collies): Two Jays Kennels began in 1963 with the purchase of Ch. Two Jays Hanover Enterprise from Carol Chapman. This prefix quickly attained noteworthy success in the breed. Enterprise sired fifty-two champions, and was Best Stud Dog at the CCA Specialty for five consecutive years; a son, Ch. Baymar's Coming Attraction was BOB in 1971, and a grandson, Ch. Two Jays Added Attraction followed in Prise's footsteps as best stud dog for the following three years. With Chuck Valentine doing the handling, the dogs continue to succeed in the ring while the two Jims are busy as Herding Group judges.

Among the more successful up and coming kennels are Leslie Jeszewski's Highcroft Collies. Aided by husband Don, the prefix has sprung to national prominence. Their Ch. Highcroft Quintessence is leading all-time dam with no less than thirteen champions.

Louis and Pam Durazzano (Starr's Collies): The Durazzanos, of New Hampshire, succeeded royally with the offspring of their two Hi Vu purchases, Ch. Hi Vu Madresfield Molly and her daughter, Hi Vu Silver Mystery. They have continued to produce consistently attractive Collies which have taken top honors at the National Specialty and many other important shows. Co-owning with Dan Cardoza of Providence, Rhode Island, and combining talents with New Hampshire neighbor Jan Wanamaker of Candray, whose start was with Hi Vu foundation stock, they have set a hard-to-beat winning record over the last fifteen years. They have put the related dogs of Tartanside and several outcrosses to good use, cobreeding the 1992 CCA BOB, the Stringer-Haslett owned Ch. Sealore's Grand Applause by outcross Ch. Applause Parader Persuasion, out of Starr's Dark Crystal, a Breezy daughter. Another Breezy daughter, Ch. Starr's Painted On Jeans, by Ch. City View Advantage, was BOS and their granddaughter, Ch. Candray Brilliance, was Best Of Winners enroute to her championship at that show.

Eng. Ch. Babette of Moreton (1900), the top Smooth bitch of her time in England.

Eng. Ch. Laund Lynne (1917) distinguished herself in the showring with numerous outstanding wins and as a working stock dog of great ability. *Hedges*

Chapter 3

History of the Smooth Collie

The popularity of the Smooth Collie has increased significantly all over the United States in the past thirty years. The improved quality of Smooths has enhanced their success in intervariety competition at Specialty shows and among all breeds in Groups and Best in Show classes. Rough and Smooth Collies are still being interbred today and it is not surprising to find the two varieties becoming more competitive in the showring. The Smooth Collie has also gained greater recognition as a companion, obedience, guide, hearing and helper dog.

The Smooth Collie differs from the Rough Variety only in coat. The correct coat is as important to the overall quality of the Smooth as the full coat is to the Rough. The Smooth Collie is a double-coated dog with a short, soft, dense undercoat required for insulation, as in Roughs. The outercoat should be straight, harsh and close to the body and of sufficient length to cover the undercoat. The head and ears are smooth, as are the forelegs and hind legs below the hock joint. The neck is furnished with slightly longer, thicker hair forming a slight ruff. The hair forming the pants, or skirts, on the hindquarters is slightly longer and more abundant than the body coat. In breeding and judging both varieties of Collies, an understanding of the correct coat characteristics is imperative.

EARLY SMOOTHS IN ENGLAND

During the mid-1800s the Smooth Collies of Northern England were, in general balance and conformation, closer to today's type for the Variety than were the Rough-coated dogs of Scotland. These tended to be short-legged and long-bodied, with short, forward-thrust necks. Rough/Smooth crosses were common.

H. E. Packwood wrote in *Show Collies Rough and Smooth-Coated*, published in 1906 in Manchester, that Smooths had made good progress in the previous ten years and were equally as good for show or shepherd work as their Rough brothers. He noted that the Smooth was not so popular with the public and entries at shows were small.

The show history of the Collie had begun in 1860 at the Birmingham National dog show, where one class for dogs and bitches of all sheepdog varieties was offered. By the 1870s the Variety had taken hold and enough Smooths were being exhibited for a few large shows to offer separate classes for them. One of the first Smooths bred for the showring was Ch. Pickmere, a tricolor dog from a Rough/Smooth cross, bred by F. Hurst and exhibited by A. H. Megson.

Another early influence on the Smooth Variety was Ch. Heathfield Dot, sired by a Rough brother of Ch. Metchley Wonder, the well-known winner, from a blue merle Smooth working bitch, Blue Light. Packwood wrote that Dot was . . . "an ideal quality blue merle with a perfectly chiseled head, nice ears, pleasing expression and a coat that is seldom equaled."

Ch. Babette of Moreton (1900) was the top Smooth bitch up to that time. She was a great-granddaughter of Heathfield Dot and was almost entirely of Smooth breeding. In 1902 she won the Challenge trophy for Best Collie of Any Variety at the Collie Club show. Babette has been described as ideal, a lovely true type, an exquisite quality bitch with hardly a fault in her conformation. In 1906 at the same show, Ormskirk Venice won the championship, repeating the performance of Babette by winning the Challenge trophy.

A particularly beautiful and versatile Smooth was the blue merle bitch, Ch. Laund Lynne (Hetman ex Primly Primula), owned by W. W. Stansfield. Whelped in 1917, Lynne herded sheep and cattle, retrieved and also had an illustrious show career. She was the winner of sixteen Challenge Certificates, and was placed Best in Show all-breeds or Best Bitch in Show an amazing ninety-five times. Her record included the cup for Best of All-Breeds at the English Kennel Club show. She also won outright the silver jardiniere of the Kennel Club for Best Bitch in Show by winning it for three straight years. Lynne was never bred during her youth owing to the demands of her show career. Remarkably, at ten years of age she successfully reared a litter of seven puppies.

EARLY SMOOTHS IN AMERICA

The earliest record of Smooths being shown in the United States is found in the catalogue of the 1888 Westminster Kennel Club dog show. There was a class at that long ago event for "Smooth-coated Collies and BOB-tailed Sheepdogs," sexes combined, which attracted five entries. By the 1890 Westminster, Rough and Smooth Collies were mixed in all classes except for open, which was divided by coat, but in Smooths combined in sexes. In the next decade four champions appeared: Ch. Clayton Countess (1901) finished in 1906, Ch. Ormskirk Mabel in 1907 and her daughter, Ch. Ormskirk Lucy, the

Laund Laventer, by Black Donovan ex Merrion Blue Dorrit, was the foundation sire of Margaret Haserot's Pebble Ledge Smooths. Imported from Laund Kennels in England, he was a brother to Laund Blue Peter.

Little Dorrit, by Laund Laventer ex Laund Larchfield, the dam of Halmaric Trilby.

Ch. Christopher of Pebble Ledge (1946), by Harline's Son of Cainbrooke, a Rough, ex Ch. Pebble Ledge Bambi. Christopher and his litter sister, Ch. Pebble Ledge Inc, CD, were instrumental in the foundation of American Smooths.

following year. Then came Ch. Warren Patience in 1909. Smooth entries later declined, with no record of the Variety being shown at all from 1923 to 1940.

During the golden age of Collies in America, the popularity of Roughs rendered the Smooth Variety all but extinct. In an attempt to overcome this condition, a syndicate was formed in 1939 consisting of prominent fanciers H. R. Lounsbury of Halmaric Kennels, Mrs. Clara M. Lunt of Alstead, Robert G. Wills of Alloway, Arthur Foff of Tamalgate and Mrs. Genevieve Torrey Eames of Torreya. They imported Laund Blue Peter, a blue merle Smooth male, and Laund Loftygirl, a Smooth tricolor bitch, from the Laund Kennels in England. The pair were bred twice with the members drawing lots for the puppies. Unfortunately the syndicate disbanded after a few years due to lack of interest and the progeny of the pair scattered, but their influence remains today.

Due to a lack of competition, there were no opportunities to make up Smooth champions during this period. However, Hewmark Hallmark, an imported tricolor bitch, won Best of Breed over Roughs for three points and went on to place second in the Working Group at the Hampton Roads Kennel Club show in Norfolk, Virginia in 1941.

EARLY SMOOTH BREEDERS

Miss Margaret Haserot (Pebble Ledge Farm): The Ohio fancier, Margaret Haserot, whose interest in the Variety went back to the 1920s, was attempting to breed Smooths on her own at Pebble Ledge Farm. Disappointed in several early imports, she finally succeeded in getting a litter from the blue, Laund Laventer, out of her tricolor, Laund Larchfield. From this litter came Little Dorrit, a tricolor, which was bred to Halmaric Baronet, a blue Smooth from the syndicate pair. The resulting tricolor Smooth, Halmaric Trilby, was bred to the sable Rough, Ch. Halmaric Scarletson, to produce the first Smooth champion since 1909—a span of thirty-eight years! Ch. Pebble Ledge Bambi, whelped in 1944, was a sable bitch of superb quality. She was Best of Variety every time shown and could easily have been a top winner today. In 1946 Bambi was bred to the sable Rough, Ch. Harline's Son of Cainbrooke, to produce the next two Smooth champions, littermates Ch. Christopher of Pebble Ledge and Ch. Pebble Ledge Inca, CD. Bambi and her children laid the foundation of modern Smooths in America.

Miss Haserot was breeding Smooths on a small scale at a time when there was scant interest in the Variety. She was nonetheless determined to continue alone, if necessary, until the spark of interest was fanned into a flame. She was instrumental in forming the American Smooth Collie Association, Inc. At its formation in 1957 there were only twenty-six members; in 1995 there was some ten times the original number.

Margaret Haserot walking in the woods at Pebble Ledge Farm. Virginia Holtz, whose Cul-Mor Smooths trace back to Pebble Ledge, writes of this photo:

"Pebble Ledge Farm was originally bought to house the horses during winter. It later became home for Margaret and her father. The acreage behind the house included . . . great ledges of black stone, in which are embedded tiny white pebbles. The ledges lead to the Chagrin River which flows through the property and provided enjoyment for the dogs during hikes. Because the river and surrounding woods trap moisture, the pebbled rocks at ground level are covered with blankets of lush moss, through which moist, granite-like pebbles show a lustrous glow. . . . The mild humidity keeps the leaves soft underfoot so that the place has an other-worldly quality. A few hours there were as refreshing as a week's vacation. We all loved the place.

"Margaret was by nature a giving and generous person. She always welcomed her many friends to come and stay at Pebble Ledge Farm. Her sense of fair play, integrity and good sportsmanship did alot to set the tone for the Smooth Fancy."

SOMETHING ABOUT SMOOTHS

by Margaret Haserot

Back in 1933, Mr. Fred Kem, of Lodestone fame, was convinced that there were no Smooth Collies in North America, and I, too, was sure there weren't as the result of diligent writing hither and yon for two years. So, I imported a brace from Seedley Kennels. After their arrival I heard of two individual Smooths—one, by hearsay, in Cleveland, and the other from a mention in *Time* magazine of an importation to New England.

The day came when my brace and all their get were wiped out. Though days were devoted to the effort, I could not find either of the "hearsay" Smooths, which to all practical purposes left the country Smoothless again. There was nothing to do but start over. Laund Laventer finally sailed from England in 1940. He established the line of Smooths which Pebble Ledge Kennels has developed. The previous year, Laventer's brother Laund Blue Peter, and Laund Loftygirl were imported by a syndicate of Collie people. Blue Peter eventually went to California, and he may have been the progenitor of some of the Smooths there. For a couple of years, at least fourteen Smooths were mustered for the Chagrin Valley Kennel Club show in Ohio, all of Pebble Ledge ancestry.

Smooth Collies are intelligent and lovable dogs. However, without the long coat of the Rough, any body fault is immediately apparent. One who truly appreciates their litheness and grace will persist in breeding Smooths. The Smooth has a sleek, contemporary appearance and should be appreciated in these fast moving days.

Mr. and Mrs. Omer Rees (Glengyle Kennels): In 1953 the Rees of California went to England and purchased a two-month-old Smooth sable bitch from Miss Margaret Osborne of the Shiel Kennels. This puppy became Ch. Solo From Shiel and was the foundation for most Western Smooths of the 1950s. Solo's bloodlines included the Beulah and Grangetown lines.

Solo produced four champions and several other point winners, and held her quality until her death in 1965. For a decade, her son, Ch. Glengyle Smooth Sailing (1954), by the Rough Ch. Hertzville Hightop, was the leading sire of Smooth champions. An elegant tricolor, Sailor was BOB over more than sixty Roughs at the Collie Club of Northern California Specialty show and produced nine champions. Solo, Sailor and their offspring are indisputably responsible for the high quality and great popularity of Smooths on the West Coast. Many modern Smooths descend from Sailor through his son Ch. Paladin's Black Amber, CD (1957) and two daughters, Ch. Paladin's Blue Jade (dam of six champions) and Ch. Pebble Ledge Generosity (1960).

Ch. Belle Mount Bambi, CD (1953): In 1956 Bambi, owned by Tom Kilcullen, won the Dog World Award of Canine Distinction for obedience. This sable Smooth completed her championship with four Group placements, a record for the Variety at that time. Bambi was also Best of Opposite Sex to

Best of Breed at the Chicago Specialty and was undefeated against Smooths. She was a daughter of Luke of Pebble Ledge (a son of Ch. Pebble Ledge Bambi) out of the Rough, Belle Mount Rosey Future (of Noranda/ToKalon lines) and was bred by Alice Burhans.

Even greater than her show record was Bambi's producing legacy. Her five champion children include: Ch. Echo of Ebonwood, CD (1955), Ch. Cul-Mor's Kilcullen of Ebonwood (1958), sire of nine champions, and his litter sister, Ch. Cul-Mor's Babette of Ebonwood. Many of today's Smooth bloodlines can be traced to Ch. Belle Mount Bambi, CDX and her litter sister, Lulabelle of Belle Mount. They were influential in the development of modern Smooth Collies.

Irene Kneib (Glen Terrace) began in Collies in the 1930s and produced fifteen Rough and thirteen Smooth champions over the years. "That doesn't sound like a lot after fifty years," she says. "But we worked! We rarely got out of Southern California and there were never as many shows. We were lucky if there were five shows a year!"

Ch. Glen Terrace Blue Moon (1961) was Mrs. Kneib's best Smooth bitch. Bred by Mr. and Mrs. Donald Harper of Don Monte Kennels, she was the dam of seven Smooth champions, herself one of five sired by Glengyle Smooth Silver Flint out of Don Monte Joya Real, a tricolor Rough. Flint was by the Rough, Ch. Glen Terrace Silver Lining out of Ch. Solo From Shiel. Blue Moon made dog show news as part of an illustrious brace with her litter sister, Ch. Don Monte Joya Rival. At the 1964 Long Beach show she was one of the foursome that won Best Team in Show. Her daughter, Ch. Glen Terrace Half Moon (1963), by Pebble Ledge Legacy of Cul-Mor, and litter sisters Ch. Glen Terrace Blue Dorella and Joya Rival were the other members of the successful team. Mrs. Kneib's Ch. Glen Terrace El Rojo (1963), by Ch. Don Monte Señor Antonio out of Ch. Cul-Mor's Calpurnia, also made a lasting contribution to the Smooth Variety by siring five champions before he died at the early age of four.

Dr. Lee Ford (Shamrock): Dr. Ford believed in the potential of Smooth Collies as working dogs. Over thirty graduated as guide dogs for the blind, and her dogs earned over sixty obedience titles, putting the Smooth Collie in the limelight at a time when there were few fanciers. Ch. Shamrock Smooth Rocket, UD, bred by Dr. Ford and owned by Gail Thompson, was the first Collie champion of either Variety to earn the Utility degree. In addition to champions and obedience titleholders, he sired guide dogs and what are now known as assistance and therapy dogs, which received Specialty training to work with retarded and disabled children.

Myrtle Ackerman (Myrack): Myrtle Ackerman was another founding member of the American Smooth Collie Association who did a great deal to popularize the Variety. Because her first Smooth was a pound rescue, breeders would not allow their stud dogs to be used, but the descendants of She's An Old Smoothie included thirteen Myrack champions including

Myrtle Ackerman with Ch. Myrack Smooth Celebrity (1961), by Myrack Diplomatic Envoy ex Anna's Smooth Tammy of Myrack. Mrs. Ackerman was an effective, energetic supporter of the Smooth Variety during the 1950s and 1960s.

A memorable, winning team consisted of (from left) Ch. Don Monte Joya Rival, Ch. Glen Terrace Blue Moon, Ch. Glen Terrace Half Moon and Ch. Glen Terrace Blue Dorella. They are shown winning Best Team in Show at the 1964 Long Beach show under judge Major B. Godsol. *Ruml*

a CCA BOV; more than ten years later (1974) another descendant in tail-female was also BOV at the CCA Specialty.

Isabel Chamberlin (Coronation): Isabel Chamberlin established her kennel in Pennsylvania, and is now in California. She has bred and owned many champions in both varieties during her years in Collies, including the tricolor Rough, Ch. Kinmont Bobbie of Borco, sire of eleven champions. Her most famous Smooth was Ch. Glocamora Morning Mist (1963), a blue bitch by Coronation The Blue Saint out of Shamrock Smoothie O'Shadalon, bred by Vikki Highfield. Mist gained her title in 1964; along with Group placements and many Bests of Variety, including two at the Collie Club of America Specialty, she had several Bests of Opposite Sex to Best of Breed to her credit. She was the first Smooth to receive the coveted Ch. ToKalon's Blue Banner, CD bowl for the top winning blue merle of either Variety.

Coronation The Blue Saint was the great grandsire of Sombrero of Glocamora and sire of Hi Fi's Smooth Sugar, the parents of leading Smooth dam, Ch. Glocamora Evermore of Emboy. Ch. Coronation Gray Velvet, also a descendant of Blue Saint, was the dam of five Smooth champions. Ch. Coronation Tawny Trinket by the Hawk son Ch. Dorelaine Smooth Domino, was a multiple Specialty BOB winner.

Virginia Holtz (Cul-Mor): Following in Miss Haserot's footsteps, Virginia Holtz of Wisconsin has led Smooth breeders and the American Smooth Collie Association. Her Cul-Mor Collies have been preeminent in both varieties. Ch. Cul-Mor's Conspiratour was the first Rough to contribute in a major way to both; he sired twenty Rough and six Smooth champions.

A daughter, Ch. Cul-Mor's Portia, is the ancestor of Ch. David's Pride Hanover Special, dam of ten champions. Another daughter, Ch. Cul-Mor's Calpurnia, produced Ch. Cul-Mor's Autumn Haze, dam of Ch. Cul-Mor's Cordelia, one of a litter of five champions by Ch. Cul-Mor's Kilcullen of Ebonwood. Her son by Ch. Kirklyn's Bueprint was Ch. Cul-Mor's Bow Street Runner (1968), co-owned with Dorothy Kanter, sire of fifteen champions. From the Rough, Ch. Regaline's Blue Intuition, he produced for Michael Resnick Ch. Nostalgix the Changeling, dam of one Rough and six Smooth champions, and Ch. Nostalgix the Unholy Grail, dam of seven Smooth champions.

Another Bow daughter, Ch. Dokana Hoya, produced Ch. Verlor's Charmer of Lick Creek, dam of nearly a dozen champions for Vernon and Michael Esch of Illinois. Two of her daughters by the Rough, Ch. Suejim's Mr. Onederful, placed Best of Winners at the 1980 and 1981 National Specialty shows, the foundation of numerous Verlor champions. Michael and Tess Esch continue to breed successfully under the Signet prefix in Connecticut. Mr. Onederful, owned by Jim and Sue Karbatsch in Illinois, is also a leading Rough sire of Smooths, with 118, in addition to three Rough champions.

Cul-Mor's Birken Shaw (1966) was bred by Marion Koebel and Miss Holtz, and owned by Margaret Ulman. Sired by Ch. Cul-Mor's Loch Ness

Ch. Black Hawk of Kasan (1966), by the Rough Ch. High Man of Arrowhill ex Kasan's Fine and Fancy. Hawk was the first Smooth in history to win an American all-breed Best in Show, this at the York KC under William L. Kendrick, handler Leslie M. Canavan. *Shafer*

Beastie out of Ch. Cul-Mor's Sophie Western, she is one of the leading Smooth dams of all time, with eleven champions, ten in two litters by Ch. Black Hawk of Kasan. Best known were Ch. Cul-Mor's Maltese Falcon and Ch. Roydon's Miss Amanda of Jagwyn.

A NEW ERA FOR SMOOTHS—CH. BLACK HAWK OF KASAN (1966)

Among the eleven Smooths that finished in 1967 was Ch. Black Hawk of Kasan. Whelped in 1966, Hawk was bred by Sam and Ethel Singer and owned by Miss Sandra K. Tuttle in California. He was by the sable Rough, Ch. High Man of Arrowhill, out of Ch. Kasan's Fine And Fancy, a granddaughter of Ch. Glengyle Smooth Sailing.

Smooth history was irrevocably changed with the appearance of this big-bodied, sound moving tricolor from the West Coast. Hawk broke one record after another. He is the only Collie to win his Variety six times at the Collie Club of America Specialty show and, to date, the only Smooth to go BOB at the parent event. Hawk became the first Smooth to win an all-breed Best in Show *and* he is the leading producer of the breed with seventy-five champion offspring. Among Collies who have sired ten or more Smooth champions, in addition to Hawk, are two Hawk sons, Ch. Dorelaine Smooth

The Rough, Ch. Cul-Mor's Conspiratour (1958), by Ch. Teecumsee Temptor ex Cul-Mor's M'Lady Frolic. Bred and owned by Virginia Holtz, he sired 20 Rough and six Smooth champions and was one of the few sires influential in both varieties. The Smooth, Ch. Cul-Mor's Kilcullen O'Ebonwood (1958), by Ch. Bellochanty Belafonte, Rough, ex Ch. Pebble Ledge Bambi, sired nine Smooth champions and is found in many Smooth pedigrees.

Ch. Cul-Mor's Bow Street Runner (1968), by the Rough Ch. Kirklyn's Blueprint ex Ch. Cul-Mor's Cordelia, the sire of 15 Smooth champions. *Olson*

Domino and Ch. Firehawk of Kasan, and Ch. Scandia-Bayberry Night Hawk, whose dam is a Hawk daughter. Nine of the top Smooth dams show Hawk in their pedigrees. Hawk's influence was felt across the country when he was at stud in California with his owner and for a time in the East with his handler, Miss Leslie Canavan.

Hawk was more than just a great show dog or a prepotent sire. He interested people in Smooth Collies as they had never been before. Within a year the number of Smooth champions doubled. In five years over sixty Smooths finished and their number continued to climb until Smooths now surpass Roughs in the number that finish each year. Hawk put Smooth Collies into the showring—and made them contenders. Of all Hawk's achievements, his most lasting was the enthusiasm and interest in the Smooth Variety that he inspired wherever he went.

Marion Durholz (Jancada): For several years, Ch. Glocamora Evermore of Emboy (1967) was the leading producer among Smooth bitches with twelve champion offspring from five litters, ten of which were sired by Hawk. "Tawny" was bred by Vikki Highfield and Marjorie Prescott and was the foundation Smooth for Marion Durholz's Jancada Kennels in Maryland. Three of her daughters became top producing dams: Jancada Tender O'Kings

Valley (1973), dam of eight champions; her litter sister, Ch. Jancada The Wind Bird, dam of nine champions; and Ch. Jancada Blackbird, CD (1969), dam of six champions. In 1973 Marion Durholz won the CCA Breeder of the Year Award for breeding seven Smooth champions. In 1980 she won again as breeder of five Rough champions. She is the only person so far to have won the award in both varieties, which she continues to produce successfully.

Eva and Leslie Rappaport (Kings Valley): Oregon-based Eva and Leslie Rappaport founded their kennels in 1972 with Ch. King Valley's Hallellujah, CD, one of ten Smooth champions by the Rough, Ch. Blue Baron of Arrowhill. "Halley" was out of the Hawk daughter, Ch. Kasan's Katydid, and produced four champions, bred back to her grandsire. Ch. Kings Valley Hosannah was BOB at the Central Oklahoma Specialty in 1976 and her brother, Ch. The Pied Piper of Kings Valley, was Best of Winners and Best Smooth puppy at the CCA Specialty that year. The Rappaports' other foundation bitch, by Hawk out of Ch. Glocamora Evermore of Emboy, Jancada Tender of Kings Valley, produced ten champions. Their line continues successfully in both Roughs and Smooths through succeeding decades. The Kings Valley Collies are noted for having Breed, Obedience and Herding titles.

Mrs. Robert Werderman (Dorelaine): Mrs. Werderman, a veteran fancier from Long Island, bred the first Hawk champion, Dorelaine Smooth Domino, winner of the CCA junior sweepstakes in 1970 when his sire went Best of Breed. In addition to winning two Groups, Domino sired twelve champions including intervariety winners. Mrs. Werderman has been president of the Collie Club of America and is a Herding Group judge.

Scandia-Bayberry to Curtacy and Seawood: Ch. Scandia-Bayberry the New Look, a Hawk daughter owned by Janet Leek, was bred to Ch. Valley View's Whirlaway and among her champion offspring was Ch. Bayberry Lucretia of Genesis, foundation of Hannah Cook's Curtacy kennels. Her son, Ch. Curtacy Ebony Scene Stealer, produced eight champions in two litters. Her granddaughter, Ch. O'Corra's Jet Judy, was a multiple group and BOB winner.

Lucretia's litter brother, Ch. Scandia-Bayberry Night Hawk, sired seventeen champions and was BOS at the 1976 CCA Specialty show where his son, Kismet's Black Knight, was Best of Winners. Black Knight produced champions for Robert and Roberta Tedford of Massachusetts and his line continues through Nancy Greenwood's Oakhill Smooths.

Thelma Brown Spears (Skyline): An early Specialty winner was Ch. Skyline Captivating Smooth (1965), bred and owned by Thelma Brown Spears. Her granddaughter, Ch. Skyline A Star Is Born was bred to the Rough, Ch. Misty Valley's Cherokee, to produce the winner of the largest Smooth entry at a CCA Specialty to date—119 in 1978. Ch. Skyline Wooden Horse was the first Smooth to win two BIS, as well as more than ten Group firsts and 150 BOV. His son, Ch. McMaur's Diamond Jim, was BOV in 1981 and also an all-breed BIS winner.

Ch. Curtacy Swing Time, CD
(1975), by the Rough Ch.
Laurien Afterhours Blues ex Ch.
Bayberry Lucretia of Genesis.
Tehon

Ch. Curtacy Ebony Scene Stealer,
CD, a litter brother to Swing Time
and a successful sire in his own right.
Klein

Ch. O'Corra's Jet Judy
(1978), by Ch. O'Corra's
Blue Lightning ex the Rough
Clayland's Khe Serra (out of
Ch. Bayberry Lucretia of
Genesis) was a multiple
Group and Specialty
winner. *Tehon*

Marianne Murray (Ledge Rock): In 1976, Marianne Murray owned the first Smooth to take a Best of Opposite Sex to Best of Breed at the CCA. Bred by Judith Howansky, by Roydon's Struck with Thunder, out of Elmwood's Tantalizing Echo, Ch. Ledge Rock's Simply Smashing produced one Rough and eight Smooth champions. Her son, Ch. Christopher of Ledge Rock, owned by Alice Burhans, breeder of Ch. Bambi of Belle Mount, was the first Smooth to place in the Working Group at Westminster, going third in 1982.

The second Smooth bitch to go BOS to BOB at a CCA Specialty was the elegant tricolor, Ch. Windamere's Firstimever, bred by Susan Nance and owned by Emma Slusser. The dam of five champions, her son by Ch. Firehawk of Kasan, Ch. Romek's Trojin Masquerade, was Reserve at the same show. Her litter sister, Firstimever, has Specialty BOB wins as well. They were by Blue Haven Streaker, grandson of Ch. Cul-Mor's Bow Street Runner out of Windamere's Kanebriar Kachet, by Ch. Antrum Alltheway II.

Barbara and Mel Ridgway (Mel-Bar): The Mel Ridgways began in 1964 with two Collies from Drelms bloodlines. Their foundation bitch, Kasan's Show Me, came from Sandra Tuttle; from her they bred over twenty Smooth champions.

In 1972 history was made when Ch. Mel-Bar's Brandwyne Bobbi, CD (1968) won an all-breed BIS, the first Smooth bitch to accomplish this. She had two other Group placements and was the dam of ten Smooth champions. Bobbi was bred by the Ridgways and owned by Dianne Washburn. Her daughter, Ch. Mel-Bar's Mischief Maker O'K-Lor (1970), was BOB over 120 Roughs at the San Diego Collie Club Specialty. Mel-Bar's Kara Mia was the dam of five champions including Ch. Mel-Bar's Murmur In The Night (1975), BOV at the 1980 CCA Specialty. Ch. Mel-Bar's Kerry On, CD (1971) was also the dam of five champions. A blue son, Ch. Mel-Bar's Blu Streak (1974) built a strong record which included six Group placements. Ch. Mel-Bar's Powder Pouf O'Tremont, a blue Rough bitch owned by the Ridgways, and bred by Emma Slivkoff was BOS at the 1979 CCA Specialty show.

Fran and Carol Coleman (Merrytime): The Colemans of California finished the Rough Ch. Valley-Hi Tri Again (1959) in 1963. Bred by the Jensens, he was a son of their Ch. Lewellen Watch My Line, CD and became the first champion at Merrytime. Since then the Colemans have bred or owned numerous Rough and Smooth champions, including the leading sire Ch. Lisara Merrytime Rainmaker, sire of over twenty champions and a National Specialty BOV winner.

The Colemans' Smooth foundation was Pebble Ledge Generosity (1960), a daughter of Ch. Glengyle Smooth Sailing, purchased from Miss Haserot. They finished her in 1966 and bred her to Ch. Glen Terrace El Rojo, which produced Ch. Merrytime Merry Mary, whose daughter, Ch. Merrytime Felicity, is the dam of Ch. Jim Pat Copper Dust O'Merrytime (1971), sire of seventeen champions. He had fifty-four BOVs and six Group placements.

His litter brother, Ch. Lisara's Merrytime Drambuie, was owned by the Leonards and was the sire of thirteen champions.

Carmen and Larry Leonard (Lisara): Not until 1980 did another bitch surpass the record of Ch. Glocamora Evermore of Emboy. Ch. Lisara's Seaview Nightingale (1975), was bred by Florence Lippman and owned by the Leonards, then of California, now living in Illinois. The dam of thirteen champions, she was sired by the Rough, Ch. The Blue Baron of Arrowhill, out of Ch. Seaview's Lark O'Kasan, a Hawk daughter. Lark, bred by Sandra Tuttle and Florence Lippman was dam of one Rough and seven Smooth champions.

Ch. Lisara's Merrytime Drambuie, bred by the Colemans, sired six champions in two litters from the sable Rough, Tawny Miss of Glenayre. They then bred a Nightingale daughter, Ch. Lisara's Cover Girl, to the Rough, Ch. Windrift's Blue Knight. This combination produced Ch. Lisara's Afterknight Delight, dam of thirteen champions including one Rough. From breedings to Ch. Sunkist Midnight Flyer, Delight produced Am. & Can. Ch. Lisara's Morning After, known as "Dutch," and ten more champions, including one Rough.

Dutch is the dam of nine champions, including three Roughs, and winner of nine all-breed Bests in Show, fifty-three Group firsts and sixty-four other Group placements. She was Best of Breed over Roughs at sixteen Specialty shows and Best Opposite Sex at another fourteen. She was twice Best of Variety at the National Specialty and twice Best of Opposite sex to Best of Breed; she was also top Smooth in the United States on all systems for two years.

Dutch's Smooth son "Bear," Ch. Aryggeth Lisara Liaison, was BOS to his mother at the 1984 National Specialty and won two all-breed BIS. His daughter, Ch. Cortner's Two Timer o' Chris Mik, was also a National Specialty BOV (1984) and his son, Ch. Lisara's Once in a Blue Moon, was BOS in 1992, when he also won the stud dog class. Among those get was Ch. Lisara's Music of the Night, BOV at the 1993 Specialty and top winning Smooth all systems for 1992 and 1993 with ten Group Ones and five Specialty BOB. In all, Bear sired twenty-one champions including two Roughs. Ch. Lisara's Slick Chick is a multiple Group winner owned by Louann Young and Debbie Price.

Dutch's Rough son, Ch. Lisara's Knighty Knight, sired the 1991 National Specialty BOS Rough, Eddy and Lingenfelter's Ch. Glenorka's All Night Affair, and was grandsire of Ch. Lisara's Naughty Knight, 1992 CCA BOV Smooth owned by Rosalie Money and Kenneth Fallis.

Bred to her son, Ch. Lisara's Blueprint, Afterknight Delight produced Ch. Lisara's Merrytime Rainmaker, WD in 1986 and BOV at the 1989 National Specialty. He has sired twenty-four champions for Carol and Fran Coleman.

Additional Smooth winners bred by the Leonards include Ch. Lisara's Hanky Panky, Winners Bitch at the 1986 Centennial national and dam of ten champions including the 1992 BOV; her daughter Ch. Lisara's Oops a Daisy, winner of many Specialty Bests, Ch. Lisara's Shear Madness and Lisara Shear Magic. These last two have helped their owner, ten-year-old Randi Moore, win many Best Junior Showmanship honors and ten Best Brace in Show awards.

Suzanne Keehn and Pat Santaga Lessard (Storm): A daughter of Ch. May-Lor's Silver Spark, bred by Anna May Taylor, was the 1963 foundation of Storm Collies. Suzanne Keehn kept a Rough blue Spark daughter and bred her in 1975 to Ch. Black Hawk of Kasan, producing Ch. Storm's Silver Falcon. The other foundation line was a gift from the Turners, Robet's Smooth Party Doll, a sable which, bred to Storm's Silver Cloud produced the 1974 CCA WB, Ch. Storm's Rain Dance. Three years later, Silver Falcon was BOS, and since then there have been numerous other wins by Storm Collies at the National Specialty show.

A Tremont bitch of Brandwyne background was bred to Silver Falcon to produce Ch. Storm's Bright Notion. In her first litter by Ch. Sunkist Midnight Flyer she produced Am. & Can. Ch. Storm's Command Performance, sire of seventeen champions and BOW at the 1982 CCA Specialty. He produced two top-siring sons, Ch. Storm's TNT, owned by Jan Wollett, sire of twenty-four champions, and his younger brother, Ch. Storm's Grand Slam, sire of nineteen champions. Jan Wollett, Pat Lessard's sister, became a partner in the kennel in 1980. Grand Slam's sons include the BIS-winning Ch. Tedjoi D'Artagnan, third in the Westminster Herding Group in 1994, while TNT's noted get include Ch. Natural Explosion and Ch. Storm's Dancing in the Light, a multiple Specialty BOB winner and BOS at the 1995 CCA Specialty. These are among the hundred-plus champions produced at Storm in the past thirty years. Their Collies are noted for head and eye quality as well as elegance and arch of neck. In addition to the families mentioned here, Abbeyhill, Tempest and Nordic have benefitted by infusions of Storm inheritance.

Fred and Carol Schaub (Mareisridge) in Maryland owned Mareisridge Moonstone, whose influence continues through numerous lines today, was the foundation for this successful Maryland-based kennel. Her daughter Tara, by Ch. Wickmere Reveille, owned by Joyce Beddow, founded the Tedjoi line. One of five Moonstone champions by Hawk, Ch. Mareisridge Rippling Water, was bred to her half brother, Ch. Dorelaine Smooth Domino to produce Ch. Tedjoi Nightingale, dam of Ch. Shamont Drambuie and Ch. Shamont Black Orchid. Both have won over Roughs and Orchid is the dam of five champions. Drambuie has 100 BOV wins, and his daughter, Ch. Meridian's Taste of Honey, was also an intervariety winner for Barbara Pickrel of Ohio.

Joyce Beddow (Tedjoi): Purchased in 1967, Ch. Kimblewyck Tara of Tedjoi was the foundation for Tedjoi Kennels in Maryland. Her background was Wickmere, Hazeljane and the English Peterblue; she was BOW at the

Ch. Storm's Silver Falcon (1975-88), by Ch. Black Hawk of Kasan ex Keehn's Starshine, owned and bred by Suzanne Keehn. *Larsen*

Ch. Storm's T.N.T. (1983-94), by Ch. Storm's Command Performance ex Storm's Dyna-Mite, bred by Pat Lessard and Sue Keehn and owned by Jan Wollett. *Larsen*

Ch. Storm's Grand Slam, by Ch. Storm's Command Performance ex Storm's Moonshadows, CD, bred by Pat Lessard and Suzanne Keehn and co-owned by them with Joyce Beddow. *John Ashbey*

Am. & Can. Ch. Natural Explosion (1990), by Ch. Storm's T.N.T. ex Ch. Storm's Natural Spice. A top winner and noted sire, he was bred and is owned by Thomas and Sharon Frampton. *Bernard Kernan*

Ch. Storm's Dancing in the Light (1989), by Ch. Storm's T.N.T. ex Ch. Crossheart's Camlin Caper. Bred by Pat Lessard and Jan Wollett, and owned by Jan Wollett, she was Best of Opposite Sex to Best of Variety, at the 1995 CCA National Specialty. *Rich Bergman*

Ch. Christopher of Ledge Rock (1978) by the Rough Ch. Kimoke's Crusader ex Ch. Ledge Rock's Simply Smashing. He made history as the first of the Variety to place in the Working Group at Westminster, scoring a third. The year was 1982—one year before the Herding Group became established. The judge was Joe C. Tacker and co-owner Rebecca Burhans, who co-owned Christopher with her mother Alice Burhans, handled him to this great win. *Ashbey*

1968 CCA Specialty and first Smooth to place in an Eastern Working Group. Tara also passed along a strong producing ability. Her son Ch. Tedjoi Silver Knight, BOS at the 1976 national, sired five champions; Knight's son Ch. Tedjoi Gallant Squire fathered eight. Squire's son, Ch. Tedjoi Squire's Page, sired seven that became champions.

Going back to Wickmere for soundness and substance, thirty-one champions have been bred at Tedjoi. Ch. Storm's Grandslam, a top ten winner in 1987 and 1988, was brought in to add elegance, and has produced seventeen champions, six out of Group-winning Ch. Tedjoi Diamond Tiara. Their son, Ch. Tedjoi D'Artagnan owned by Duncan and Elizabeth Beiler, is a multiple Group and BIS winner, in turn sire of six champions out of Ch. Olympus Toresray Odessa. His brother, Ch. Tedjoi Rider on a Storm, bred back to Tiara's litter sister, Ch. Beech Tree Farm Encore, produced four champions including Ch. Beech Tree West Sunday's Child, a multiple Group placer.

Tom and Sharon Frampton (Natural Collies): The Framptons have created their own successful line of winning Smooths, also based on Storm lines. After several heartbreaking false starts, they acquired and finished Ch. Storm's Natural Spice, and bred her to Ch. Storm's TNT, the dog who had led to their enthusiasm for Smooths. The tri male, Ch. Natural Explosion, finished his championship at seven months with four Specialty majors, and went on to win over 150 BOV, four Specialty BOB and an all-breed Best in Show. In only five litters before his untimely death he has sired thirteen champions up to the time of this writing.

This review of other very successful breeders must also include Lynne Fox and Barbara McBride of Florida. Their Foxbride's Collies have produced numerous winners for others including Kilkerran, Cherica, Azalea Hill, and Glen Hill. Foxbride's Fairly Obvious was bred to Ch. Charmant's All That Jazz, resulting in multiple champions, most famous of which is Ch. Foxbride's McLaughlan, owned by Debbie and DeHaven Batchelor, DVM. He has sired over thirty Smooth champions, many with outstanding winning and producing records for the Batchelors' Olympus Collies and others. One of his dozen Specialty and Group winning offspring, Ch. Row-Bar's Southern Exposure, has been campaigned to top honors by her owners, Robette and Steve Johns.

THE SMOOTH-ROUGH POINT SCALE

While in some years more Smooth Collies have completed championships than have Roughs, and they are judged by the same Standard except for the paragraphs about coat, they receive points under very different scales. The number of Smooths required for a major has been rising steadily, but for 1995–96 it still takes only five dogs and six bitches in Division 2, the Northeast, compared to sixteen and eighteen, and five and seven in Division 9, California, compared to fourteen and sixteen Roughs. Smooth Collies have made great strides forward in quality; many are competitive with Roughs as increasing wins between varieties, in Group and Best in Show competition attest, but entries and enthusiasm among the general public are not yet equal.

Ideal type male Collie (full profile view).

Ideal type female Collie (full profile view).

Chapter 4

Official AKC Standard for the Collie

ROUGH

General Character—The Collie is a lithe, strong, responsive, active dog, carrying no useless timber, standing naturally straight and firm. The deep, moderately wide chest shows strength, the sloping shoulders and well-bent hocks indicate speed and grace, and the face shows high intelligence. The Collie presents an impressive, proud picture of true balance, each part being in harmonious proportion to every other part and to the whole. Except for the technical description that is essential to this Standard and without which no Standard for the guidance of breeders and judges is adequate, it could be stated simply that no part of the Collie ever seems to be out of proportion to any other part. Timidity, frailness, sullenness, viciousness, lack of animation, cumbersome appearance and lack of overall balance impair the general character.

Head—The head properties are of great importance. When considered in proportion to the size of the dog, the head is inclined to lightness and never appears massive. A heavy-headed dog lacks the necessary bright, alert, full-of-sense look that contributes so greatly to expression. In both front and profile view the head bears a general resemblance to a well blunted lean wedge, being smooth and clean in outline and nicely balanced in proportion. On the sides it tapers gradually and smoothly from the ears to the end of the black nose, without being flared out in backskull (cheeky) or pinched in muzzle ("snipey"). In profile view the top of the backskull and the top of the muzzle lie in two approximately parallel, straight planes of equal length, divided by a very slight but perceptible stop or break. A mid-point between the inside corners of the eyes (which is the center of a correctly placed stop) is the center of balance in length of head.

CORRECT FOREQUARTER ASSEMBLY (viewed from the side)

(Top) Shows the relationship of the bone structure to the outline of the forequarters. The various large bones and the groups of smaller bones are labeled with both their Latin names and the terminology in common usage.

(Middle) Detail drawing of forequarter angulation. The keystone of the forequarter assembly is the Scapula (shoulder blade), although it has no skeletal linkage with the Vertebrae (backbone) but is held in its flexible position by sheets of muscles and a few ligaments. (The dog has no collarbone.)

Approximately 67 to 70 percent of a Collie's weight is supported by and distributed equally between his or her forequarters—being directed to and concentrated on the "Vertical Center of Gravity" (shown on drawing by a solid line which intersects the axis of the shoulder and the center of the heel pad as it touches the ground when the dog is standing at ease). When the dog moves, the blade rotates through a small arc upon an imaginary pivot or axis. (The blade does not have an actual pin upon which to rotate, the axis being that point which remains stationary when the pull of the muscles controlling the forward and backward movement is equalized.)

The Scapula should be set on the Collie at an angle of 45 degrees (X) to the Horizontal when viewed from the side, and should slope downward from the highest elevation (d) to the shoulder joint (a) which is the junction of the shoulder blade with the upper arm, or Humerus. All that is meant by the expressions, "a good layback" or "shoulders well laid back," is that the slope of the shoulders should not be less than 45 or more than 50 degrees with reference to the Horizontal line. (Imaginary) An imaginary line extended from the top of the shoulder (d) and continuing through, or passing over, the Olecranon (elbow) should intersect the plane of the shoulder at 90 degrees to form angle "Y." This line is theoretical because the Humerus (upper arm) is not a straight bone, but the axis are parallel to each other and therefore parallel to the line shown.

The length of the Scapula (a-b) should equal the length of the Humerus (a-c). The angle of the attachment of the Radius-ulna (lower arm) is not important, provided the bones are straight and stand vertically as observed from either side or front. The pastern is sloped in order to place the heel pad directly under the center of gravity and to provide additional length of reach of foreleg and increase the gripping power and leverage of the foot.

It is difficult to measure the value of forequarter angulation when neither the bones nor angles can be seen, so the "Visional Approximation of the Center of Gravity" can be judged along the dotted line (d-e). The highest point of the shoulder should be in line with the rear section of the elbow joint and this line should strike the ground behind the heel pad as shown on the drawing.

In action, Collies conforming to these basic principles of forequarter angulation when observed from the side move correctly. (Assuming, of course, that the rear assembly is also correctly put together.) The reach, or stride, is long; the feet are lifted only far enough to clear the ground; the gait is smooth and even; and the ground is covered with a minimum of muscular effort.

(Bottom) Correct forequarters as observed in life.

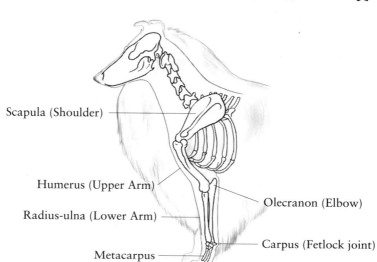

Scapula (Shoulder)

Humerus (Upper Arm)

Radius-ulna (Lower Arm)

Olecranon (Elbow)

Metacarpus

Carpus (Fetlock joint)

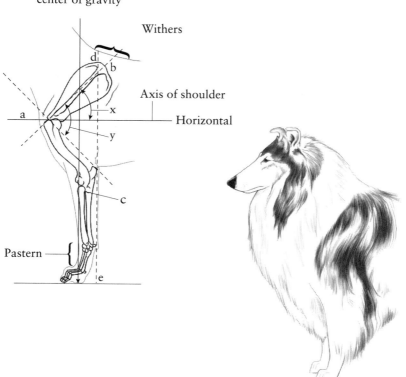

Vertical line of
center of gravity

Withers

Axis of shoulder

Horizontal

a

d b

x

y

c

Pastern

e

The end of the smooth, well-rounded muzzle is blunt but not square. The under jaw is strong, clean-cut and the depth of skull from the brow to the under part of the jaw is not excessive. The teeth are of good size, meeting in a scissors bite. Overshot or undershot jaws are undesirable, the latter being more severely penalized. There is a very slight prominence of the eyebrows. The backskull is flat, without receding either laterally or backward and the occipital bone is not highly peaked. The proper width of backskull necessarily depends upon the combined length of skull and muzzle and the width of the backskull is less than its length. Thus the correct width varies with the individual and is dependent upon the extent to which it is supported by length of muzzle. Because of the importance of the head characteristics, *prominent head faults are very severely penalized.*

Eyes—Because of the combination of the flat skull, the arched eyebrows, the slight stop and the rounded muzzle, the foreface must be chiseled to form a receptacle for the eyes and they are necessarily placed obliquely to give them the required forward outlook. Except for blue merles, they are required to be matched in color. They are almond shaped, of medium size and never properly appear to be large or prominent. The color is dark and the eye does not show a yellow ring or a sufficiently prominent haw to affect the dog's expression. The eyes have a clear, bright appearance, expressing intelligent inquisitiveness, particularly when the ears are drawn up and the dog is on the alert. In blue merles, dark brown eyes are preferable, but either or both eyes may be merle or china in color without specific penalty. A large, round, full eye seriously detracts from the desired "sweet" expression. *Eye faults are heavily penalized.*

Ears—The ears are in proportion to the size of the head and, if they are carried properly and unquestionably "break" naturally, are seldom too small. Large ears usually cannot be lifted correctly off the head, and even if lifted, they will be out of proportion to the size of the head. When in repose the ears are folded lengthwise and thrown back into the frill. On the alert they are drawn well up on the backskull and are carried about three-quarters erect, with about one-fourth of the ear tipping or "breaking" forward. *A dog with prick ears or low ears cannot show true expression and is penalized accordingly.*

Neck—The neck is firm, clean, muscular, sinewy and heavily frilled. It is fairly long, carried upright with a slight arch at the nape and imparts a proud, upstanding appearance showing off the frill.

Body—The body is firm, hard and muscular, a trifle long in proportion to the height. The ribs are well-rounded behind the well-sloped shoulders and the chest is deep, extending to the elbows. The back is strong and level, supported by powerful hips and thighs and the croup is sloped to give a well-rounded finish. The loin is powerful and slightly arched. *Noticeably fat dogs, or dogs in poor flesh, or with skin disease, or with no undercoat are out of condition and are moderately penalized accordingly.*

Legs—The forelegs are straight and muscular, with a fair amount of bone considering the size of the dog. A cumbersome appearance is undesirable. Both narrow and wide placement are penalized. The forearm is moderately fleshy and the pasterns are flexible but without weakness. The hind legs are less fleshy, muscular at the thighs, very sinewy and the hocks and stifles are well bent. *A cow hocked dog or a dog with straight stifles is penalized.* The comparatively small feet are approximately oval in shape. The soles are well padded and tough, and the toes are well arched and close together. When the Collie is not in motion the legs and feet are judged by allowing the dog to come to a natural stop in a standing position so that both the forelegs and the hind legs are placed well apart, with the feet extending straight forward. Excessive "posing" is undesirable.

Gait—Gait is sound. When the dog is moved at a slow trot toward an observer its straight front legs track comparatively close together at the ground. The front legs are not out at the elbows, do not "cross over," nor does the dog move with a choppy, pacing or rolling gait. When viewed from the rear the hind legs are straight, tracking comparatively close together at the ground. At a moderate trot the hind legs are powerful and propelling. Viewed from the side, the reasonably long, "reaching" stride is smooth and even, keeping the back line firm and level.

As the speed of the gait is increased the Collie single tracks, bringing the front legs inward in a straight line from the shoulder toward the center line of the body and the hind legs inward in a straight line from the hip toward the center line of the body. The gait suggests effortless speed combined with the dog's herding heritage, requiring it to be capable of changing its direction of travel almost instantaneously.

Tail—The tail is moderately long, the bone reaching to the hock joint or below. It is carried low when the dog is quiet, the end having an upward twist or "swirl." When gaited or when the dog is excited it is carried gaily but not over the back.

Coat—The well-fitting, proper-textured coat is the crowning glory of the Rough Variety of Collie. It is abundant except on the head and legs. The outcoat is straight and harsh to the touch. *A soft, open outcoat or a curly outcoat, regardless of quantity, is penalized.* The undercoat, however, is soft, furry and so close together that it is difficult to see the skin when the hair is parted. The coat is very abundant on the mane and frill. The face or mask is smooth. The forelegs are smooth and well feathered to the back of the pasterns. The hind legs are smooth below the hock joints.

Any feathering below the hocks is removed for the showring. The hair on the tail is very profuse and on the hips it is long and bushy. The texture, quantity and the extent to which the coat "fits the dog" are important points.

Color—The four recognized colors are "Sable and White," "Tricolor," "Blue Merle" and "White." There is no preference among them. The "Sable and White" is predominantly sable (a fawn sable color of varying shades from

CORRECT HINDQUARTER ASSEMBLY (viewed from the side)

(Top) Shows the relationship of the bone structure to the outline of the hindquarters. The various large bones and groups of smaller bones are labeled with both the Latin names and the terminology in common usage.

(Middle) Detail drawing of the correct hindquarter assembly which will provide the Collie with a maximum drive, lift and power for propulsion. The mechanical efficiency depends upon several features of angulation which experience has shown to be correct for the breed.

The hind leg is firmly attached to the skeletal framework through an articulated attachment to the Ilium (pelvis). The pelvis should be sloped at an angle of 30 degrees (Angle X) to the Horizontal as shown on the line (a-b). The axis of the Femur (thigh or upper leg) should intersect the pelvic slope at 90 degrees (Angle Y) as indicated by the typical axis line (c-d). The stifle, consisting of two bones, the Tibia and the Fibula, is articulated with the Femur and should be distinctly angled at the "stifle joint." (This is referred to as "good bend of stifle.") At the lower end, where it meets the hock "joint," the line of the stifle (o-f) should intersect the vertical line of the Hock-Metatarsus (g-h) at an angle of 45 to 50 degrees (Angle Z). The overall length of the stifle should at least equal the length of the thigh bone, and preferably should exceed it. ("Hocks well let down" is indicated by the shortness of the hock—i.e., close to the ground—in relation to the long stifle bone.)

Leverage exerted by the stifle and a short, straight hock, in action with the tendons and muscles, produces lifting action and, with the Femur, the power to move the Collie smoothly and without wasted muscular effort. (Assuming, of course, that the front quarters are also correctly "angulated.") When moving at a fast trot the combined forces reach maximum thrust along line "A" and not over the Center of Gravity "B" as might be supposed.

Line "A" dropped vertically from the Ischium (buttock) should parallel the inside of the hock and bisect the foot. This is the position assumed when the Collie stands "four square" at attention. When at ease, a Collie will often shift one or both feet up to the normal center of gravity. This is not to be confused with a bent or "sickle" hock which is an anatomical defect due to an abnormal curvature of the Metatarsal bones below the Os Calcis, or "hock joint." A "Sickle Hock" cannot be straightened by the dog when in action and is faulty because it opposes the principles of leverage.

(Bottom) Correct hindquarters as observed in life.

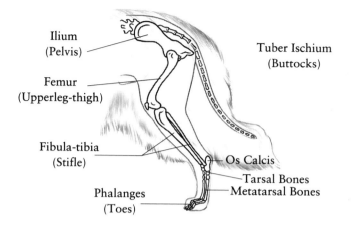

Ilium
(Pelvis)

Tuber Ischium
(Buttocks)

Femur
(Upperleg-thigh)

Fibula-tibia
(Stifle)

Os Calcis

Tarsal Bones

Metatarsal Bones

Phalanges
(Toes)

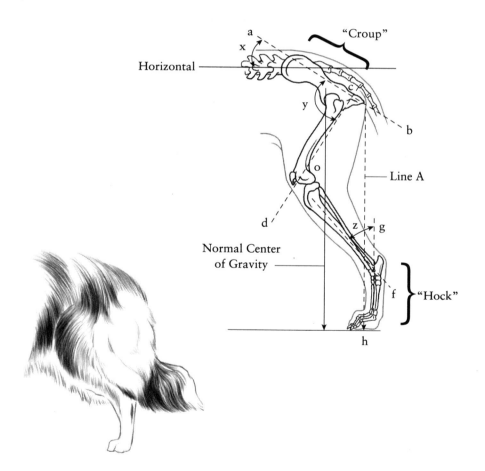

"Croup"

Horizontal

Line A

Normal Center
of Gravity

"Hock"

light gold to dark mahogany) with white markings usually on the chest, neck, legs, feet and the tip of the tail. A blaze may appear on the foreface or backskull or both. The "Tricolor" is predominantly black, carrying white markings as in a "Sable and White" and has tan shadings on and about the head and legs. The "Blue Merle" is a mottled or "marbled" color, predominantly blue-gray and black with white markings as in the "Sable and White" and usually has tan shadings as in the "Tricolor." The "White" is predominantly white, preferably with sable, tricolor or blue merle markings.

Size—Dogs are from 24 to 26 inches at the shoulder and weigh from 60 to 75 pounds. Bitches are from 22 to 24 inches at the shoulder, weighing from 50 to 65 pounds. *An undersize or an oversize Collie is penalized according to the extent to which the dog appears to be undersize or oversize.*

Expression—Expression is one of the most important points in considering the relative value of Collies. *Expression,* like the term "character," is difficult to define in words. It is not a fixed point as in color, weight or height and it is something the uninitiated can properly understand only by optical illustration. In general, however, it may be said to be the combined product of the shape and balance of the skull and muzzle; the placement, size, shape and color of the eye; and the position, size and carriage of the ears. An expression that shows sullenness or which is suggestive of any other breed is entirely foreign. The Collie cannot be judged properly until its expression has been carefully evaluated.

SMOOTH

The Smooth Variety of Collie is judged by the same Standard as the Rough Variety, except that the references to the quantity and the distribution of the coat are not applicable to the Smooth Variety, which has a short, hard, dense, flat coat of good texture, with an abundance of undercoat.

Approved May 10, 1977

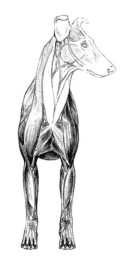
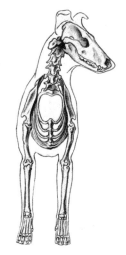

Correct front.   Superficial muscles of front.   Skeleton.

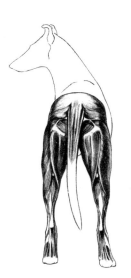
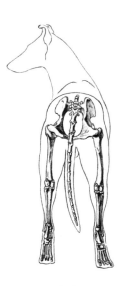

Correct rear.   Superficial muscles of rear.   Skeleton.

Correct front.

Narrow front.

Front too wide.

Out at elbows and
toes in.

"East-West" front.
Narrow and pinched
at elbows and chest;
feet turn out.

"Fiddle front." Legs
give bowed, weak
effect above pasterns,
turn out below.

Correct hocks.

"Spraddle" or bowed hocks.

"Cow hocks."

Narrow, weak rear.

THE BITE

A. Correct "Scissors Bite."
The upper front incisors slightly overlap the lower front incisors, and the inner surface of the upper incisors touch the outer surface of the lower incisors.

a. Detail Drawing of "Scissors Bite."

B. Even Bite (Incorrect).
In this bite the upper and lower incisors fit evenly one atop the other. This type of bite causes the incisors to wear down—in older dogs they may be clear to the gums.

C. Undershot Bite (Incorrect).
In this bite the lower front incisors project beyond the upper front incisors. Also, note that the alignment of all of the teeth may be affected. In counting the teeth in this diagram you might feel that one tooth is missing in the lower jaw—however, in the specimen used as model for this drawing all teeth were present, but the teeth are so out of line that the first molar is hidden from view by the upper canine tooth.

This type bite is most often found in connection with a "Roman" head or a "Roman" nose.

D. Overshot Bite (Incorrect). In this bite the upper front incisors project beyond the lower front incisors. The rest of the teeth may also be affected but usually not to the extent that they are in the "Undershot" mouth.

This type of bite is often, but not always, found in a head where the foreface is long in proportion to the rest of the head. Usually produces a "chinless" appearance.

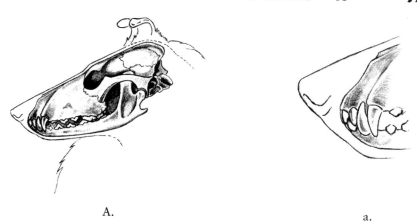

A.   a.

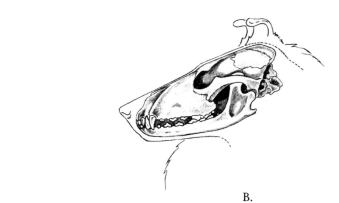

B.

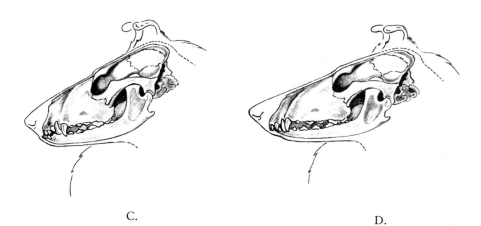

C.   D.

See page 80 for an explanation of these illustrations.

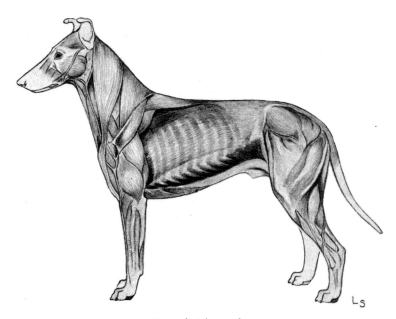

Superficial muscles.

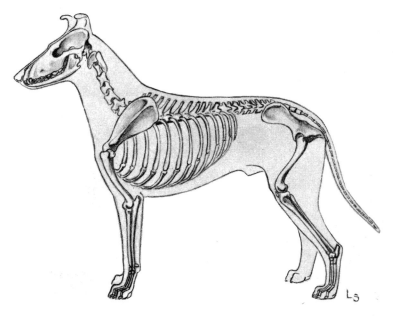

Skeleton.

Headstudy of ideal type Collie (profile view).

Head Faults (profile view)

 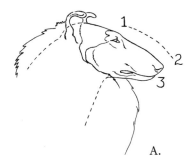

A.

A. Roman nose and undershot jaw. (1-2) Shows a pronounced arch of muzzle rather than desired straight line. (3) shows jutting out of lower jaw, produced by the lower incisors protruding beyond the upper. Commonly accompanies a "Roman Nose."

 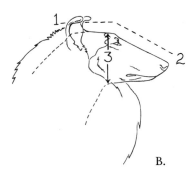

B.

B. Two-angled head. (1-2) Skull and muzzle form two lines at angles to one another instead of being approximately parallel. Also, produces a "deep through" the cheek effect (3).

 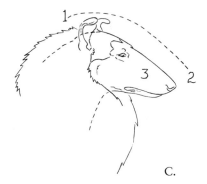

C.

C. Borzoi-type or foreign head. (1-2) The relation of skull to muzzle forms a curving effect throughout. Foreign to true Collie-type and reminiscent to another breed entirely. (3) Foreface too long in relation to skull.

Head Faults (profile view)

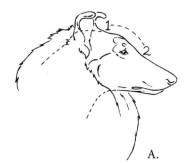

A. High over and between the eyes. A "lump" above and between the eyes (1-2) gives an "alligator"-like appearance to the head. Spoils the expression as well as the planes of the profile.

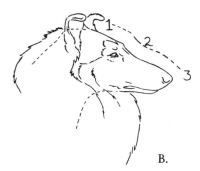

B. Wavy profile. Presents a wavy appearance rather than the desired straight line of the skull, slight drop at stop, then straight line of muzzle. Caused mostly by long stop (2), and a "drop-off" at the end of muzzle (3).

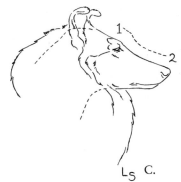

C. Dish face. Here the muzzle presents a scooped or "dished" effect (1-2) rather than the desired straight line.

Head Faults (profile view)

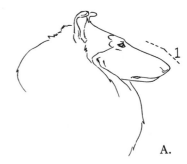

A. "Drop-off." A very acceptable head except for "drop-off" at the end of muzzle (1).

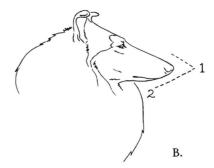

B. "Shark jaw." Here a lack of chin (2) gives a weak, "shark-jawed" effect to this head. Bite may be correct and fault lie in absence of chin, or it may accompany an overshot bite.

C. "Slack jaw." Here the lower jaw gives a slack and hanging effect (1). In the correct jawline the lower lip should fit tightly over the teeth and meet the upper lip. The "slack" lipped appearance often comes with old age.

Head Faults (profile view)

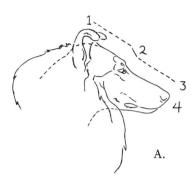

A. "Farm shepherd type." The head presents a "common" appearance. Too much stop (2) and a short, blunt muzzle (3-4).

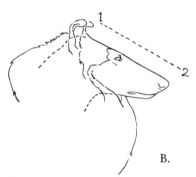

B. Straight line profile (No Stop). At first glance this appears to be a good type head, but close inspection reveals total absence of stop (1-2). The stop on a Collie is slight, but it should be there, nonetheless.

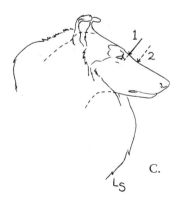

C. Long stop. The stop on this head is too far down the muzzle (dotted line 2). Correct location of stop should be at solid line (1).

REFERENCES

The drawings used in this chapter are from *Illustrations of the Collie, His Character and Conformation,* by Lorraine B. Still, Copyright © 1961 by the Collie Club of America.

The Collie Standard as prepared by the Collie Club of America, Inc., and approved by the American Kennel Club, Inc.

Calderon, W. Frank. *Animal Painting and Anatomy.* London: Seeley Service & Co., Ltd., 1975.

Cooley, B.B. *Structure of the Shetland Sheepdog and the Collie.* Issued by the Pacific Northwest Shetland Sheepdog Club, Inc.

Ellenberger, Baum and Dittrich. *An Atlas of Animal Anatomy for Artists.* New York: Dover Publications, Inc., 1956.

Lyon, McDowell. *The Dog in Action.* New York: Howell Book House, 1950.

THE A B C'S OF
COLLIE COAT
COLOR INHERITANCE

by Dot Gerth

The four basic coat colors in collies are sable, tricolor, blue merle and white. With certain crossings of the merle factor, two other colors can be produced . . . sable merles and defective white merles. Deviations from the normal due to mutations or linked recessive genes in certain individuals can also result in the lethal grays, the maltese, the sable faced tricolor, the chinchillas, etc. However, it is the purpose of this article to provide the reader with a simple reference chart concerning the more common color crosses as well as some of the less common crosses involving the merle factor. Thus, we shall eliminate the rarer combinations as well as genetic technicalities. The percentage ratios (1:1, 1:2:1, etc.) of the resulting POSSIBLE progeny are factual, but not necessarily a POSITIVE end result of each breeding as Nature's whimsies cannot be computer programmed due to the Laws of Chance.

For simplification, the following letters represent colors.

I. S . . . . . . SABLE, dominant over tricolor. Shadings may run from straw thru red to dark mahogany.

        a. PS . . . . PURE SABLE. Usually a clear shade of straw or orange red without dark masking or fringes. These individuals carry no tricolor gene and can produce only sable color regardless of what color is combined with them. (Charts I, II, III, X, XIV, XVI, XIX)

        b. ^{t}S . . . . TRIFACTORED SABLE. Sable collies carrying the tricolor gene in conjunction with the dominant sable gene. Usually (but not always) a dark orange to a very dark mahogany in color with dark masking and fringes. (Charts II, III, IV, V, IX)

II. tri . . . . . TRICOLOR, recessive to sable. Black collies with white and tan markings on sides of muzzle, above eyes, sides of checks, chest and inner margins of legs. (Charts II, IV, VI, VII, XI, XII, XV, XVII)

III. M . . . . . MERLE. A dominant dilution gene which in combination with sable or tri genes produces merled collies.

        a. BM . . . . Blue Merle. Bluish gray with black splotching, carrying sable markings in the same pattern as the tricolor. Color results from the interaction of the dominant dilution gene (M) with the tricolor gene (t). (Charts VII, VIII, IX, X, XVIII)

Chapter 5

Collie Breeding—Challenge and Reward

To the serious dog enthusiast, breeding to bring about improvement in his or her chosen breed is the ultimate gratification and the logical consequence of keeping fine animals. To the outsider looking in, breeding sometimes appears an easy way to earn extra income and, in some cases, to be one's main source of livelihood. But, as Oren D. Kem observes in this chapter, "It isn't that easy."

Breeding and raising fine Collies costs. This is an activity that represents large amounts of money spent and, more often than not, never recovered. Over and above the money factor, there is the matter of time and work. The amount of both components a serious Collie breeder devotes to producing and developing the next generation is staggering. It is not unusual for a breeder's ideal to be on the mental drawing board while its mother is still a puppy herself. Researching pedigrees, evaluating potential studs, arranging and consummating the actual mating, providing nine weeks of scrupulous care to the in-whelp bitch, all take time—lots of time. Whelping and raising a litter take time. Endless hours of observing puppies individually and as a group are imperative to select a future standard-bearer, and once that selection is made, more time and effort are needed to hone and polish the youngster from a silly puppy to a regal show dog.

But to the truly dedicated breeder and Collie lover, seeing his own creation standing alone in the winner's circle is worth all the time, work, money and frequent tears involved. That's the way it is with all creative endeavors.

Breeding Collies successfully requires proper physical facilities, and a knowledge of genetics and canine husbandry. This is truly a challenging way of investing one's time, but it's also rewarding in the sense that the breeder

Ch. Cainbrooke Clear Call (1937), by Royal Majesty II ex Corogal Joan, by Ch. Cock Robin of Arken, was the dam of seven champions—four in one litter by Lodestone Landstar.

Ch. Kitsap's Shadow O'Shane (1961), by Ch. Sandamac's Mr. Sandman ex Collevoy's Kit-N-Kaboodle, was a Best in Show winner and dam of five champions. *Horton*

is repaid by his partnership with nature in the creation of living beauty. Perhaps it is this last reward that keeps the true breeder at it year after year and what inspired great Collie fanciers of yesterday to lay the foundation for the genetic picture of both Varieties for their modern counterparts to work with now.

IT ISN'T THAT EASY

by Oren D. Kem

Everyone is exposed to Mendel and his green and yellow peas in Biology II these days. How simple the laws of inheritance appear. They beckon us to put them into operation, Colliewise. Apply a few simple rules and you're in. Mate best to best. Then clean up your bad recessives. Very simple. Those old chaps floundering around . . . they must be really dumb . . . or maybe so kennel blind they can't see the mess they're making. Yeah. We thought that, too. Speedily we find out that while there are many simple dominant and recessive traits, much more time should have been spent on those few embarrassed paragraphs, minus all the fancy formulas and mathematical proofs, entitled *Incomplete Dominance,* and half-hidden toward the end of the book. These attempt to account for the exceptions to the ironclad rules . . . explain why you don't *always* get the black and white of dominant and recessive but rather the various shades of gray. Why the higher mammals don't always bound from extreme to extreme like the famous peas but rather tend to move sluggishly in between. Sometimes they behave suspiciously as they were supposed to do in that heresy called *Law of Blending Inheritance.* One suddenly realizes that breeding is more like playing the slide trombone than choosing between previously truly tuned notes and chords on a piano.

An excellent example to use at the start is the average sable Collie with a mask and contrast and a white collar. This is very far from being a "pure color"—being a brindle and a piebald brindle or roan at that. And a roan is the classical example of incomplete dominance—where two colors mix instead of one being dominant and apparent and the other recessive and hidden. The piebald factor is an erratic factor that can never be tamed down to giving duplicates of markings by any known method of breeding, but continues to break collars and hearts of breeders by its freaks.

There are other methods that vary the beginning simple formulas. Instead of two genes, length of rabbit's ears are controlled by six genes, each one making the ears twenty millimeters longer or shorter, depending on whether it is a "long" or "short" type gene (other animals' lengths, breadths and measurements are possibly controlled by a similar process). Or consider the "good disposition." It is the happy balance of all the genes of intelligence, nervous and glandular systems and even the digestive system. But one bad gene can spoil the whole balanced structure.

Top: Ch. Two Jay's Hanover Enterprise (1966), by Ch. Parader's Country Squire ex Ch. Cul-Mor's Highland Holly. *Susan Larson*

Right: Ch. Tartanside the Gladiator (1969), by Ch. Hi Vu The Invader ex Tartanside Tiara. *Susan Larson* These two dogs are among the breed's leading sires with numerous champions in both varieties.

Enough of warnings of complexity. The purpose is to persuade that breeding is not like a railway system where payment of fare puts one aboard a surely-moving, timetabled freight or express according to the cost. It is rather like the sea, apparently trackless, yet with prevailing winds and currents that reward keen study and observation with startlingly fast progress in full sight of others becalmed. Most geneticists freely admit only the general rules of their craft apply to large show mammals—experience and observation must supply the rest.

The first requirement of a capable breeder is the ability to recognize a good Collie. He or she cannot measure his or her material or progress otherwise. He or she will soon see that the ideal Collie has on each side extremes from which it has been compounded, virtues modified and kept, faults cast away. He or she will also run into the practical difficulty that the faults and virtues of the extremes are hard to separate and that most good dogs lean to one extreme or another as these points have been only partially separated. Let's look at the two obvious extremes and their groups of interlocked good and bad qualities. The old-fashioned or common type is first—look at pre-1890 pictures of typical Collies. These are closer to the ground and cobbier in body, usually heavier coated with a tendency to short neck, broad coarse skull, light muzzle but relatively good profile and stop. Their eyes often inclined to be large and light and ears were often wide and even heavy.

The other extreme is the foreign extreme type, tending to be rangy and slab-sided, lighter in coat, generally easier in movement and more stylish. Head is longer, sides cleaned up with a stronger, smoother muzzle and underjaw but much more inclined to a full stop, Roman nose and receding skull. Thus the ideal type is a balance between the two in some ways, and in others the virtues of one side held intact. We want some of the size, style and freer gait of the extreme dog to combine with the better rib, loin and coat of the conservative Victorian model. The length, cleanness and stability with age of the extreme dog's head needs combination with the better profile, balance and stop of the older type. From this description you can readily see why all the experts implore the budding breeder *not* to go overboard in his or her affection for one particular point. This infatuation may well blind him to the whole train of attendant evils that come along, barring strenuous efforts to prevent them. Balance is the crowning achievement of the breeder's skill. If you get hepped up on gait, you will find that the narrow bodied, light-boned dogs that are active and "hard keepers" move easiest and give fewer gait faults—but look at the other headaches. If you go all out for flat skulls, you'll also end up with wide skulls, and if elegantly lean, clean-sided heads are your passion, watch for skulls that are likely to recede and stops that fill up. The competition at the present time is so keen that no one dares deliberately sacrifice for single points and still expect to win.

Ch. GinGeor Bellbrooke's Choice (1960), by Bellbrooke's Master Pilot ex Gayheart Golden Miss, is the sire of twenty-eight Rough and two Smooth champions.

Ch. Twin Creek's True Grit (1977), by Ch. Lochlomun's Interlock ex Ch. Lee Aire's Amazing Grace, is the sire of forty-five Rough and two Smooth champions.

No matter what system in regard to ancestry you use: in-, out- or line-breeding—you have a choice of breeding together Collies that look alike, or breeding some degree of opposites. You can see that breeding like to like will probably bring you to one of the extremes sooner or later. That is the reason an inbred mutant is so valuable to stop the drift and hold the line in balance. The history of the breed has related a series of famous balanced dogs—Collies from matings of opposites that have hit the middle equilibrium. These have often been mated to like dogs and have founded "lines," until

Ch. Laurien Afterhours Blues (1972), by Ch. Clelland's Blue Yonder ex Laurien Black Satin, sired nine Rough and five Smooth champions.

Ch. Lewellen Cali-Collaire (1952), by Ch. Lewellen Summer Escapade, CD ex Parader's Grand Girl, the sire of eighteen Rough champions.

a definite drift to an extreme has appeared, at which time another "unlike cross" was needed to bring them back into midstream again. The success of this matter of balance is what appeals to the old-time breeder or judge— not matters of trifles of color: dirty sables, rusty tris, white haws or funny markings or other similar points, which deserve consideration only when, in exaggerated form, they damage the dog's beauty.

Mating opposites does not work well with many individual points. Low ears to high ears usually is a disastrous mating. Ears are complex. Proper carriage is a matter of shape, size, texture, placement, temperament, not to mention environment. A bad rear should be analyzed and improved by a mating stressing excellence in the weak points. Rarely does mating of two faults create a virtue.

The broader one's knowledge of the type in an individual Collie's ancestry and the type of its siblings and other offspring, the better one can choose a proper mate. Obviously, no formula for mass-producing champions will be offered. It is enough to urge use of the best obtainable foundation and formation of a sharply focused, well-balanced picture of the ideal Collie in one's own mind early in the program, and constant acquisition and digestion of all information not only on one's own Collies but on all Collies. Fortune may give you one great dog or even one great litter, but skill can keep marching a steady procession of good ones.

THE BROOD BITCH

by Mrs. George H. (Bobbee) Roos

It takes imagination to create anything of significance and lasting importance in dogs. It also takes patience, strength and perseverance. Quality can dissipate rapidly when the breeder can see no further than his or her own kennel or the current show season. Those who look forward to posterity are usually the ones who looked first to their dogs' ancestors. Answers to many questions and problems can be found in the past.

In the 1933 *Collie Club of America Yearbook*, Dr. O. P. Bennett included these observations in an article, "Collie Bloodlines":

> Some years ago I prepared and published an Ancestral Tree of Leading Collies, Past and Present. Considerable work was entailed in its preparation and in making a study of the various dogs, the names of which appeared therein. I gained a great deal of information which made me feel that in our calculations we give altogether too much credit and place altogether too much importance to the male line in our breeding operations. Perhaps it would be more correct to state that I do not believe sufficient significance was placed on the female line.

In order to get a correct opinion of the value of any dog, the name of which appears in any genealogical scheme, one must know more about the females he was bred to and be better informed about the dams of the sires carrying on such a tree. It is my honest opinion that much of the good found in certain Collies can be more properly attributed to their dams than to their sires. As an example I mention a dog which I own. Ch. Alstead Eden Emerald, which report goes, has sired more champions than any dog living. He was sired by Ch. Poplar Perfection and Perfection was sired by Ch. Magnet. Emerald's dam was Ch. Eden Elenora, one of the most perfect Collies seen in England for many years. While Perfection was a good dog, even superior to his sire Magnet, neither compared in quality to Emerald's dam, Elenora. Is it quite fair to attribute all of the good in Emerald or even most of it to his sire or grandsire rather than to his dam? Many such instances could be mentioned.

Instruction and advice to those joining the ranks of breeders is to search for a good female from a good line. Choosing wisely and then breeding astutely reduces uncertainty to a minimum.

From many years of experience, Mrs. Benjamin Butler of Kinmont Kennels comments:

We say to a young breeder. "Go buy the best bitch you can find." But what is that? How do you define best? For all our pontificating, there is such an element of luck involved! Star of Arrowhill, for example, was in Florence Cummings' words a plain bitch; in mine, a good, honest bitch. Her sister had the style to burn, the showmanship—a good show bitch. Yet of the two it was Star who was the real producer, having large litters of incredibly uniform quality. From Star came Arrowhill Ace High, one of the great producers of the decade, Ch. Kinmont Kiltie and Ch. Kinmont's Enchanted Flame. There were other lovely Collies from her not so well known. She produced not only champions but outstanding Collies. Her sister had breeding problems and I do not believe she produced anything of note. Yet if one could have had either of the two bitches, one would have almost automatically taken the better show prospect.

If I were buying a good brood bitch today. I would want one that was linebred or inbred from a good producing line that came from a strain or branch of a strain which produced good-sized litters without whelping difficulties, that had normal seasons and were not breeding problems. I would rather breed from a bitch with one or two faults and heavy plusses than from a bitch who was indifferently correct.

Another contemporary, Oren D. Kem of Lodestone, covered "The Importance of the Brood Bitch" in a special article for the 1957 *Collie Club of America Yearbook*. The following excerpt adds significance to Mrs. Butler's opening remarks:

When we go to outline the ideal brood matron, defined in terms other than those of past proven successes, terms by which anyone should be able to recognize her on sight, we run into great difficulty. No matter how she is defined in absolute terms like large or small, someone can and no doubt will bring up an outstanding example of a matron who has done extremely well and is opposite in every direction from our description. All kinds have turned the trick just as (and because) there are all kinds of studs which have produced winners.

Some say top brood matrons should themselves be champions or capable of winning the title. Ch. Halbury Jean of Arken and Ch. Cainbrooke Clear Call are outstanding examples of great winners producing a great number of winning offspring. Yet when one considers the number of champions and show bitches bred to Ch. Honeybrook Big Parade, and then stops to think that the line of descent from him most prominent today is through Silhouette of Silver Ho (who was no top show dog) it becomes clear that we cannot be dogmatic on the point. Percentages may favor the likelihood of getting a winner out of a winner more often than from a nonwinner, but the exceptions are so numerous and respectable that we cannot insist on the point as a hard and fast rule.

Ch. Magnet is accepted by most as the most influential sire of this century but neither his sire nor his dam were champions and we cannot recall offhand, from a rather wide browsing through Collie writing and conversation, anyone commenting on their type or saying they had seen them at a show. Presumably they were obscurities on an island where no deserving Collie needed to stay obscure.

One final point: these more obscure Collies were *not* common Collies from common breeding. They were close up in breeding to the top dogs of their time. You cannot make a silk purse from a sow's ear—quality has to come from somewhere, and not spontaneous combustion. A Collie with extreme qualities and a few faults may not show so well as it produces, but it will bring lots of useful things with it to any mating.

Mrs. William H. Long, Jr. of Noranda Kennels was asked to present her views on "The Importance of the Brood Bitch" at the 1960 Seminar of the Collie Club of Maryland. Mrs. Long emphasized some of the doctrinal statements made by so many of our well-known predecessors and added some of her own personal theories, as follows:

The importance of the bitch as a producer for the kennel cannot be emphasized too strongly. She controls the overall type to be found in any given kennel. Out of her each time she is bred comes the stock to go on with. If the first sire used is not a success, another can be used and so on until we have found the quality of our bitch *plus* the quality for which we bred. There is nothing to prevent the kennel from keeping males, potential show and stud dogs, but beware the kennel that cannot show you a line of bitches, important bitches that have produced their like with added improvements. This does not necessarily mean champion bitches, but it does imply bitches of championship quality. The job of a stud is to add a given quality with positive assurance. The asset of a good bitch is to be able to absorb that quality and add it to the growing list of good points in her puppies. With a good bitch and today's easy transportation, no stud is out of reach.

Whether we think in terms of a kennel of thirty bitches, or the owner of three, there is the same opportunity to create. With bitches we can do just that. The framework of the Standard is written as a yardstick, not, thank goodness, like the specifications for a house with so many feet here and the cube there. Each one of us has a mental picture of what the words of the Standard mean. We can, within general bounds, create our own image, emphasize the points we appreciate, mold our ideal.

Don Lyons, in a speech before the Tri-State Symposium in 1959 made the biggest little statement I have heard in a long time, and I quote, "If there is one stark truth in all this business of breeding, it is this—there is no easy way." Nor, may I add, is there only one way. Two of the biggest winners I have ever had were the products of chance, not thought. The first owed its actual sire to the fact that the planned sire had eaten a rabbit and was more concerned with his queasy stomach than the business in hand. The other was the well-known hole in the fence! When we have a stud dog, we are committed to him, for better or worse, and we acquire our bitches with him in mind. But the owner of a bitch has the stud force of the country at his disposal, and has a chance to learn from his mistakes and try to correct them all within the life expectancy of one bitch.

Mrs. Long was a close friend of Mrs. Florence Cummings of the Arrowhill Kennels. Mrs. Cummings was as generous with her time and advice as she was with words of praise for those who had helped her. She was still active in Collies at the time of her death, which has left a permanent void. Her life spanned over half a century in breeding and exhibiting Collies and many of her personal letters were kept and savored by recipients because they contained such philosophical comments as:

When someone comes saying they want to start breeding Collies and want a good bitch, I always ask them if they want to start showing and winning— in other words, become an exhibitor—or if they want to build a line of truly fine Collies. There is a great difference, and the two ends are attained by entirely different methods. Much, much more thought, care and dedication, *and* time is needed being a breeder than in becoming an exhibitor.

Mrs. Clara Lunt taught me a brood bitch was the most important thing in any breeding program. I have always followed this rule very closely and never use a bitch that could not go in the ring and win in good competition. She must also be in top physical condition and of very sound disposition. I am talking about long-range breeding, not getting a flyer or two for showing. This can happen from two poor ones, but in long-range breeding or building up a line, the result is only as good as each dog in it. Mrs. Long always said I had the best bitches in the country and sent me no end of customers wanting good brood bitches for a good start in Collies.

A winning family from 1970: (from left) Ch. Arrowhill Bee Beautiful (Ch. Parader's Country Squire ex Promise of Arrowhill) owned and handled by Nina Campbell; her son Ch. Arrowhill Oklahoma Tornado (by Ch. Cul-Mor's Conspiratour), handled by Jo Buckingham; his son Ch. Sunnyhill Mr. Hershey and daughter Ch. Sunnyhill Dyanne's Delight (out of Ch. Sunnyhill Dyanne), owned and handled by Lawrence and Bonnie Schwed. The judge, Mrs. Florence Cummings, stands behind the group. *Don Petrulis*

Ch. Tartanside th' Critic's Choice (Ch. Tartanside Heir Apparent ex Ch. Briarhill Midnight High), bred by Terri Pattison and owned by John Buddie. As of the mid-1990s, he is the leading sire of the breed with over fifty Rough champions to his credit as this book goes to press. *Krook*

It is not difficult to breed a champion. The difficulty comes in keeping it up year after year. Look at your ads—new kennel names, advertising the best in the world, etc., and in two years this kennel is gone, never heard of again.

Aspiring breeders may overlook a potential breeding prospect or even a show specimen because of minor faults. During sessions of reminiscing, there are always stories of the good one that got away. One that could top the list appeared in the August, 1964 issue of *Paw Prints* when Editor Claudia Schroder asked Stephen Field for information to eulogize Ch. Parader's Bold Venture:

> Venture's dam was Parader's Cinderella, winner of the bitch division of the Collie Club of America Futurity and of two five-point majors. Cinderella was once sold by Field to a breeder who rejected her because of one prick ear and a light haw. A few weeks after her return to Parader Kennels, she whelped Ch. Parader's Bold Venture and Ch. Parader's Dancing Girl!

Mrs. Robert Hamilton addressed the ACCONEUS Collie College in Niantic, Connecticut in 1962. Mrs. Hamilton related events leading up to the creation of the foundation American Collie families:

> While Strongheart was the dominant American sire of his day, he did not create a producing tail-male line which, to my knowledge at least, has survived. His two most interesting sons were Ch. Bellhaven Stronghold and Ch. Bellhaven Bigheart. It is through Stronghold that the Strongheart tail-male line descended furthest and strongest. Stronghold himself sired five champions including a litter with three in it out of a bitch named Beauty Girl V. Beauty Girl V goes back in her pedigree to King Hector in tail-male lines of her parents and her maternal granddam goes back to King Hector in both of hers. Bigheart sired a single champion, Poplar Playboy out of Ch. Alstead Aida. In this same litter we find the bitch, Gaily Arrayed of Arken, who was to become the dam of Ch. El Troubadour of Arken. The interesting point here is that Stronghold was in one of the three-champion litters sired by Strongheart (the Seedley Solution litter of 1923) and Bigheart was in the other champion litter of three whelped in 1924 out of Nowdrop. This is an interesting example of the *transmission of quality through litters where there is a concentration of quality.*

THE IMPORTANCE OF THE BITCH IN THE BREEDING PROGRAM

by Tom Coen

My advice to others has always been to look to the dams of stud dogs. Tail-male charts are interesting, but they leave out a very important element of the story, and that is the bitch. It is the bitch who provides the complement to the sire and determines the distinction among his offspring, in both quality and producing ability.

Breeding dogs is a creative process that combines the eye of the artist with the laws of nature. Also included must be a large measure of common sense. Breeding dogs is a process of building generation after generation, of constantly gaining in one area and losing in another. The breeder is like a juggler trying to keep the pins for correct type, stable temperament and good health all in the air at the same time. The bitch is the building block utilized in the process of creative breeding.

When selecting a foundation bitch or planning a breeding, there is one principle I have witnessed as law. *As ye sow, so shall ye reap.* If you don't want something to show up, don't start with it or add it to the gene pool. Recessive problems will slip by through lack of information, but knowingly adding a serious problem to your program shows no common sense. You may try to close your eyes to something, but Mother Nature will provide a wake-up call at some point up the road. Quirks of temperament, tendencies toward physical weakness and reproductive problems are inherited as well as physical characteristics.

Not all show bitches are great brood bitches. We had a multiple Best In Show bitch who looked as if she would be a tremendous producer as well. She had exceptional quality, substance, and great attitude. We bred her several times and each time she whelped perfectly formed but stillborn puppies. This was particularly frustrating since we could feel movement a few days earlier. Trying to outsmart Mother Nature, we had a Caesarean section performed several days prior to her next due date. We saved one bitch puppy, which was bred and produced a beautiful daughter who finished easily. When this bitch was bred, she whelped litters of perfectly formed, stillborn puppies. This was our wake-up call, and the bitch was culled. Keep in mind that tendency toward skin and thyroid problems and bloat are also heritable.

When evaluating a bitch from a breeding standpoint there are several key areas to consider: health, temperament, physical quality (phenotype) and pedigree (genotype). The ideal bitch should be an easy keeper and doer. A hearty appetite that keeps her in good flesh with no coaxing is of great importance. A bitch who won't eat, especially when she has a new litter depending on her, is not well suited to motherhood and can make your life miserable. Avoid bitches from families that require medication and supplementation to maintain condition and fertility. The goal is to produce healthy, good-sized litters to provide selection within a creative breeding program and to keep the process as natural as possible. Veterinary medicine has become quite sophisticated in the area of reproduction. Thyroid medication and hormone therapy make it possible for bitches who would not ordinarily do so to come into season and produce litters. There are tests to monitor silent or irregular seasons to pinpoint ovulation so that problem bitches can

Ch. Highcroft Quintessence, (1985) bred by Sandy Prazak and owned by Leslie Viken Jeszewski, holds the all-time record as the top-producing dam in breed history with thirteen champions. She is by Twin Creeks Hot Property ex Sarellen's Adventuress, CDX.

Ch. Tartanside Animation, (Ch. Sealore's Grand Applause ex Tartanside Caress), bred and owned by John G. Buddie, is the dam of six champions. *Joe C*

Ch. Starberry Belle of Georgia (1979), owned and bred by Jennifer Futh Deneault, is by Ch. Hanover's Flaming Legend ex Starberry Rachel, Rachel. Belle was Winners Bitch at the CCA Specialty and scored a Specialty Best of Breed from the classes. *Connolly*

conceive and produce offspring. Although it is impressive that we can over-come Mother Nature, I question the benefit in the long run. Do we really want what are now considered irregularities to be the norm? If we continue such seeming triumphs over nature, all naturalness of the reproductive pro-cess and vigor of the breeding force will be lost.

Ideally, the bitch should be as free as possible from hereditary defects. In this area, common sense should be employed. Don't breed bitches with eye disorders such as entropion, or with family histories of testicle problems, bad hips or a long list of woes unless you are willing to deal with more of the same.

The ideal bitch possesses a stable, sensible temperament with intelligence and trainability. These qualities of correct breed character not only make good show dogs but are what has drawn the pet-buying public to the Collie for years. The bitch is the role model for the puppies, and in temperament counts for more than her genetic 50 percent. There is no excuse or place in a breed-ing program for a shy, flighty or nervous Collie bitch.

When selecting for physical quality it is important to keep in mind which qualities are most difficult to achieve and maintain. While not every bitch can be a Halbury Jean, purchase of a foundation bitch requires extensive study, followed by careful thought and selection. This is not the time to become frugal. Go for the very best bitch you can find, as she can save you years of disappointment, frustration and wasted time.

Head qualities are of great importance in the brood bitch. All will have some deficiencies, but degree of fault must be considered. It is extremely difficult to correct severe lack of skull, snipey muzzle, depth, lippiness and certain bite problems. Be wary of a narrow underjaw, missing premolars and inverted molars. The virtue of flat frontal bone, clean sides to the skull, tight lip line and roundness of muzzle will definitely increase your chance of producing exceptional quality. The greater the degree of virtue your bitch possesses, the better are your chances of producing a great one from her.

It is almost impossible to radically change body type and structure through breeding in only a few generations. Therefore it is necessary to select and maintain bitches who approach your mental picture of the ideal described by the Standard. Correct body type is a matter of proportion and angles of the skeletal structure. While abundant coat is a real plus in a breeding program for Roughs and can enhance a good outline, it is still only the icing on the cake. It is what is under the coat that is important, i.e., arch of neck, strong back, well-laid-back shoulders, long stifles, good definition of the hock joint and sloping croup. These are the qualities an ideal bitch would possess, that create the picture of correct Collie type, standing and in motion. It is these qualities that make individuals stand out in the huge classes at the National Specialty. Since soundness and elegance are priorities in our program, we continually select for curvaceous and sweeping body lines, with deeper angulation and more neck. Just as the head naturally reverts to commonness, so do body and outline.

Unless you have had firsthand experience with the dogs in a pedigree, the document is of little more value than a list of names. With study, a pedigree becomes a valuable tool for creating and predicting quality. Nowhere on the pedigree does it say which dogs were strong producers and which were producers of problems that still haunt us. The title of Champion means little when evaluating producing ability.

It is your responsibility to study and research individuals and family lines and to choose those whose "look" appeals to you and whose shortcomings you can abide. The qualities a bitch possesses should reflect the qualities of her ancestors. She should be the physical demonstration of her pedigree. Bitches who are the exception for a family rather than the rule cannot be counted on for predictability.

It is impossible to place a value on a bitch of extreme virtue and strength of pedigree without taking into account breeder judgment. However, when used in a creative way by an astute breeder, it would be fair to say that her value is nothing less than the future of the Collie.

Chapter 6

Influence of the Showring

Some Collie fanciers regard the showring as the arena in which to gratify their competitive urges, while others look on the showring as the place to bring their young stock to be evaluated by an impartial expert. The first mentioned is primarily interested in competition for the sake of winning prizes; for the pleasure of owning the winning dog. The second shows to measure the results of his breeding program against that of other breeders.

The reason the Collie owner exhibits is less important than the fact that the shows exert a tremendous influence on the breed. Recognizing the potential for influencing future generations will help any fancier get more from any level of participation in any form of dog show competition.

The lure of the shows is like a siren's song. It beckons invitingly, tempting the fancier with its carnival-like atmosphere. This is a stage upon which one can strut for the price of an entry fee. How much further the exhibitor takes his or her level of participation is a personal choice. Few people come into showing and remain with it all their lives. Many more take up the sport for only a few years, giving it up when immediate success is not forthcoming or when the allure and novelty wear off.

For the "lasters," showing dogs never loses its aura of excitement. There's always a new puppy to bring out, a new judge to try, and the company of a host of companions from far and near, representing lifetime friendships and a meaningful human relationship in a personally rewarding sport/hobby.

SELECTING THE BEST COLLIE PUPPY

by Stephen J. Field

Ability to anticipate and evaluate probable show quality of Collie puppies at an early age is an important attribute of the successful breeder. Nothing can bankrupt a kennel faster than indefinitely supporting scores of half-grown

Sheyne as a puppy.

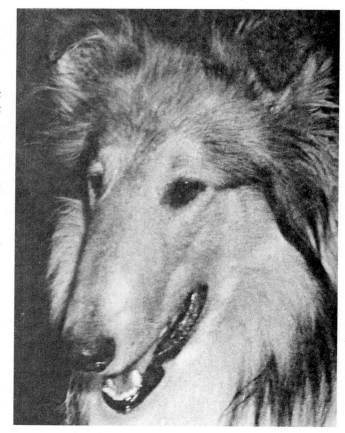

Ch. Kinmont Sheyne as an adult (1946), by Ch. Parader's Golden Image ex Ch. Parader's Pamela. Sheyne's get includes Ch. Country Lane's M'Liss, 1960 CCA Specialty Best of Breed; Ch. Kinmont Kerry, a BIS winner; and Arrowhill Ace High, a sire of 16 champions. *Johnson*

pups that should have been sold as pets during the roly-poly two-month stage. Nothing can destroy confidence in a breeder like unqualified, glowing promises of future quality that never can materialize. Any serious breeder should produce a percentage of puppies that rate above pet level of quality, and it is to the advantage of buyer as well as seller that these puppies be as accurately evaluated as possible at an early age. Needless to say, no system for predicting future quality of Collie pups is 100 percent accurate and no fair-minded buyer of a puppy has a right to expect it to be completely accurate. But here are a few observations that will help:

1. Although individuals may rise above mediocrity of origin, such specimens are the exception rather than the rule. Do not look for top prospects in a litter unless the quality and breeding of parents and grandparents and the skill with which they are mated to correct their faults will warrant high expectations. Pups from common parents frequently show promise at two and three months, but, as they mature, the gap widens and the pups from the better parents develop into better specimens.

2. Study the good and bad points of both parents, and consider them in evaluating the pups. For example, if one parent tends to coarseness, I would view a heavy-headed puppy with more concern than if parents and grandparents did not have this fault. If cow hocks are a family characteristic, I surely would inspect all pups more carefully for bone structure and movement than if the bloodline were noted for soundness.

3. Have a definite aim in mind as to type and as to what you wish to improve, correct, or emphasize. If your bloodline is shy of coat, you will pay more attention to that. If heads need improvement, pay attention to head properties. If eyes need improvement, you can usually select the pups with the best eyes at two or three months of age. Emphasize color if you want to, but that is not the way to improve show quality. Perhaps no puppy in the litter will excel in all features and you will not find the perfect puppy any more than you will find the perfect grown Collie. However, one thing is quite sure—you will be disappointed in development more often than pleasantly surprised, so avoid over-optimism or you will eventually be due for a let-down.

4. Color is not as important in the selection of Collies as in some other breeds. Personally, I do not pay as much attention to color in a female pup as in a male that might later be used at stud. Full, white collars are not necessary. Neither are regular white markings on front legs. Large white spots on the body are undesirable unless you intend to breed for white. At present there is a prejudice against the large uneven blaze in face or on muzzle, but there is nothing in the Standard against such markings and I think discrimination against the blaze is justified only to the extent that

the blaze might detract from proper Collie expression. A narrow blaze properly centered should be no handicap. Blazes in face or on muzzle usually narrow as the pup gets older.

Proper color in blue merles and also proper marking of white pups will be considered more important than in sables and tricolors. The Collie Standard does not imply that great emphasis should be placed on color, but, in actual practice, you will find that dark masks on sables, rich tan cheek markings on tricolors, and other features of color that add to beauty and proper expression will be of value. At least it is something that can be recognized in a relative way, at an early age. However, color shade can change—usually for the better—especially in sables. Many of the beautiful mahogany sable Collies were drab "grizzled-sable" pups at three months of age. Color at the five, six, and seven month stages is usually lighter than it will be at maturity. For example, Collies that are golden sable at four months will be orange sables at maturity. This is a point that is hard to convey to the novice: Color should not be given too much emphasis in evaluation when making a selection for show type.

5. It is surprising in how many litters the best pup can be selected at a glance, strictly on the basis of general appearance. The best pup need not be the largest, but special attention should be given to the bold, friendly, alert, vigorous fellow, with style of posture and with a long, stand-out coat, good rib spring, and good legs that are free from cow hocks or evidence of rickets. Especially important is the sweet eye and expression that just radiates personality. It is virtually impossible to list all the head properties that influence expression, but if you have an eye for a Collie, you will know good expression when you see it. Examine such a pup carefully, keep your eye on him as he develops, and unless you find some very bad features such as poor skull, poor eyes, monorchidism or cryptorchidism, do not drop the pup from consideration.

6. Unless the bloodline is noted for undersize—and very few are—you need not disqualify a puppy for being below average in size. But one fault I wish to caution against is a peculiar type of genetic, dwarf quality often associated with a head far too refined, occasionally with small beady eyes with poor sight, and bone far too light. Such pups can be detected at whelping by the expert and at three months are evident to anyone. The sooner they are eliminated the better. The condition is a recessive characteristic and can be produced by normal-size parents. Fortunately, this fault appears early, so it can be eliminated easily.

7. The shy puppy can be detected early, especially if the bloodline or parents suggest a history of the same fault. Be sure to penalize shyness heavily in evaluation of any puppy. Try a few weeks of kindness and special attention with shy ones, for many will respond to special love and attention. If they do not, then they are of no value even as pets, much less for show

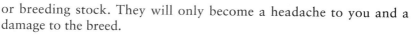

or breeding stock. They will only become a headache to you and a damage to the breed.

8. Eyes can often be evaluated as early as three weeks of age. They seldom improve. Color of the haws can often be observed at three weeks by noting presence or absence of dark pigment on the rim of the haw. Small dark haws are desirable but not necessary. Shape and placement and color of eyes can be better evaluated at two or three months of age. Most successful breeders place a great deal of emphasis on eyes, because eyes are the key to correct expression. The eye should be dark and not too large or full; neither should it be too "piggy" or round. It is possible for eyes to be too small and beady, but the opposite extreme of too great size and fullness also seems common. The merled eye is permissible in blue merles but is not desired. A good eye is difficult to describe, although the better judges know it when they see it. Breeders would do well to cultivate the ability to recognize the sweet, attractive, true Collie expression that is dependent on proper size, placement, shape, and color of eyes.

9. Evaluation of skull and muzzle is most important and, unfortunately, most difficult. Regardless of claims to the contrary, no bloodline is pure genetically for perfect skulls and there will be variations. Consider the parents and ancestors as well as the individual puppy in making predictions on head properties. Some bloodlines tend to keep good skulls through puppy stages—other bloodlines show good indication of backskull development at three months of age, then recede in skull during the fourth through seventh months, but then improve later on. Improvement of skulls usually continues until the dog reaches one year of age, and in some bloodlines until two years. In other bloodlines coarseness of skull may appear after one year, or receding backskulls may never be corrected. At birth, head properties should be observed. Oblong heads, suggestive of a brick placed on edge, are usually preferable, though there will, of course, be some tapering to the nose. A blunt, well-rounded nose is preferable to a snippy, "shark-pointed" head. Tight cheek bones are preferable to protruding ones, especially in lines where you might expect to encounter coarseness. The profile of the head of a newborn pup should be fairly flat, free from highness over eyes, and free from receding ("fall-off") of backskull.

When the pup is two or three months of age, the head properties should be observed again. If the head is not promising then, it probably never will be good. The backskull should be free from marked receding and the muzzle should be quite full and well rounded, almost like a little stove pipe, fairly blunt at the end. Beware of muzzles that are too full or arched, and avoid highness over the eyes. Remember that muzzles may appear satisfactory at three months of age and become "Roman" later on.

Many Collies are too long in foreface, and unless the head is balanced properly at three months of age, it will seldom be balanced later. Heads will lengthen with age, so pups that appear too stubby in head at three months usually will be nicely balanced at maturity. Pups that appear too fine at three months usually will be entirely too fine at maturity. The puppy with a fine, snippy muzzle seldom matures into a quality Collie. Accuracy in evaluation of heads depends somewhat on familiarity with family patterns of development.

10. Most bloodlines have a greater tendency toward overshot than toward undershot mouths. Pups with blunt, short muzzles naturally are less likely to become overshot in bite. A high percentage of pups will go one-eighth inch or more overshot during the third-through-seventh month stage and then even out to the scissors bite. So do not be alarmed provided the upper jaw does not protrude more than one-eighth inch in half-grown pups. I have seen mouths one-fourth inch overshot that evened out properly to a scissors bite at maturity. The shark muzzle is to be avoided, regardless of whether the bite is overshot or not.

11. Ear properties are the result of at least six hereditary or genetic factors (size of ear, shape of ear, placement of ear, texture of ear, temperament of dog, growth of hair on the end of the ear). Also, ears are influenced by numerous environmental factors (injury, ear mites, training of ears, and possibly feeding and exercise). These complicating factors, plus the fact that final ear carriage is not determined until a rather late age, imply that ear carriage is difficult to predict. Placement that is fairly high on the skull is desired and can often be observed very early. At three months of age I prefer to see ears that have raised somewhat, tips arched up and over, but breaking lower than one would desire on a grown Collie. Perfect ears at three months are likely to be prick ears at maturity. In a bloodline inclined to slack or low ears, beware of large ears that are hanging flat and low at two months of age.

Many ears that are poorly carried at four, five, or six months of age may still be satisfactory at maturity. Ear pattern of parents and grandparents is about as accurate a means of prediction of ears as study of three-month-old pups. Both are subject to great error. However, if the puppy is good enough in quality, it is worthwhile to spend some time in legitimate forms of ear training. Most ears go through some bad stages, especially during teething age.

12. At two to three months of age, an abundance of long, coarse guard hairs on the back and chest is an indication the puppy may mature into a heavy coated Collie. After four months, these guard hairs seem to be lost. The puppy coat at ten months should be abundant and not too fine in texture and should fit the body contour properly. Texture will often be too fine or slightly wavy the first year, and color (of sable particularly) may

lack richness the first year. These faults often improve by the third year. Second-year coats, especially in males, may sometimes be inferior in quantity to first-year coats. This may be due to lack of condition or other indirect factors.

Bear in mind that the perfect Collie has yet to be whelped, and most selections of "promising" pups develop into disappointments. Do not plan to breed or buy Collie puppies unless you are emotionally capable of adjusting to such disappointments, yet will still keep enough enthusiasm so you will try again. If you can improve one or two features each generation and occasionally produce an outstanding show winner, you may properly consider yourself a successful Collie breeder.

THE COLLIE IN THE SHOWRING

by John Buddie

While little can be done genetically to make a large eye small or a short head long, a good handler has the ability to bring out the best in his dog. He can transform a sullen expression to one that sparkles or a drab outline to one of elegance. Showing a dog to his best advantage is an art that can be easily learned, and it can make the difference between a good dog and a great one.

Early Training—The Formative Months

The first step in establishing owner/handler rapport occurs in the whelping box where the puppies become accustomed to being picked up and played with. As the puppies grow older, they learn to respond to your voice. Later training sessions with lead and collar cement the final bond between puppy and handler.

Bringing a puppy into the house will enhance its outlook on life and prevent it from becoming panic stricken at its first indoor show. It is in these familiar surroundings that a puppy should first learn basic ring manners.

On these frequent visits indoors begin to train the puppy to "bait," or stand foursquare and bring up his ears for a tidbit. You can use table scraps or boiled liver for this. A readily-available, dehydrated liver product is excellent to keep on hand. It does away with the odor and inconvenience of cooking fresh liver at regular intervals.

Leadbreaking

Twelve weeks is an ideal time to begin leadbreaking. The easiest method is first to introduce the puppy to the choke collar. These collars are manufactured in various lengths and thicknesses of nylon or chain. The collar you choose should be of the lightest weight and have about two inches extra length

High Man as a young dog.

Ch. High Man of Arrowhill at eight years (1959), by Arrowhill Ace High, by Sheyne, ex Arrowhill Janie of Crag Crest. High Man sired the legendary Smooth, Ch. Black Hawk of Kasan. *MikRon*

to accommodate growth. Let the puppy wear it for several days before you put the lead on.

For its first venture on the lead, let the puppy take charge; let it go wherever it chooses. Later teach the puppy to respond by giving gentle tugs on the lead. Encourage the puppy with your voice to go in the direction you want. A bit of food can also be an incentive, but never, under any circumstances, drag the puppy or use force in training.

Make your training sessions fun, with lots of praise. Train your puppy to walk on a loose lead at your left side. The puppy should also be taught to put up its ears and set itself up in a foursquare position when bait is presented.

Remember throughout these early months of training that Collies are intelligent and responsive. Praise is important. The puppy should always be rewarded, either verbally or with food, when it has done well. A harsh word, in most cases, is all that is necessary if the puppy has done something wrong. To strike a puppy or continually jerk it around on a lead can demolish any rapport you have established, and ruin the puppy for showing.

The Grooming Table

The puppy should also learn good manners on the grooming table. There is no greater frustration than to take a puppy to a show and have it writhe in mock agony when it is lifted onto the table to be groomed. Getting a puppy accustomed to the grooming table is as integral a part of training as leadbreaking.

The puppy should learn to stand to have its whiskers clipped, its feet trimmed and all other necessary preparations for the showring. It is helpful to have someone hold the puppy while you concentrate on grooming. Start with short sessions, making the puppy hold still for only a few minutes at a time. Use abundant praise and rewards when the puppy does well and it will soon look forward to these grooming sessions.

Match Shows

Match shows are excellent experiences for both puppy and handler. Entries can be made on the day of the show and while actual show conditions are simulated, the atmosphere tends to be more informal than "point" shows. All events sanctioned by the American Kennel Club are governed by AKC rules, and it becomes very important to learn them. Write for a free copy of *Rules and Regulations Applying to Registration and Dog Shows* from the AKC, 51 Madison Avenue, New York, NY 10010.

Match shows accustom puppies to what they will experience at point shows both indoor and out: loud noises, crowds, stairs, slippery floors, mats and, of course, being examined by a judge.

Some clubs also sponsor handling classes, another excellent training opportunity for dog and handler. If you are interested, ask an active fancier in your area where such a class is being offered.

Conspiratour at age six months.

Ch. Cul-Mor's Conspiratour (1958) as an adult, a dog that exerted a tremendous impact as a producer of quality in both varieties.

Gwyneth at five and a half months.

Ch. Rudh'Re's Gae Gwyneth at two years, by Ch. Cul-Mor's Conspiratour ex Rudh'Re's Shiel Bri. *Olson*

Short, frequent trips in the car are important to help your puppy adjust to traveling as well as to new people and surroundings. Car breaking gets your puppy over travel distress before you begin to show him.

Knowing When to Show

Many people think of handling solely in terms of knowing the tricks of the trade. They completely overlook the most vital aspect: knowing *when* to show.

A dog is ready to win when it is in full bloom, its head is completely developed, it is in good weight and physical condition and it has that sparkle that makes it stand out. It is rare to see a professional handler showing a dog that is not ready to win.

The waiting game is the most frustrating aspect of showing dogs. Many people leave the sport because they lack patience and perseverance. Quality dogs are taken out before they are ready to win and their owners become easily discouraged.

There is no generalization about the best time to show a dog. Every family develops differently. One bloodline, for instance, is noted for having a fully-matured, heavy coated puppy flyer at eight months while another bloodline shows signs of receding skulls and lack of coat at the same age. At two years the latter is fully matured and ready to win. It would be ill-advised to push this dog as a yearling.

Condition is extremely important. As your young hopeful is growing it must continue to receive a balanced diet and regular checks for parasites. Your puppy should be kept in top physical shape and its coat—its crowning glory—must be maintained in luxurious form. The best dogs, regardless of their quality, are not worth the price of an entry fee if they are not in top condition.

For some reason first impressions tend to leave a giant mark in the minds of breeders. A bad first impression becomes a lasting one no matter how well the dog develops later on. Therefore, taking out a potential stud dog when it is not ready to win may turn off future potential stud services to the dog. Do not subject your dog to needless defeat and criticism due to lack of maturity and condition. Leave it at home, let it grow and coat up. Then take the dog out and campaign it fearlessly against all comers.

Your Collie's First Point Show

Entries for point shows must be made prior to the closing date—usually two and a half weeks prior to the show. Write to the superintendents listed in the bibliography for premium lists of the shows in your area. The premium list will include names, addresses and assignments of judges, location, prizes, entry forms and other pertinent information about the show. By now you should also be thoroughly familiar with AKC requirements for each of the classes.

Mediator at eight weeks.

Ch. Berridale Mac-Dega Mediator as an adult (1973), by Ch. Tartanside The Gladiator ex Ch. Glen Hill Silver Lace. His two most celebrated offspring were Ch. Tam-isett's Golden Dream and Ch. Shamont Stormalong. *Gilbert*

It is a good idea to go to a few point shows prior to entering as you can see if your dog measures up to the competition.

Remember that the judge is there to see the dog, not the handler. A good handler is as inconspicuous as possible. Dress accordingly; be modest in what you wear in both style and color, so you don't distract the judge from viewing your entry—which is the real reason you are present.

Get your dog to the show early. Give it plenty of time to adjust and feel at ease. It is a good idea to feed your dog only lightly the night before so it will be responsive to bait and not get carsick. Carry fresh tap water from home or bottled spring water with you to shows. Water to which your dog is unaccustomed may upset its system and cause diarrhea.

Allow yourself a solid hour for grooming. This means, aside from driving time, you should include twenty minutes in your schedule to unload your gear and park as well. Be at the ring promptly at the scheduled judging time.

Unless the judge requests everyone to assemble in numerical or catalog order according to armbands, it is up to you whether you get into the ring first or last. Usually it doesn't matter, but there are times when being first or last into the ring has its advantages.

If your dog tends to chase the tail in front of it, try to be first so it has no other dog to follow. If your dog is distracted by dogs behind it, try to be last into the ring. If your dog needs time to feel at ease before beginning to show, being last will allow you extra time to work with the dog while the judge is going over the other entries.

Ring Procedure: What Is the Judge Looking For?

When evaluating a class the judge looks for different things. An allover picture is the most important. When the dogs first walk into the ring this is what the judge wants to see. It is important to have your dog present an elegant, graceful picture of balance. This is *not* the time to worry about little things like a hair out of place or a flying ear. Get your entry standing foursquare and showing off, first.

After looking at the overall picture the judge will ask exhibitors to gait the dogs. Listen carefully for the direction in which he or she asks you to move. Always keep your dog between you and the judge. Collies should be moved on a loose lead—never on a tight lead. If your dog tends to pace, take a few short steps in one direction, then quickly and suddenly change direction. This will eliminate the pacing problem if you catch the dog off guard.

It is easy to find a dog's fault in the ring when a handler continually draws attention to it. For example, if you are constantly setting up a dog's front, the judge will know you are trying to cover up something. You are drawing attention to the fault.

Animation is important. Collies were not meant to stand like statues and stare at liver as if they suffered from malnutrition. They must show that they are full of life and interested in their surroundings.

Be sure you know where the judge is at all times and know what he or she is looking for every moment. Should the judge make a noise, he or she wants to see your dog's expression, so turn your dog toward him or her. Don't stand between the judge and your Collie so that the judge is forced to peek over your shoulder or walk around you.

Some dogs are natural show dogs. They don't need to be baited because they show all the time for noises or people around the ring. If your dog will do this, don't distract him with liver. Let your dog show itself off. This same advice applies to a dog which shows for liver but is suddenly distracted by a noise outside the ring. If a noise attracts your dog's attention and draws its ears up, take advantage of the situation and capitalize on its showmanship.

Accent the Positive

By now you should have established an individualized style of showmanship. Each dog has its own faults and virtues. You want to accent the positive and minimize the negative. Knowing your dog's good points and being honest about its bad ones is an advantage. While a competent judge will usually find a dog's faults, at least he or she does not have to stare at them throughout the judging.

If your dog is strong in expression but wavy in profile, show it on a three-quarter view, showing its expression as much as you can. If your dog is too large in eye but excels in good stop, flat backskull and clean lipline, show it in full profile. If your dog's eye is too large or too light, try baiting it with its head angled down. This will help to make its eyes look more oblique. For an eye that is not dark, stand the dog in front of you with the light directly behind you. This will cast a shadow over its face and shadow the lightness of the eye. At outdoor events, show your dog with its back to the sun; its eyebrows will cast a shadow.

If your dog is not in full coat, lacks belly hair or depth of brisket, never show it with the light directly behind it. This will exaggerate its height. Show your dog directly into the light and try to keep it from presenting a full profile view of its body.

A knowledge of judges and their tastes is helpful in planning the campaign of your dog. Find out as much about as many Collie judges as possible. *The American Kennel Gazette* and other breed publications listed in the bibliography carry show reports. These will give you an idea of what type of dog or bloodline judges prefer. Try to learn which judge will appreciate your dog and show under him or her. If you are not showing, visit as many shows as possible to watch the judges and learn their preferences.

If you feel your dog is ready, campaign it to the fullest. As one famous breeder remarked. "You can't win if you don't show." If your dog is well on its way to its title, keep it going. Bitches should not be retired for litters or males for any reason when they are only a few points away from their championships. Many things can go awry while waiting for a new coat to grow. Some dogs only sparkle in full bloom during one coat season.

Ch. Stoneypoint Spartacus (1972), by Ch. Antrum Alltheway II ex Mistyvale Doll O'Stoneypoint, the sire of seven Rough champions.

Ch. Stoneypoint Stalwart (1975), by Ch. Merrill's Honest Abe, by Spartacus, ex Stoneypoint Merry Hill Gypsy, the sire of four Rough champions. *Schley*

When showing males, be wary of bitches in season. They will cause most males to stop showing and begin sniffing around the floor trying to pick up the scent. A drop of vanilla extract on the end of the male's nose will help eliminate this problem. It also helps with dogs that drop their heads to the ground in search of food.

There has always been a controversy over whether champions are born or made. I prefer to believe it is a combination of both. While many puppies are chosen as potential champions, if they are not given proper feeding, grooming, handling and ring exposure, they are going to fall by the wayside.

An owner who familiarizes him- or herself with all aspects of the showring, who knows his or her dog's virtues and faults and who advantageously makes use of both in showing, can make the difference between a good show career and a great one.

GROOMING THE COLLIE

by Rosslyn Durham

Collie breeders and handlers are becoming increasingly conscious of the value of proper grooming for the showring. An average Collie can look good and a good Collie can look great when the coat is skillfully prepared.

In close competition, presentation is often an important factor— sometimes even the deciding one!

Collies do not require excessive trimming nor should they be subjected to it. Trimming on the head is done to achieve a light, neat look. The head should never appear to have been freshly trimmed, and should look as if the hair grew that way naturally, untouched by scissors.

Before Trimming

Before you begin trimming, you must know all your Collie's strengths and weaknesses. The words of the Collie Standard must be so familiar that a mental picture of the perfect Collie is formed in your mind. Look at your dog and note how it meets the requirements of the Standard. Learn where your dog excels and where it is weak in head properties. In trimming the head you will accentuate your dog's best qualities and minimize weaker areas. Always work in a positive fashion when you groom. Every Collie has some good features. Your job is to make them more prominent.

Your first experimental trimming should be done on a dog not being shown. Once the hair is removed, it cannot be replaced. It is much better to undertrim the dog the first time and do a little more trimming the next, than to take too much hair off at once.

The dog should be placed on a sturdy table with its head at your eye level. Be sure your table is on firm footing so the dog feels secure. You will probably want a helper to hold and steady the muzzle so you will have both hands free to trim or you can invest in a proper grooming table fitted with a ribbed rubber top and an adjustable grooming arm with collar. This arrangement will be comfortable for the dog and allow you the freedom of both hands if you are working alone.

Have all your tools close by: a very fine-toothed comb, a pair of sharply tapered barber shears, double-edged thinning shears, blunt-edged curved scissors and a stripping knife.

The head is the first major objective in trimming the Collie. Study your dog's head before you begin. Get its ears alert so you can make a mental note of the areas needing the most attention. Remember that trimming will not eliminate your dog's faults, it will only minimize them. The appearance of a properly-thinned head will last several weeks, and require just a little smoothing work with a stripping knife as new undercoat grows in.

Trimming the Ears

The ears are the most essential part of trimming the head. Their size, shape, set and carriage will determine how they are trimmed. The finished ear, correctly carried and well used, is, with the eye, the determining feature for correct Collie expression. The finished ear should not look closely stripped. It will be soft in appearance, gently rounded at the tip and free of ragged hairs coming from the back or sides.

Ear carriage will create impressions of head qualities, whether or not they are actually present. For instance, a high, tightly set ear will give the impression of an excellent backskull. Low-tipping, wide set ears give the head a heavy, common look.

For normal, properly set ears, begin by inserting the fingers of your free hand into the ear and cupping it as it will be held when alert. Fold down the tiny flap of skin at the inner base of the ear and cut all that hair down to slightly above the skin line. Comb the hair on the back of the ears toward the outer edge. Take off the excess with thinning shears. Be sure that you taper those outer hairs so they are shortest at the top and longest at the base. Clean out the hair inside the ears with the blunt scissors. *Never* take any hair off the tip from the break upward! This hair acts as weight to keep the ear tipped. Its removal can cause a naturally-tipped ear to become pricked overnight.

If you are working with very high ears that barely tip, take no hair from them except to clean up the ragged edges. When working on the skull, leave most of the hair right in front of these high ears. This will give the desirable illusion of less height.

If your dog has the opposite problem—heavy, low-breaking ears—you break the basic rule of not taking hair off the tips. These ears must be trimmed all the way around the edges with thinning shears as close as possible to the skin without bare patches showing through. Clean out all the hair inside, and use the stripping knife to clean off outside hair, working with the direction of coat growth so you don't leave ridges. Remove all skull hair in front of the ears, allowing you to look directly into them. This will give the illusion of more length.

For wide set ears, leave most of the hair on the inner edges. Just trim the outer sides and be sure the inner edges are neat; even them up where necessary. This will give the impression of the ears being held closer together.

Trimming Skull, Throat and Whiskers

When the ears are done, start on the skull. The following method can be used successfully on all Collies. It will enhance lean skulls and flatter those with wider heads, making them appear leaner.

Trimming on the skull is done in a triangular area which runs upward from each eye to the inner and outer edges of each ear. With thinning shears work along in parallel rows, taking out full hairs. The color of the hair in the mask area is lightest at the base and darkest at the tips. If half a hair is removed, the remaining part will be a different color than the whole hair lying next to it. If many hairs are cut this way the result would be a salt-and-pepper effect. If the full hair is cut at skin level, there is no color variance and the skull remains its original shade when trimming is completed. As with all trimming, comb out the hair after you have trimmed a little. Go over and over an area working slowly. Stop when it looks and feels right. You will see the hair beginning to lie in an upward direction on the sides of the skull and a curve appearing that forms a frame around the face.

When the skull is trimmed down as close as you wish, go under the hair behind the jawbone and in front of the ear with the thinning shears and take out some hair. This will emphasize the curve even more and form a deeper frame for the face. When you groom the dog for the showring, comb these hairs upward. You will be amazed how the expression and skull definition will have improved.

The most important thing to know in head trimming is when to stop. The hair cannot be glued back. It is easy to take one more cut if needed later. That is why I believe in taking plenty of time with this. The resulting smoothness of finish is well worth the extra effort and patience.

On a Collie with a full stop, careful thinning with the shears can minimize the problem a little. Part the hair at a point in line with the upper eye, and between the eyes take the tiniest snips close to the skin—almost one or two hairs at a time. You will usually find quite an amount of hair there when the stop is full. You can back-comb it straight up with the back edge of the trimming knife, so you'll know what you are working with. Take a couple of cuts on each part and work downward to the lowest part that bulges. Then smooth the hair back with the thinning knife. If done carefully, you will see no dents, just a loss of some of the hair that was helping to build up the bulge.

Ch. Arrowhill Oklahoma
Redman (1954), by
Arrowhill Ace High
ex Arrowhill Miss
Oklahoma, the sire
of eleven Rough
champions.

Ch. Wickmere Silver Bullet (1976),
by Ch. Wickmere Battle Chief ex
Kemjo's Sweeper's Moon Shadow,
winner of the Stud Dog class at the
1981 CCA Specialty. *Shelly Roos*

All that remains is to neaten the lip line with the straight-edged scissors and to clip all facial whiskers with the blunt-edged scissors. If you plan to show the dog, clip whiskers the night before the show. They grow very quickly and will be stubbly when the dog is alert if they are trimmed earlier. The whiskers are trimmed one by one with tiny, curved nail scissors. Cut them right at the skin. Trim the eyebrow and cheek whiskers this same way, too. Stripping out the throat line can do much to enhance a short neck or emphasize a long one. It also makes a good place to lay the lead in the ruff. Using the stripping knife, take straight strokes downward with the direction of the hair, blending it into the chest hair. Trimming the throat and underjaw as described will also make a head look less deep.

On a tricolor head, more attention must be given to the brown eyebrows which should be neatened with barber shears, hair by hair, to form identical brown half-moons over each eye. With thinning shears, trim the brows off straight in line in profile with the backskull and muzzle.

On a blue merle head, too, the trimming becomes more difficult. Along with minimizing faults you must trim with the pattern, which will vary with each dog. Never cut off blue hairs in a straight line next to black ones; it will look choppy and make your trimming obvious.

Fine sandpaper does a good job of smoothing the whole head trim. Sand in one direction only, from nose to earset, in the direction of the hair. Then a *tiny* drop of oil or Vaseline may be rubbed into the palms of your hands and rubbed *well* into the hair over the entire head, again with the coat growth. A tiny smear of Vaseline applied to the nose before going into the ring brightens it a bit too and adds to the overall picture.

Correcting a Topline

Sometimes a young Collie may look quite soft in back because of an excess amount of hair on the rump. This hair can spoil its all-over appearance and should be taken down with thinning shears. Layer the coat on the rump from the hip bone back and go far under to take out hair. Never cut into the outer hairs; they can be combed back down over the thinned part. If enough is taken out gradually the appearance of a smooth topline should be achieved from the shoulder back.

Trimming Legs and Feet

The rest of your time will be spent on the legs and feet. With the thinning shears, take off the hair from pad to first joint on the back of the front legs. Do not skin the leg; leave enough hair to keep the back of the bone well rounded. You can vary this basic trim for each dog. A tall, rangy dog will look best with all the front leg hair left intact, with just a tapered line from pad to feather. Look at the whole dog and try to balance his body into a symmetrical unit when trimming and grooming.

Either straight shears or thinning shears can be used to trim the hocks. Comb the hair out directly backward. Line up the shears either parallel to the hock bone or slightly out at the top and cut down to the pad. Leave enough length of hair to round out the bone. How much you leave at the top will depend on how much your dog's stifle is bent. The straighter the stifle, the more hair at the top. Cow hocks can be improved in appearance by cautiously trimming the inner hair of the hocks very close at the top and leaving it fuller at the bottom. Leave a rounded leg, not squared off.

All four feet are trimmed in the same way. Try for a neat, catlike foot. You can choose either to have nails exposed when the foot is trimmed or leave them hidden by hair. If the dog's nails are so long they cannot be brought into proper length by show time, leave them exposed. If hair were left around the long nails, it would look as though the foot itself were long and pointed instead of high and compact. The hair around the pads is easily taken off with the blunt, curved scissors. Do not trim the hair in between the toes, as this leaves hollows. Nails should be cut or ground back every week so the quick continues to recede. The nails will be at the correct length when they cannot be heard "clicking" as the dog walks on a hard surface.

The Finishing Touches

The work you do in grooming your Collie for the showring will be most obvious in contrast to what you did in trimming it. It goes without saying that you will exhibit a clean dog. Whether to bathe his full coat is an individual decision depending on condition and how near the coat is to shedding. Usually we advise washing just the white areas. For the colored areas consider any of the excellent dry or liquid cleaning preparations on the market. The use of chalk is favored less nowadays than it used to be, simply because of the stricter enforcement of the dog show rules concerning foreign substances in the coat that will cause a dog to be excused from the ring. If you chalk the white collar, do it a day or so before the show so that every trace of it will be gone. Dampen the area and work in the chalk. It absorbs the water as it dries and will fall or shake out of the coat. The excess must be brushed out.

When you attend a dog show, all that is ahead is the dog's final grooming. The dog is trimmed, clean and ready for the last-minute touches. Bring your grooming table and all essential grooming tools and preparations. When the dog is on the table, dampen its coat all over. This is done in layers, brushing the moisture into the undercoat with the pin brush as you spray. Be careful not to wet the outercoat very much. By wetting the undercoat, you allow it to expand with the moisture. This will hold the outercoat away from the body and look much as it does when the dog is out in early morning dampness. Brush the coat against the grain from the back of the neck to the tail.

How you finish brushing your Collie will depend on its general body outline and the amount and length of coat it carries. Generally you follow the dog's body outline in layering the coat, with the exception of the neck, which is left to stand off as a frill all around the face and neck. The pants and tail are left brushed outward after dampening.

Finish off the head by moistening your hands with some coat dressing or other grooming preparation and rubbing them along the sides of the head, setting the hair in place. Comb the hair framing the face forward into a curve.

Brush the leg hair upward and comb the feathers straight backward. Brush the hair on the hock upward. Some people put chalk into the legs at a show to clean them and give the hair extra body. Be sure, if you do this, that every speck is removed before entering the ring!

Now stand back and view your finished creation. It should be the best dressed Collie at this party, a picture of perfect balance. When your Collie steps into the ring, it should rate the admiration of all who behold it. Even if it is not the best Collie in the class, it can be the best-groomed Collie, the one which proclaims to all at ringside: Here is a Collie presented as a Collie should be—proud, noble and beautiful.

DEGREE OF FAULT

by Gustave Sigritz

It is accepted that physical perfection has never been achieved in the Collie, yet throughout the history of the breed certain individuals have gained the classification of *Greats*. Undoubtedly the breeders and judges who knew these dogs would alter them to meet their concept of the ideal of perfection if given the opportunity.

There is little reason to believe that this picture has been changed today; nor can it safely be forecast that the future will bring forth a Collie that is perfection in the eyes of *all* who view him. The Collie Standard and ideal are generally considered one and the same, yet I believe there is a variance. The Standard is a blueprint put into the most meaningful and explicit words possible. Admittedly, black or white is of universal interpretation, but combinations of words might well give you a different mental picture than me.

The forthcoming illustration of the Standard is a step in the right direction, to be sure, and it will undoubtedly be a great aid in our quest toward the ideal. However, I will hazard the statement that it will be most unusual if it meets with the approval of *all*.

I believe there is a difference between the *Standard*, words or pictures, and ideal. Ideal is individual . . . your ideal is not necessarily my ideal. In essence this is the basic reason I believe there will always be a variance in type, in breeding theories and practices, and that identical variance is desirable. I am convinced that this will always be a part of the game in spite of all we might do in an effort to pull it into a tighter sphere.

I want to retain the same variance of type that we find running through the Collie today. I am sure this disturbs many breeders and exhibitors, but I say that this is not only healthy and normal, but adds interest to the breed. One can safely say that these variations in type all fall within the specifications of the Standard, yet each in itself can be a thing of beauty. I hope that in our quest for perfection we never reach the point where our Collies look alike, as though they had been stamped out with a cookie cutter. I think it will be a sad day when our Collies are so uniform and so well defined that it will be unnecessary for us to have dog shows.

The Collie ideal is synonymous with beauty. And beauty is synonymous with art. Beauty and art can have many variations yet be achieved over the basic pattern. If there is a doubt in your mind, think momentarily of the great beauties of the movie screen. Are they look-alikes? Identical? Maureen O'Hara might be your ideal of beauty while I may say that to me Ava Gardner is the essence of womanly perfection. Yet someone else might say that a particular feature on neither was perfection and so they chose Marilyn Monroe as their beauty queen.

So beauty is variable to the extent that it dictates your tastes in your choice of clothes, your home and its decor, and your choice of cars. One could well say that the Collie Standard calls for classic beauty, but that too has its variations.

As long as there is art, we will have art critics. There will be those with a natural talent for creating art, and those who possess the ability to evaluate it. A certain number of people will develop, through years of hard work and concentration, both abilities while others may struggle a lifetime and achieve nothing more than mediocrity. These things cannot be achieved or evaluated by a slide rule. Experience has proven that there is a measure of truth in the traditional adage, *One is born with an eye for a dog.* This is vague and meaningless to a neophyte—as much as the astounding statement, usually beyond the grasp of most non-breeders, that each dog is an individual with an individual personality.

The Standard is a blueprint, or pattern to be followed. But within that pattern variations can be made with *great* Collies emerging . . . Collies which still have *faults to a degree.* Consider momentarily the one place on a Collie that seldom seems to reach perfection. In my time I have seen only a few Collies that seemed to reach perfection in stop. This one point expresses all I feel about degree of fault—a Collie can be faulty to a degree in stop yet superior in other departments to win, and be considered a top specimen of the breed.

I vividly recall a dog I judged. He was generally a good dog—good everywhere but in stop, with a fullness that was the first thing one saw from the front, three-quarters or side view. In profile the stop was nearly a perfect arc—so it was a disturbing and distracting area that spoiled the entire dog. *Whereas,* had this fault been of a lesser degree the dog could have won the class and possibly gained consideration for higher ribbons. Of interest is the fact that this dog later finished to his title, but I would assume that he had improved in this department before he began serious winning. I never again saw or judged the dog, but subsequent photos told me that he had improved in stop, which is indeed possible.

One may say that a dog can be faulty in ear placement, skull development, angulation, or in any department, but only to a degree before it becomes so jolting to the eye that it offends. And, *a combination of faults to a degree can be assembled in one dog, yet that dog may win in the ring and be considered a good dog by top authorities. Conversely, a dog can analyze well, department by department, yet in the overall be a "Nothing."*

A number of years ago a friend and fellow-exhibitor greeted me at the door of a show building to tell me what a good dog he was showing that day. He took me to his bench, going over the dog point by point, and his reasoning was understandable. Then I asked him to take the dog off the bench and after one glimpse I said that I would beat him that day. I did. That dog failed to make the overall picture; the component parts did not fit, although point by point he analyzed extremely well.

The degree of fault is of concern not only in evaluating your own stock, but is involved in judgment in the showring. Again the human element is involved and regardless of specifics set down in our Standard, there will be variables. The criticism of judges and inconsistency in judging is the main cry of the uninitiated or unschooled. Those who cannot achieve the rewards they expect must feel the rules of the game are wrong. Instead of playing by the rules, the rules need altering to fit.

Let us not be lulled into the belief that there will ever be a cure-all for the ills of discontentment. However, one of the most interesting and enlightening experiments is one I have advocated for years, to introduce our fanciers to the problems of judging. This is a function of the local club, since education must begin at the roots, and most clubs hold matches, the ideal time for this experiment of "Any number can judge." Hold your regular match with the judge undetermined. Each member is required to draw straws with three to five persons designated to judge. Everyone has the opportunity to judge the entire match in turn, without the following judges at ringside. You'll be surprised at the results and the interest in discussions following. This "laboratory experiment" forces these members into the position of being entirely objective in their thinking, giving them a keener appreciation for the task before a judge at a regular dog show. This begins to show them the reasoning a judge must use in evaluation and good judgment. It will do as much as any method devised to educate and yet eliminate some of the unjustified and loose criticism of judging. A few experiences in the ring as a judge will give anyone a different perspective of his or her own dogs, too: how to evaluate objectively, eliminating sentiment—and developing a better understanding of the problems.

When we think in terms of evaluating a dog, invariably the adult comes to mind. The problem most of us face is in first evaluating or selecting our puppies. Much has been said and written about selection of puppies and it remains the enigma of the breeder. The successful breeder has a "feel" or "sense" about the selection of puppies just as he or she does in the selection of an adult specimen. One angle frequently overlooked is that perhaps there is nothing to select from in the first place. A sound mating is made, with every reason for success, yet even the best is often not good enough. Also, the complexity is that each mating is different, and although repeat matings generally produce a certain level of quality, no two individuals are identical. Puppies should be evaluated the same way as adults, with a dozen or so "Ifs"— if it holds in skull, maintains its good bite, retains its good eye and expression and so on. Here again is the matter of considering the degree of fault, which cannot be overlooked in evaluating the three- or the six-month-old puppy.

I cannot conclude this discussion without further introducing the relationship between breeding the good specimen and showing it. After fourteen years of breeding and exhibiting I am still inclined to favor the specialty judge, on the whole, as opposed to the all-round judge. The all-round judges who know the Collie best are the ones most likely to appreciate a good one. And when I say know, it is invariably proven that those judges at one time owned, bred or were associated with the breed. So my conclusion is that few can know or appreciate the breed from reading and learning through the Standard alone.

I've found that a stock question asked of judges is: "If you had a good-headed Collie in the ring which was cow hocked and a poor-headed one beside him with a good rear, which would you put up?" This hypothetical question throws me, because in my experience in the ring I have never been up against such a situation. Just as I must admit I have never been up against the number two stock question: ". . . if you had two dogs that were equal . . ." To the first question the reply is: "Tell me to what degree the dog is cow hocked and to what degree the other dog is bad in head. Then if you can specifically tell me or show me the two dogs, I could give you an answer that would suffice or be in a better position to pass judgment."

Kyle Onstott, in *The Art of Breeding Better Dogs,* says that breeding dogs is an art and a science. I say that breeding dogs is an art with a pinch of science and good common horse-sense thrown in. But breeding fine dogs is very heavy on the art side; hence my constant reference to it and the parallels I invariably draw to those who will listen to me.

I believe the true breeder is an artist. He or she either has a natural gift for it or must learn through experience. He or she learns through litter after litter just as the artist must paint and paint and paint. Regardless of God's gift of talent, an artist seldom paints a masterpiece the first time he or she puts brush to canvas. This comes through years of effort and is achieved only after many paintings have been done. The true breeder is an idealist just as the artist is.

The artist must have materials just as the breeder must have stock with which to work. The better the paint, the better the picture.

"The art so long, the life so short."

AN EXHIBITOR'S EXPECTATIONS

by Mrs. Winston T. (Barbara) Kellogg

Fundamentally, exhibitors want a judge to be an expert and to have a thorough knowledge of the Standard, coupled with an expert and experienced "eye" for a Collie. They want him to place the dogs as he evaluates them that day, completely erasing from his mind the memory of their past records or wins, or how they looked another day. We expect the judge to put out of his mind any prior knowledge of the dogs, their handlers or their pedigrees. Thus, honesty, integrity and an "eye for a Collie" should be the basic prerequisites for any Collie judge.

This is only the beginning. Next comes the judge's technique in handling his assignment. What does the exhibitor expect when he puts on his armband and enters the ring? The judge under whom the exhibitor likes to show is often the one with considerable ring experience who knows how to bring out the best in all the dogs presented to him regardless of their quality. He shows consideration for the dogs and their handlers in many ways. He makes their directions plain and well-understood in regard to gaiting and posing the dogs. He is patient with the novice exhibitor and takes time to help him, recognizing that his job is in part educational—he is there to encourage, not to tear down, the exhibitors of the future. He speaks to the dogs and approaches them gently but handles them firmly when going over them.

On the other hand, there are times when a judge fails to examine some of the dogs in the ring. All exhibitors like to feel they have been accorded equal time in the judge's individual examinations. A favorite complaint heard from those who fail to win is that, "He didn't even put his hands on my dog!"

The considerate judge does not demand that the dogs show excessively. He tries to help those that are loath to put up their ears by attracting their attention in various ways. The judge does not demand that they be kept showing overly long. If there are delays in starting the class or it is an unusually large one, the judge will tell the exhibitors to let their charges relax at times instead of maintaining the *qui vive* pose too long.

Exhibitors like judges who are thoughtful of their entries. Judges who watch them carefully to see they are not crowding each other too closely. Ones who see that they stay spaced so as not to interfere with each other. They do not ask that the dogs be posed in such a way that the space available does not really suffice. Many all-rounders are guilty of this. They often ask the exhibitors to "set their dogs up" in profile so that each dog is nearly touching the one ahead of it and there is no room for the exhibitor except at the side. Our Standard frowns on excessive posing and asks that the dog come to a natural stop, not stand like a statue indefinitely after having its feet placed by its handler. It is impossible for a dog to come to a natural pose if, in effect, it has to fit itself into a slot.

The thoughtful judge is aware of all that may affect his or her entries giving of their best. If it is an outdoor show the judge does not demand that the dogs be posed facing a strong wind as he or she knows this will force a dog with good ear carriage to fly its ears. If the sun is scorching hot the judge will try to find a shady spot for the dogs. If the floor or mats provided at an indoor show are slippery and cause some dogs to feel uneasy, the judge will have them stand where they feel most secure.

As to ring procedure and the particular routine the judge follows with his or her entries, it is a help to the handler if the judge is consistent and follows the same pattern in all classes. They know better what will be expected of them and their dogs. Also, most exhibitors and ringsiders prefer a judge whose thought-processes they can follow by the way he changes the line-up as the class progresses. Especially in a large class, the exhibitor prefers to have an inkling of how his dog is standing up to the rest before the class is over.

Many judges like to indicate by various gestures (such as placing their hands together at an angle to illustrate a receding backskull), that a dog may be deficient in certain respects. The value of this to the exhibitor can be somewhat limited, as, if the gesture is plain to him, he may feel that it is also obvious to the point of embarrassment. The judge may be getting the message across to the ringside as well and thus advertising his dog's faults.

On the whole, the exhibitor is an overly sensitive, demanding type and a judge has the impossible job of trying to make him happy. If all the foregoing adds up to an impossible ideal let us at least say it is a desirable one from the exhibitor's point of view and the popular judge is the one who can keep the most exhibitors happy even when they don't win!

Chapter 7

Owning a Collie

To be the owner of a Collie or any other dog is a two-sided proposition. There is the pleasure of a dog's company on the one side and the ongoing responsibility for its total well-being on the other.

Fortunately for us Collie owners, our breed has a depth of character and sense of loyalty that make our responsibilities small payment for what our dogs give in return. Since the first dog herded the first sheep for the first shepherd, dogs always gave of themselves in unlimited measure. Some things never change. We always seem to get the best of the bargain.

For most, owning a Collie starts with the acquisition of a puppy. What kind of Collie that puppy grows into depends, to a certain extent, on its heredity. For the rest, environment will be the determining factor. The care provided embraces physical as well as emotional needs and when these are right and the puppy is one of stable temperament, a wonderful dog and a source of pride to all is bound to result.

Yes, a Collie is a very special dog and owning one is a very special experience. In this chapter, you'll read why this is so and you'll also learn of some special needs every Collie has and how best to meet them.

WHAT IS A PUPPY?

by Mrs. Robert P. Hamilon

A puppy is the whelp of a bitch. It comes into the world wet and slippery, so undeveloped it can neither hear nor see, but able enough to smell its dam's teats, strong enough to crawl to them and nurse, and intelligent enough to do it.

A Collie puppy is a part of a plan in a breeder's mind. The eager circle which waits for him may be looking for a dog to work sheep or lead the blind, a show dog, a pet, a breeding prospect or an obedience dog. The purpose

Ch. Merrie Oaks Humdinger (1951), by Merrie Oaks Gallant Lad ex Wesbara's Wedding Belle, the sire of fifteen Rough champions.

of the puppy's existence has been determined before his arrival. In other words, litters are not born just to produce more Collies.

But predestination does not always work—as most everyone knows—in dogs any more than it does in anything else. The new arrivals, however inexperienced they are in life, have a way at times of settling their own destinies. A great show dog will emerge from an unexpected corner, a litter born to the purple (and one had devoutly wished to purple rosettes) finds its way to separate homes to be companions, and two pets which met by chance at the propitious moment spawn a great obedience Collie.

What does all this tell us about puppies?

Of course they are the future of the breed. Selected from their midst are the ones that will carry the breed forward, or backward. So, in a sense, a puppy bears a responsibility—or rather, its owner bears a responsibility to see that it is used most wisely for the breed.

A puppy is hope.

CARE OF YOUR COLLIE PUPPY

by The Collie Club of America Education Committee

Selecting Your Puppy

The best place to purchase a Collie puppy is directly from a reputable breeder. There are many dedicated breeders throughout the United States who are

Lynn Hyman

Until a puppy is four months old, it will eat 10 to 15 percent of its weight daily in order to support explosive growth. This is one of the reasons that proper feeding is so important to its future development. *Karen Phelps*

striving to improve Collies by carefully planning their litters. Puppies that are not show quality are sold to make healthy, happy pets. The Collie Club of America, the American Kennel Club or your nearest all-breed dog club will be able to give you names of reputable, local breeders.

Your new puppy should be at least eight weeks old before you bring it home. Be sure to pick one that seems outgoing and ready to trust you. It has been proven that the human contacts a puppy has had from ten days of age on will be of lasting effect. If you are looking for a show or breeding prospect, be sure to make this clear to the breeder. He or she may suggest that you wait or buy an older puppy so that you may be more certain of its appearance at maturity.

In any case you will want a healthy, alert youngster showing no signs of discharge from the nose or eyes. His coat should glisten and be free of bare patches. (Scratching may be a sign of skin trouble or parasites.) His bone should look solid and fairly heavy and he should move soundly. Some awkwardness and waddling are natural to any plump little puppy.

He will have started his inoculations against distemper, hepatitis and parvovirus, and should have been wormed at least once for roundworms. He should also have had an eye examination by a canine ophthalmologist. If you plan to breed your puppy, you may wish to make your purchase contingent upon an examination by a mutually agreed-upon specialist in this field. This is important, because a small percentage of Collies are born with defective vision in one or both eyes and many others, even though their vision is satisfactory, have eye conditions indicating that they should not be used for breeding. Read the section on "Your Collie's Eyes" in this chapter for additional information.

In addition to the health record of the puppy, giving data on shots, worming and eyes, you should also receive a three- or four-generation pedigree of your puppy's ancestors and a blue registration application form from American Kennel Club made over to your ownership and signed by the breeder. (This shows that the puppy is a member of a litter already registered by AKC.) Later, when you complete this form and mail it back to AKC, you will receive your dog's individual registration with his own number, showing you as owner. If, for any reason whatsoever, the breeder is unable to supply you with this form, be certain to demand a bill of sale giving the puppy's birth date and names and registration numbers of both parents. Some breeders register their puppies individually, naming the puppies themselves. If the puppy you purchase is already registered, the breeder will give you the registration certificate, signed over. You must complete "Section B" and mail the certificate to AKC with the proper fee and a new certificate, showing you as owner, will be sent to you.

Bring Your New Puppy Home

You must make preparations for your puppy. If you already have a fenced yard, fine. Otherwise a small amount of your property should be fenced off for your puppy so that it will be safe when you can't be out with it. Then plan on a good-sized run for it when it is grown. A dog will get sufficient exercise in a four- by twenty-foot run. Your dog should always be a good citizen. In most communities it is illegal as well as dangerous for a dog to roam at large! Never chain a Collie puppy, however, as this can be extremely frustrating to the puppy and can adversely affect its disposition for life.

You will decide whether the new puppy is to sleep inside or out. If it is to spend much time outdoors, it will need a draft-free, insulated house in its run. In cool weather provide your puppy with a thick layer of dry bedding. If it will share its quarters with another dog, be sure that the older dog lets the new puppy inside, or the pup may be forced to spend the night in wet or on the cold ground. It is hard for a puppy's system to adjust between a heated

A Collie is a devoted family dog and is never happier than when it can be with those it loves. *Lynn Hyman*

The Collie's legacy as a herding dog allows him to live in harmony with other animals. *Lynn Hyman*

house all day and a cold doghouse at night so, although it can adjust to living outside at extremely low temperatures, it should be allowed indoors only for short visits.

If you decide you want an indoor dog, prepare a nice box in a quiet, draft-free corner. If the puppy is lonesome and cries the first few nights, try putting a warm hot water bottle in beside it or place a ticking alarm clock nearby.

When you bring the puppy home, let it make the first advances. It will soon be eager to make friends and play but, like any baby, it must have lots of time to rest and sleep during the day. Make sure that children do not handle it too roughly. Don't allow the younger ones to carry the puppy about, since a puppy can be seriously injured by a fall. Older children can be taught to carry it by placing one hand under the chest and the other under the hindquarters to support it.

Housebreaking

Since a Collie puppy is eager to please, housebreaking should be comparatively simple. It is a naturally clean animal but, being young and small, lacks self-control.

If your puppy is to live indoors, you will have to take it out at frequent intervals: after each meal and every hour or so between. Always take it to the same spot and praise it when it does what you want. The intervals between trips can be gradually lengthened, but try to get the puppy out before it makes a mistake.

At night it should be confined to a small area; being naturally clean it won't want to soil its bed. A wooden or wire dog crate, or an old baby playpen are valuable aids in housetraining. They can also be used to keep the puppy out of mischief when you aren't able to watch it. At night put several layers of newspaper down and if you find the puppy can't make it through the night without soiling, shred more on top for absorbency. Never reprimand it unless you catch it in the act. Its memory is still very short and it won't understand why you are scolding it.

Leash and Collar

The puppy's lead training should begin as soon as you get it. It will be easier if you start it as young as possible. Get a small, lightweight collar and light lead. To start with, just slip the collar on and off several times until the puppy is used to it. Before long you can pick up the lead and try to get the puppy to follow you. It may trot right along after you, or it may refuse to follow. Talk to it and coax it along if necessary. You can also use a tidbit of bread or cheese to encourage it. When it follows, reward the puppy with the tidbit and be sure to pet and praise him.

By about four months of age you can start using a light chain or nylon collar for training. A choke collar will do less damage to your Collie's ruff than a leather or plastic one and it can be worn comfortably loose without slipping over its head when the puppy is leashed. Never leave it on the puppy without a snap to hold the rings together, as it could choke the puppy.

General Health—Your Veterinarian

As soon as you have your new puppy at home, call your veterinarian and tell him what inoculations the puppy has had and on what dates. The veterinarian will advise you when the next injection is due and will probably suggest that you bring in a small stool sample at the same time. This will let the veterinarian know if the puppy is worm-free. If worms are present, the veterinarian will give you the medicine to take care of the problem. After the puppy has had all the recommended inoculations for distemper, hepatitis, leptospirosis, kennel cough and parvovirus, it should be given rabies protection at three months. As a rule, your veterinarian will then recommend an annual booster shot to maintain immunities against these diseases.

INTERNAL PARASITES (WORMS)

Many dogs harbor internal parasites at one time or another and an annual stool check is recommended. Puppies are especially prone to roundworms, but hookworm, tapeworm or whipworm as well as coccidia (a protozoan) may be present. If allowed to go unchecked these can cause many undesirable symptoms along with general debilitation. Hookworm, for instance, can cause severe anemia. Never worm your puppy on suspicion. This can be dangerous, especially if it isn't feeling well. There are many medications suitable for treating parasites, but they should be administered or prescribed by your veterinarian after microscopic examination of the stool.

You should also check into preventive medicine for heartworm. This mosquito-borne plague, once confined to the South, has spread throughout the United States. After an infected insect has bitten a dog it takes from six to eight months for adult worms to develop in the heart. By this time it is both dangerous and expensive to treat. Ask your veterinarian for daily medication as a preventive, before, during and after mosquito season. The once-a-month treatments are not recommended for Collies.

EXTERNAL PARASITES (FLEAS, LICE, TICKS, FLIES)

External pests not only make a dog uncomfortable but can start severe skin problems. Fleas and lice can carry tapeworm eggs and when the dog bites at them it may swallow the eggs and develop tapeworm. Ask your veterinarian about suitable dips, sprays or powders to combat skin parasites. The dog's sleeping quarters must be treated at the same time. Although most ticks are present outdoors just during the summer months, some breed indoors year-round. They will keep appearing on a house dog to complete their life cycle unless places where the ticks drop off are sprayed at frequent intervals.

Lyme disease, a serious disease borne by the tiny deer tick has made its unwelcome presence felt in recent years. Humans and dogs are both susceptible to this painful malady. Dogs that have been in heavily wooded areas should be carefully examined for deer ticks. Happily, a preventative inoculation is available. Consult your veterinarian for his or her recommendations and be guided accordingly.

During, warm weather various flying insects may plague your dog. If your dog lives outdoors you should treat it every morning with a repellent spray or ointment, especially on its ears. Flies can bite and draw blood, causing great pain and discomfort. Keeping its yard scrupulously clean will prevent much of the fly nuisance.

Feeding—General Rules

Proper feeding for your puppy is important to its future development and health. A puppy requires more food for its weight than a grown dog, and its protein, mineral and energy needs are higher. He will use up to 100 calories per pound of body weight per day; until it is four months of age it will eat 10 to 15 percent of its weight daily.

The puppy should be fed the same meals at the same hours each day. Be sure to increase amounts as its appetite grows. If it is licking its dish clean, feed it more. If it fails to clean it up in ten or twenty minutes, remove the dish and feed less at the next meal. Food should be fed lukewarm or at room temperature—not ice-cold from the refrigerator.

Keep a dish of water available throughout the day. If your puppy likes to play in it and spills the water, buy a nontipping dish or one that can be fastened to the wall with a clamp. For the outdoor puppy use the same type or a small pail clipped to the fence by the handle.

Whenever your dog has excessively loose stools or does not eat well for a few days, consult your veterinarian. In case of severe diarrhea or vomiting, withhold food for the rest of the day, but get in touch with the veterinarian immediately. Viral enteritis can be cured, but only if no time is lost.

SOME HELPFUL DON'TS

Don't make an abrupt change in the dog's diet. New foods should be introduced gradually over several days. For this reason it is best to start your new puppy off on the same diet its breeder has been feeding it.

Don't feed an all meat diet; this could be very harmful. (See next section.)

Don't feed steak, chicken or chop bones. They can splinter and cause internal injury and bleeding. A beef knuckle or shank bone—cooked

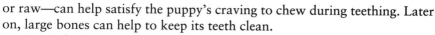

or raw—can help satisfy the puppy's craving to chew during teething. Later on, large bones can help to keep its teeth clean.

Don't feed raw egg whites. These are hard for a dog's body to digest and remove vitamins from the digestive tract.

WHAT TO FEED AND HOW OFTEN

Weaning to Three Months: Feed three times daily at well-spaced intervals. At eight weeks, if you don't have a diet from the breeder, try: ³/₄-cup of puppy food, ¹/₄-cup ground beef or canned meat, mixed with enough warm (not hot) water, milk or broth to make a fairly moist mixture. Increase the amount weekly as long as the puppy cleans it up shortly after feeding. Don't leave food out for it to nibble and thereby get finicky; put it away until the next meal, after an hour at most.

Three Months to Six Months: Feed three times daily until appetite drops off, same foods as above but in larger amounts. Add less liquid so that the mixture is drier and more crumbly. When it no longer relishes it, cut out the noon meal and offer the puppy a biscuit or two instead. Don't forget that at least three-fourths of the diet should consist of a good grade of commercial food. The other quarter may consist of ground meat (fresh or canned) or table scraps such as meat trimmings and vegetables. Small amounts of fat such as vegetable oil, bacon grease or suet, added to the ration are beneficial. These should never exceed 15 percent of the diet and be sure they don't cause loose stools.

Six Months to a Year: Feed twice daily. By this time good eating habits should be well established. Your dog should be eating two meals a day eagerly until it is ten to twelve months old. When its period of most rapid growth is over it won't need as much food and you can cut back to one meal a day, unless the dog is thin, plus a second snack or biscuit. You can change now from puppy food to a maintenance diet. Most Collies are fed twice a day throughout life and seem to do better on it. Continue with a good commercial food with no more than 15 percent of its weight added in the form of meat and fat. The amount of food your dog requires to stay in good flesh varies with each individual, climate and the amount of exercise it gets.

DIET SUPPLEMENTS—VITAMINS AND MINERALS

Ask your veterinarian about adding supplements to your puppy's diet. Most commercial foods present a balanced diet, so it is risky to add extras without his advice. Modern medicine has shown that more harm than good can be done by over-supplementing.

Grooming

Frequent grooming benefits a puppy's coat, keeps it free of dirt and prevents loose hairs from settling about the house. A puppy usually sheds its first, fuzzy coat at three to five months. It will look quite naked until it is about seven months old and grows a longer outercoat and a new undercoat, which will make the outercoat stand away. As a rule, a dog will shed just once a year, for a few weeks, once it is grown. Daily brushing is important at this time in hastening removal of dead hair.

Use a bristle brush on your puppy and brush against the lie of the hair. In this way you can get close to its skin and help prevent mats. Watch for mats behind the ears, where the hair is finer, and on the insides of both front and hind legs near the body. Your puppy should soon enjoy being groomed and it will rarely be necessary to bathe him. A bath will help to hasten shedding, using mild soap and warm water. Rinse out every bit of soap and make sure your puppy is completely dry before you take it out in cold weather.

A puppy's nails should be checked at least every two weeks and cut back to the quick. This is the pink vein you can see going down the center of a light-colored nail. If its nails grow too long, they will cause its feet to become long and flat.

If you plan to show your puppy, you will be interested in detailed grooming instructions in the pamphlet "Your Collie from Kennel to Showring," which you can purchase from the Collie Club of America. Check the appendix for more information.

Although there is much to remember in raising your new puppy, you will be repaid many times over for the love and care you give it. Its life and well being are in your hands. We hope that you and your Collie have many happy years together!

YOUR COLLIE'S EARS

by Barbara M. Kellogg and the Collie Club of America
Education Committee

Inspect your puppy's ears regularly and keep them clean with cotton slightly moistened with lukewarm water or alcohol. Be careful not to drip any down into the ear.

The correct ear carriage for a Collie is three-fourths erect. In other words, the top fourth should tip forward. During the teething period, from three to seven months, ears may go prick (stand up straight and stiff like a German Shepherd Dog's) or hang low (like the ears of a hound or spaniel).

Many a fine Collie has lost out in the showring because of poor ear carriage and many a pet is less attractive because its ears do not conform to the Collie Standard.

Some ears are hopeless from the start. No amount of attention will help, due to their basic structure and placement. However, this is rare and hard to determine when the puppy is young. If it shows promise it is worth the effort to help its ears.

However, over-correction can be as detrimental to final ear carriage as none at all. Low ears can be glued so tightly to the top of the head that there is little opportunity for the puppy to develop natural use of muscles at the base and get the ear standing higher by itself. High ears can be over-weighted so that a break is formed too low down. Most breeders agree that by a year of age it is too late to train ears. However, it is necessary to help some grown dogs temporarily when their ears go up due to shedding or when a bitch comes in season.

If the ears do stand up straight, get after them right away; apply some glycerine, cuticura ointment or lanolin. Rub the material into the top half of the ear inside and out. This will help soften the cartilage and also add weight to bring the ear over.

Antiphlogistine is undoubtedly the most widely-used substance for training the Collie ear. It is similar to chewing gum in appearance but is water soluble. It may be obtained at country drug stores and comes in a tube or jar. Apply a small dab on the inside of the ear tip; add more as needed to bring the tip over, and coat with dust or sand or a bit of paper towel to prevent stickiness. Dogs just love licking it off, so don't use it unless the puppy can be isolated, or, if you have more than one dog, add pepper to discourage removing the material.

If the ear is hanging too low or off to the side of the head, try trimming some of the hair off the inside, back and edges of the ear. This will lighten it and help the puppy to carry it higher. You can also try massaging the inside of the ear daily with alcohol. If this doesn't work, some form of prop may be needed. It is best to get help from the puppy's breeder on this.

If you can't get help locally, send for the Collie Club of America pamphlet, "Your Collie's Ears," which will give more detailed information on ear training. See the appendix for more information.

When grown, your Collie will present a more pleasing appearance if it carries it ears correctly, so do everything possible to help them develop correctly while your dog is still growing.

YOUR COLLIE'S EYES

by Barbara M. Kellogg and Sue Barlow,
Collie Club of America Education Committee

Dogs, like people, are subject to a large number of inherited eye diseases. Two which affect the Collie's eyes should be of concern to all breeders.

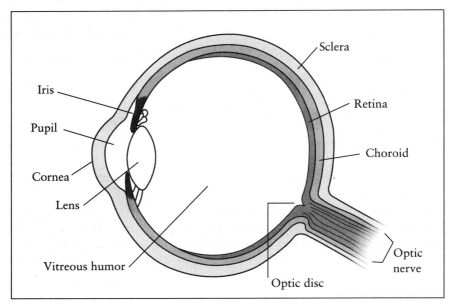

Cross section of the canine eye.

The most common is called **Collie Eye Anomaly,** although it is also found in other herding breeds, notably Shetland Sheepdogs, Border Collies and Australian Shepherds.

Collie Eye Anomaly

Veterinarians first noted this problem at least thirty-five years ago. It was later found to exist in most Collies. This so-called syndrome, meaning a group of conditions which appear in conjunction with each other, is present prior to birth. It can be diagnosed by a trained observer, i.e., a canine ophthalmologist, when a puppy is just a few weeks old. Drops are given to dilate the pupil and the interior of the eye is examined with an ophthalmoscope. The eye is then graded as "clear," not affected, or as affected, showing signs of the syndrome listed below. (More than one term is often given as there is no uniform nomenclature used by veterinarians.)

Staphyloma, Coloboma, Ectasina: While not completely synonymous, these terms all refer to a cupping or bulging in the eyeball, usually in the area of the optic disc.

Choroidal Hypoplasia, Chorioretinal Change: These refer to abnormalities in the pigmentation or coloring of the choroid, or central layer of the eye's lining.

There are variations even in normal eyes. These correspond somewhat to a dog's coat color. Thus it is often difficult to judge the pigment in a blue merle's eyes, as it is diluted along with his coat color.

Retino/Vascular Disease, Tortuous Blood Vessels: Defects in the vessels of the eye which are responsible for its blood supply or "nourishment." These may be malformed, undersized or even lacking.

Retinal Detachment: Loosening or separation of the inmost or retinal layer from the wall of the eye. This may involve a tiny area or the entire retina. The latter is termed a complete detachment, the result being blindness in that eye.

Can the Collie's eyes become worse? Might it later go blind? The basic answer is "No" as CEA is present prior to birth. However, a dog born with a severe Staphyloma or with Retino/Vascular Disease may later suffer loss of sight if detachment or severe hemorrhage occurs. The majority of dogs which are slightly affected have perfectly adequate eyesight during their lives. Even a dog with one blind eye will cope perfectly well with his surroundings. It should be noted that CEA can exhibit such subtle variations that, among mildly affected dogs, we find differences of opinion among experts as to which are clear or not.

What have breeders done to improve Collie eyes? Because CEA has involved so much of the breed, eradication had to be slow in order to keep other desirable qualities. Even among dogs that are examined clear, most are carriers of the gene. They have a hidden gene for the condition and will transmit the gene to half their offspring.

Two other conditions *not* part of the syndrome and which occur in other breeds also should be mentioned:

Hypoplasia of the Optic Nerve: An undersized nerve, which is noted where it enters the eyeball. In extreme cases, this can cause blindness.

Corneal Dystrophy: This condition comes on when the dog is mature, often during stress. Opaque spots appear centrally on the surface of the cornea. It is often confused by the layman with cataracts which occur in the lens.

Originally there was a pronounced lack of veterinarians trained to examine eyes. In 1972 the American Veterinary Medical Association formed the American College of Veterinary Ophthalmologists (ACVO), providing specialists in the animal eye field.

The Collie Club of America encourages its members to have all their puppies checked as young as possible by a qualified ophthalmologist. When there is none in the area, the alternative is to sell a dog contingent on a later check. No dog should be used for breeding until examined and found to be above the examiner's standard. The most accurate readings can be made when a puppy is young. Minor symptoms often become inapparent later on. Such cases are referred to as *Go-Normals* and will produce as if affected.

What pattern of heredity is involved? Specialists cannot agree. For a dog to show symptoms, both parents, even if they show no signs themselves, probably carry a gene for the condition. Evidence exists that some other parts of the syndrome are handed down separately. Staphyloma rarely occurs except in the presence of chorioretinal change. Dogs recommended for breeding will vary according to the standard set by the individual examiner. The ideal, of course, is to eliminate all but the clear, noncarriers from the breed.

Progressive Retinal Atrophy

Unlike CEA, this disease occurs in many breeds of dogs. PRA is a term which describes retinal degeneration resulting eventually in total blindness in both eyes. The most common form is Generalized PRA.

Generalized PRA has proven to be a simple recessive in all breeds studied. This means that, even though the condition is not present at birth, *both* parents *must* have been involved as carriers. Early signs of the problem may be noticed by the owner as night blindness. The dog has trouble seeing in dim light. An expert may detect early signs in the eye at three to four months. By two years, if the Collie shows no ophthalmoscopic signs, he may be assumed to be permanently safe from PRA. We have pointed out that puppies should be examined for CEA as early as possible. They should be looked at again for the onset of PRA at six months or so, especially if they are to be used for breeding. A final check can be made at one and one-half to two years of age.

Make sure if possible that there is no evidence of PRA in the dogs produced by those directly behind yours in its pedigree. Hopefully, you can rely on the breeder and owner of the sire to give you the facts on its eye pedigree. No reliable breeder would carelessly use a dog capable of producing PRA puppies. If any reasonable doubt exists, the breeder can request that a puppy be neutered. This will in no way reflect on its worth as a family pet.

For further information see the appendix.

Chapter 8

The Collie at Work

The Collie is a working dog. There can be no argument about this simple fact. The breed owes its very existence to early man's need for a means of protecting and controlling flocks and herds of food animals. As noted earlier, the Collie is Scotland's development of the sheepdog. In other countries, dogs working with sheep took other forms depending on local conditions. In this way the entire stock dog family developed.

In our modern world, most purebred Collies never have the opportunity to work with sheep. Indeed, countless thousands never see a living sheep all their lives. Still, the instinct is there and many amazing stories are on record of untrained dogs falling back on instinct to do what Collies have done so well for centuries.

Those interested in doing something useful and interesting with their Collies have often turned to obedience training and competition to gratify this wish. The breed has done well in obedience and can boast a good number of champions with Obedience degrees in both varieties. Beauty *with* brains is always a good combination.

Suffice it to say that today's Collie can still work when given the opportunity. An individual owner may never need to have a working stock dog, but it's good to know most Collies today, if called upon, could perform in this capacity as well as their field-wise forebears.

THE COLLIE IN OBEDIENCE

by Mrs. Inga Holm

Obedience Degrees

An Obedience degree is awarded by the American Kennel Club when a dog has earned three qualifying scores at AKC licensed or sanctioned Obedience

Ch./OTCH Shoreham Dubious Delight, TD (1974), by Ch. Shane MacDuff of Koani ex Shoreham Enchantee, CD. "Dubie," owned and trained by Jennifer Julander had the distinction of becoming the breed's first OTCH.

Trials under three different judges. A qualifying score is at least 170 points with over 50 percent of the available points earned in each required exercise. The initials of these degrees are added as a suffix to the dog's registered name.

A must for any working dog should be the Companion Dog degree (CD) which requires heeling on and off lead, recall, stand for examination, long sit and down. For the Companion Dog Excellent degree (CDX) exercises include

OTCH Walstone Impulse, TD (1974), by Ch. Wickmere Chimney Sweep ex Walstone Woodmouse, owned and trained by Madeline Loos, was the breed's second OTCH and the first bitch to achieve this coveted title. *Loos*

Ch./OTCH North Country Wildfire (1975), by Ch. Alteza Aureate ex North Country Winsome, was owned and trained by Sandra Hall to become the third OTCH Collie in history.

retrieving on the flat and over the high jump, drop on recall, heeling, broad jump, sit and down with the handlers out of sight. A Collie must jump one-and-a-half times the height at his shoulders for the high jump and three times that height for the broad jump. The Utility Dog degree (UD) is the most difficult. This degree requires the dog to pick out an article bearing his handler's scent from a group of identical, unscented articles, perform a signal exercise, directed jumping and retrieving and group stand for examination. During Open (CDX) and Utility exercises handlers are not permitted to touch their dogs. The CD, CDX and UD degrees must be obtained in sequence.

The American Kennel Club also awards a Tracking degree (TD) which can be obtained before or after any of the other Obedience degrees. In 1980 the TDX (Tracking Dog Excellent) degree was instituted. Before entering a Tracking Trial a dog must be certified by a Tracking judge to be capable of tracking. For the TD a dog must find an article dropped at the end of a track 440 to 550 yards in length containing at least two turns and aged for thirty minutes to two hours. To compete for the TDX title a dog must first have his TD degree. The TDX track is aged for three to four hours, has at least three turns, two cross tracks and three articles dropped along a track of 800 to 1,000 yards. All the articles must be found.

In 1978 the AKC added another challenge for obedience enthusiasts: the Obedience Trial Championship (OTCH) awarded to Utility Dogs who have obtained 100 points in Obedience competition including three first places: one in Utility, one in Open B and another in either class. OTCH points are awarded for placing first or second in Open B and Utility classes. The more dogs in competition, the more points are awarded.

The first Collie OTCH was Ch. and OTCH Shoreham Dubious Delight, UDT, a tricolor male owned and trained by Jennifer Julander of California. The second was Walstone Impulse, UDT, a tricolor bitch owned and trained by Madeline Loos of New Jersey. The third was Ch. and OTCH North Country Wildfire, UD, a sable male owned and trained by Sandra Hall of Minnesota.

A free copy of the AKC booklet, *Obedience Regulations*, can be obtained by writing to the American Kennel Club.

Early Obedience History and the Collie

Obedience was brought to the United States by Helene Whitehouse Walker, who was introduced to the sport on a visit to England during the early 1930s. Actual Obedience competition began in 1936. In 1937 Mrs. Walker and her celebrated associate, Blanche Saunders with three of their Standard Poodles left on a now famous 10,000-mile trailer tour of the country to promote dog obedience training.

Doberman Pinscher and German Shepherd Dog fanciers were the first to start a club in the Midwest to promote obedience training. Soon other breeds

Ch. Master Lukeo of Noranda, CDX (1934), by Ace of Ashtead ex Ch. Lady Lukeo of Cosalta, bred and owned by Mrs. William H. Long, Jr., was the breed's first champion CDX.

Ch. Shamrock Smooth Rocket, UD (1957), by Ch. Sharock Smooth Stream (a graduate guide dog) ex Shamrock Bee, was the first champion of either Variety to earn the Utility degree. In eight litters he sired two champions, four CDs, eight graduate guide dogs for the blind and our companions with special training for retarded or blind children.

were participating regularly, among them Collies and Shetland Sheepdogs. Helen A. Sullivan, in Los Angeles, trained her homebred Collie, Goldie of Oakwood, to the CD title in 1937. In 1939 Buster Whiteson, from Jackson Heights, New York, became the first Collie to earn the CDX title. The Utility degree, however, took more time. In 1945 Sirius Sirangus became the first to earn this distinction. Five years later a bitch named Phoebe, UD became the first Collie with a Tracking title. Lockaber Ladbuck was the first Collie to win all Obedience degrees that were offered by the American Kennel Club at that time.

Mrs. William H. Long, Jr. directed a training class on Long Island. She also helped found BUDDIES, INC., which provided obedience-trained companion dogs for blind and handicapped children. In 1939 her Ch. Master Lukeo of Noranda, CDX became the first Collie champion to finish the CDX title. Mrs. Long stressed the importance of a happy and cheerful relationship between handler and Collie. She hoped to see "every GOOD Collie the holder of an Obedience title." Collies then ranked fourth in the Working Group for the number of Obedience titles earned. In 1942 Mrs. Long founded Dogs for Defense to select and train dogs for service with the armed forces. Many of these were Collies whose ability to think and reason was recognized as superior.

Janet (Mrs. William H.) Holbrook won her first Obedience trophy in Omaha, Nebraska, in 1940 with Count of Buffington. He also went Best of Variety and on to Working Group fourth that same day. He never obtained his CD despite three firsts in competition because there weren't enough dogs competing for him to qualify for a degree. Mrs. Holbrook was an enthusiastic teacher of obedience there and in California after her move west in 1954. She published a training booklet later included in CCA's first obedience booklet, and is proud that she was able to train Collies simultaneously for breed and Obedience competition. "Our best known obedience Collie was Ch. Blazer of Buffington, CDX," she says. "Blazer was handled exclusively in obedience by our daughter, Nancy, when she was eight and nine years old. When she and Blazer finished the CDX in 1961, it was our understanding that he was the only living champion Collie with a CDX title. Fortunately that picture has changed. If Blazer and Nancy had any part in encouraging people to show their conformation Collies in Obedience, we are grateful for that."

Marion Earl, from Hillside, New Jersey, began in obedience when someone told her Collies had had the brains bred out of them. In 1949 Earlcrest Jeanie, CD gained her title and Miss Earl put many other Obedience degrees on her Collies while continuing to promote obedience in her area. She was a member of the Town and Country Obedience Club and life member of the Collie Club of America.

Cinder McDale, CDX, earned his title for Dale McMackin who became president of the Collie Club of America in 1964. Backed by Mrs. W. F. Taylor and Mrs. Florence Cummings, instructors in the Tulsa Training Club, Mr. McMackin convinced the national Club to include obedience at its Specialty shows. The two ladies put on two qualifying A-O matches and every year since 1965 obedience has been part of the Collie Club of America Specialty.

Florence Cummings became interested in obedience when she discovered Ch. Arrowhill Silver Ho of Glamis, CD responded and enjoyed it. "Nancy" also performed in a movie for children and was part of a Collie drill team with juniors.

Another active drill team was led by Mrs. Leo Sturm in Indiana and the Holmhaven team performed at the Sunnybank October Festival at Terhune home in Pompton Lakes, New Jersey, for many years.

Contemporary Obedience Activity

THE SHAMROCK SMOOTHS

The first champion Collie to earn the Utility title was Ch. Shamrock Smooth Rocket, UD bred by Dr. Lee Ford and finished to his degree by Miss Gail F. Thompson of Yonkers, New York in 1963.

More than ten other Shamrock Smooths finished their CD degrees that year for Dr. Ford. In Parkland, Washington, she raised true stock dogs and these earned a proud total of over sixty degrees in a period of only six years. Eighteen were shown to their championships, one with a blind handler. Thirty-three graduated as guide dogs for the blind, nine for blind children and others guiding the retarded, quite a record for the Smooth Collie as an efficient and reliable worker.

HOLMHAVEN COLLIES

Inga Holm and her daughter Lily H. Sayre have been involved in obedience for many years. Their first Utility degree winner, Bellhaven Enchanting Lancer, was more than a year old before starting his training, but by the time he was eighteen months old he had earned his Utility degree.

Elected Duke of Holmhaven, UD received a *Dog World* Award for earning his CD, CDX and UD titles all in less than nine months. At nineteen months he was the youngest Collie to his time to earn the title. Five years later his own son, Holmhaven Magic Flash, UD, broke that record by earning his UD at seventeen months with another *Dog World* Award.

Holmhaven Collies have won over thirty titles including five UDs and six CDXs. In 1979 the Holms moved to Fort Lauderdale, Florida, where they continued their active interest in Obedience competition.

Lily H. Mattesky and one of her Collies demonstrating the high jump during the annual Sunnybank Festival. A Collie must jump one-and-a-half times its height at shoulder in the Open and Utility classes. *Inga Holm*

An accomplished group of Holmhaven Collies practicing the five-minute long down with handlers out of sight. Left to right: Holmhaven Magic Lance, UD; Holmhaven Real McCoy; Holmhaven Blond Charmer, CD; Holmhaven Magic Flash, UD; Elected Duke of Holmhaven, UD and Holmhaven Gold Star, CD. *Inga Holm*

MARIE FORDENBACHER

In 1978 obedience training lost a tremendous champion with the untimely death of young Marie Fordenbacher. A successful obedience instructor from western Pennsylvania, she was best known for her Collie, Lori: Can. OTCH Golden Major's Lori Flyer, Am. Can. UD Lori and Marie compiled an enviable record. They reached Highest Scoring Dog in Trial more than twenty times and were twice among the top ten obedience dogs in the country. Near perfect scores of 199½ in Open B and Utility on the same day from two different judges bear witness to their splendid teamwork. Marie's Collies earned over thirteen titles in the United States and Canada, including two UDs and three CDXs.

CAROL A. KNOCK

Carol A. Knock of Warren, Ohio, teaches obedience at the local YMCA. She has demonstrated an affinity for working with Collies and develops fast, happy workers. Her pupils have trained many breeds, earning numerous titles.

Carol's Cheyenne Rebel, UD, won the *Dog World* Award for scores of 195 or better in three consecutive trials. He is one of the few dogs never to fail while qualifying for his CDX and UD titles. Can. OTCH Carol's Yankee Doodle Duke, Am., Can. UD won a *Dog World* award and was ranked among the highest scoring Collies in the United States for several years.

JAN SHIELDS

Californian Jan (Mrs. D. F.) Shields believes in calm, steady communication and lots of praise when training a Collie. Her Northfield's Amber, CDX, responded by earning a *Dog World* Award with CD scores over 195 in three consecutive trials.

Jan's next Collie responded equally as well. Ch. Antrum All-Try of Northshield came to her at three months of age and immediately started training for the breed ring and obedience. At eighteen months he completed his championship and earned a *Dog World* award for his CD record.

"Wind" needed only four trials to qualify for his CDX degree and won his UD title by the time he was two, also with high scores. In August, 1971, breed history was made when Wind successfully passed the tracking test to become *the first Champion Utility Dog Tracking Collie!*

SUSAN LARSON

"A great working dog—fast, happy and accurate" is how Susan Larson of Carmichael, California, describes her first obedience Collie, of Bellhaven background. She started him at eighteen months and he had his Utility degree before he was three. Sierra Trace, UD only once, scored below 195 and won a High in Trial award along the way.

Marie Fordenbacher and her Denmalor Flyer Collies. Left to right: Ch./Can. OTCH Golden Major's Lori Flyer, Am., Can. UD; Sandy's Cinderella Flyer, Am. CDX, Can. CD; Denmalor Master Chubbs Flyer, UDT; Denmalor June Flyer, UDT; Denmalor Honey Bear Flyer. Am., Can. CD; Denmalor Jessica Flyer, CD; Denmalor Continental Flyer, CDX; and Denmalor Mighty Joe Flyer. *Joan Brown*

A consistent Collie obedience star of the 1960s was OTCH Carol's Yankee Doodle Duke, shown here with Carol Knock (right) after scoring High in Trial with a score of 199 in Open B at the Ashtabula KC. *E. H. Frank*

Ch. Antrum All-Try of Northshield, UDT (1968), by Ch. Parader's Reflection ex Ch. Antrum's All Alone, was the first champion Rough Collie with a UDT degree. He was also a successful sire with six Rough and four Smooth champion offspring to his credit. *Susan Larson*

With but one exception, these Collies were owned and trained by Susan Larson, who writes, "I have to chuckle each time someone asks if it is a composite photograph," Sue says. "It's not—the dogs were simply put in place and told to *Stay.*" They are (clockwise from left): Valley Winds Rustic Image, UD; Sequoia's Night Wind, UD; Kirkcolm's Try Power, CDX, owned and trained by Royana Power; Sierra Trace, UD; Valley Wind's Midnight Shadow, CD; and Northshield's Windfall. *Susan Larson*

Susan's second Collie, Sequoia's Night Wind, UD, completed her Utility degree before age two with even higher scores and a High in Trial. Her son, Valley Wind's Rustic Image, UD. also earned the Utility title and a High in Trial. Sired by Mexican Ch. Vidale Valley Squire, UD, he is one of the first UD Collies from UD parents.

High in Trial seems to have become a tradition with Susan and her Collie family. Ch. Northshield's Windfall CD earned this award at her first show and her son, Ch. Windhaven's Trailblazer, CD also became a High in Trial winner during the course of his career.

JANET HOLLAND THOMASON

Janet has the distinction of achieving the first two Tracking degrees for Smooth Collies. Her first dog, Am., Can. Ch. Hollyjan's Hawkeye of Markay, Am. UDT., Can. CDX, Can. TD was less than two years old when he completed all his obedience titles. According to *Off-Lead* magazine, he was the youngest Champion UDT of any breed. In addition, he received several High in Trial awards along the way.

Janet has also won several CD degrees on other Collies and the second Tracking degree on a Smooth: Can. Ch. Hollyjan's Megan of Markay, Am., Can. CD, Am., Can. TD.

JAMES AND JUDITH SMOTREL

Jim and Judy Smotrel, from Lynchburg, Virginia, have put many Obedience titles on their Daydream Collies. Most titled is Ch. Hi Vu Black Bart the Skyhawk, UDT, HT, VX. Bart is also a Canadian champion and UD and United Kennel Club UD as well. He is a registered therapy dog, the first Collie to complete the NCDA Agility 2 title. He is a son of Ch. Aurealis Skylarking out of Hi Vu Tri Again bred by Karen Hutchinson, and was Highest Scoring Dog in the 1992 CCA Obedience Trial and received the High Combined Score in 1993.

The Smotrels are cochairmen of the CCA Certification Committee, which awards Versatility and herding instinct certificates, as well as awards for breed and Obedience titles.

We hope newcomers to the ranks of the Collie Fancy will want to follow the example of these wonderful dogs and their owners. Training for obedience cements the bond of love and trust between Collie and handler. Don't miss it!

THE COLLIE AS STOCK DOG

by Glen Twiford

(Glen Twiford has spent much of his life on ranches where Collies are used daily to work livestock. He writes from years of first-hand experience about the Collie's time-honored role as working stock dog.)

As a child I remember dogs sired by Ch. El Troubador and Ch. Cock Robin of Arken among the earliest dogs bought for me by my parents. A man in Denver had brought these bloodlines into Colorado; early Bellhaven, Tazewell, Blangsted and Kelmar were the first bloodlines we took into Wyoming. The Collies we used on these ranches in later years were linebred from these early dogs, with an occasional outcross to retain vitality and hold type. Basically the dogs we used for herding were descendants of these early lines; these were the dogs from which the Wind-Call Collies were developed.

I spent a good part of my formative years on large grass ranches in Wyoming, where a thousand head of cattle could graze, followed by bands of sheep. Sheep are not as particular as cattle about their grazing, which enables the rancher to utilize his grassland more economically. When the sheep were accompanied by herders, overgrazing was prevented, and this arrangement allowed the wonderful opportunity to train and use the Collies in the work for which they were originally developed.

The bands of sheep numbered about 3,000; we usually used two Collies to a band. Before we fenced in sections of land, the sheep were allowed to graze freely, herded by Indians from a reservation to the north. They were excellent with the sheep, and eventually with the dogs, migrating into our country during the herding season, and staying until late fall or early winter. Then they would pack up their sheep wagons, hitch them behind a truck and move back to the reservation for the long, cold winter.

At the beginning the Indians wanted no part of the Collies. They had their own ideas about sheepdogs and flatly refused to try ours. One season I was determined that the Collies would have a chance, and would not let them bring their own sheepdogs. There were too many sheep, and the Indians needed their jobs, so they agreed to let the Collies stay.

At first the Collies nearly beat us home; as fast as we took them back to the range, they would return. We could only guess at what encouragement they received. Eventually the herders accepted them and the dogs stopped coming back. Although the Indians never gave us any signs of approval the Collies seemed to work well for them and were content to remain.

One herder was indispensable, for he knew sheep and was a good influence on his fellow workers. He was the leader but had one vice. He would take something back with him when the herders packed up for the winter. When caught he would look you straight in the eye and grin; it was a battle of wits, for if he was caught, you won—otherwise he did. His wagon was always searched to see what would be cached in the storage compartments under wooden seats along the sides of the canvas-covered sheepwagon: a saddle, a calf, or whatever else would fit. He probably did not need it, but it was part of the game.

At the end of the first season using the Collies we were busy preparing for departure when we realized three Collies were missing, including one that was a particular favorite of the Indians, 01' General. A thorough search of the wagons produced nothing, until we noticed that their leader's was missing. A mile down the road it was waiting under some cottonwood trees, its owner wearing a resigned grin. Two grown Collies were crammed into the seat bins, a puppy was in a box under the bed. They were making no noise, but must have been wondering what new experience would come next. The herder knew why I grinned back at him that day.

Practical Application of the Standard

During these years of observation I became impressed with the practical aspect of the Collie Standard. We paid attention to breeding for proper conformation as well as working ability, for our Collies were also shown around the country.

The features that make a Collie a beautiful animal in the showring also make it a sound, agile, graceful and functional dog at work. Without doubt the serious breeder must ascribe due importance to structure. Proper balance cannot be obtained with a disregard for any part of the anatomy. Balance is the key word.

The proper angle of the shoulder blade to the upper arm approaches 45 degrees, with the heel of the dog's foot directly under the blade's axis. With proper length of neck this enables the Collie to keep its head up when moving and to see the target of its work in tall grass. I have watched many dogs work under the impediment of incorrect shoulder angulation, with resultant loss of time and energy. These dogs may have all the heart and working drive, but they just can't last in the field in rough country.

Forty-five degree angulation applies to the rear as well. The thigh bone must be at approximately that angle to the ground. With a straight back and proper angulation in front and rear, the body will accept the shock of motion and the jolts of rough terrain will be absorbed with springlike action. The old analogy that says if you strap a glass of water to the back of a proper-moving Collie you would spill very little is not a bad one.

On days when we would move sheep to the railroad loading pens some ten miles away, the Collies would cover fifty or more miles to the sheep's ten. Our Collies worked at a constant trot, a gait the properly proportioned, sound dog can maintain for a whole day, if weather and other conditions are right. He must have near-perfect balance and strength to keep this up. That is where our Standard proves itself.

The Collie's short hocks, combined with well-bent stifles give it endurance. Strong parallel legs front and rear combine with a straight back and croup neither too sloping nor too straight, to provide agility and further enhance the endurance so necessary to an active working dog.

The Collies with endurance had straight toplines and correspondingly straight underlines. That is, from the brisket back is a straight line well to the middle of the body before forming any tuck up, the less tuck up the better.

On days when we would move sheep to the railroad loading pens some ten miles away, the Collies would cover fifty or more miles to the sheeps' ten. Our Collies worked at a constant trot, a gait the properly proportioned, sound dog can maintain for a whole day if weather and conditions are right. He must have near-perfect balance and strength to keep this up. *Twiford*

Most of the Collies worked with sheep, but they would work cattle when necessary. At least some of them would; those kicked as puppies seldom had an interest in cattle. Some of the more aggressive dogs were excellent with cattle and horses. They were usually too rough for sheep and particularly could not be used with lambing ewes. The best cow dogs were often wool grabbers who would damage pelts. *Twiford*

Besides being parallel in the rear legs, the dogs with the greatest endurance were slightly wider behind than in front. Dogs that stood too close behind could not turn quickly and had less power.

Even in head features the Collie Standard is a practical one. We had a dog who was an excellent worker but had an even bite. He was unduly rough and was used only on wethers (castrated rams); when he took an occasional nip he came away with a bit of flesh. Dogs which use their teeth generally do much better with cattle or horses than sheep.

Other parts of the Standard also have functional purposes. Semi-erect ears catch sound better than broken ones, and the tailset influences balance.

The coat is harsh, straight and sheds water. Its profusion adds warmth. On the ranch we always had a month of thirty below zero weather every winter. In that time the Collies slept out in the snow in preference to their buildings. We never could understand why.

The sections that propel a Collie are the ones which impress you most when you spend ten hours on a horse behind a dog as he moves sheep through rugged country.

There are few parts of the Collie Standard that cannot be justified from a practical standpoint. It is a good Standard, a combination of the beautiful and the practical. Most lovers of our breed feel that a beautiful Collie head, combined with properly sound body, elegance, style and animation, leaves little to be desired in a canine companion.

Winning Father's Approval

When I first became interested in Collies, my father did not share my enthusiasm for them as potential guardians of our livestock. He didn't appreciate two lively Collies tugging on opposite ends of a dead skunk, or playing catch with a three-foot rattlesnake. The head of the rattler had been neatly separated from its body by the Collie's first furious shake; the game of catch was his reward. My father did not realize that Collies had saved the hide of his son more than once from angry bulls, protective mother cows, or aggressive sheep, because I was not supposed to have put myself into such vulnerable positions in the first place.

Later, when a young Collie was slapped over a buckberry bush by a grown black bear, he showed some interest, until she dived around the bush and lit into the bear again. She was following a pack of hounds chasing the bear. When I explained that she was the only one in the pack that would tackle the bear, he was strangely unimpressed. In time, he gradually mellowed.

My Collie friends took another step up the ladder when a herd of starving hogs found their way to our ranch. There must have been twenty in all: dark red and mean. They discovered a pen of ewes and lambs, broke in, and were literally eating the sheep alive . . . a gruesome sight, and one that called for immediate action. I yelled for the three Collies and flew into the pen. Suddenly I realized these weren't fat show pigs; they were starving animals in no mood to be disputed. They met us head on; I was out of the pen so fast I don't think I left any tracks on the ground. But the dogs were everywhere; they seemed possessed. They had never seen a hog before, and who knows what brought on such aggression. Those Collies tore off ears, split noses and in three or four minutes had that herd of hogs through what was left of the fence and on their way somewhere else.

I think what won the Collies their chance with our sheep were the coyotes. Until this time, when we ran sheep on the ranch my father had borrowed Border Collies or small dogs of that type. They were excellent herders, but not large enough to be much protection against coyotes, bobcats or the occasional lynx that wandered through the area.

We found the Collies, on the other hand, to be excellent protection against coyotes. Cyanide guns could harm the sheep and traps were not practical with other livestock or dogs around. Small dogs were killed or chased back to camp, but not the Collies. They wouldn't chase. At first they only held off the coyotes by barking and running out to meet them. Often that was sufficient, for two grown Collies could easily scatter four or five coyotes.

One day I tried an experiment. I had seen a large male coyote in one area and wondered if the Collies would chase him. I put ten dogs into the station wagon and drove out to the area. After spotting the coyote, I got as close to him as possible. I stopped the car and opened the doors; several Collies saw the coyote, and the race was on. Surprisingly, they caught him quickly. They wanted to sniff him like another dog, and that would have been the end of it. But the coyote decided he had had enough and grabbed the nearest Collie, a blue merle male last to arrive on the scene and trying to get a cactus thorn out of his foot. Perhaps he was irritated, but the fight was short, ending with the coyote's back broken. From then on the dogs rarely hesitated to attack a coyote if they were near enough. It was the perfect solution to the coyote problem. Only those which preyed on the sheep were hunted.

The Collies had finally found their place on the ranch and a supporter in my father.

Training to Herd

We found the Collie temperament ideal for working sheep, but we had to have proper personality to develop a worker: a dog which was calm and friendly with people, full of life but sensible about it. I have seen strains of Collies, the boisterous, rough, always barking and leaping kind, that were worthless with sheep. The overly-friendly, rough and aggressive dog was often bored with the work and sometimes even dangerous with sheep. That type of dog had less instinct and enthusiasm for driving, although they sometimes worked out all right with cattle or other stock.

We would put five-week-old puppies in the middle of a pen of sheep to watch their reactions. It was interesting and varied, but their ability with sheep as they matured was consistent with the interest they showed as puppies.

Our method of training the Collies was simple but effective. We started them out with sheep at six or eight months of age. Having an older trained dog made it easier, for puppies are great mimics and try to do whatever the trained dog is doing. Without an older dog we would take advantage of the pup's natural desire to follow and to move back and forth behind the sheep. The next step was to teach him arm signals, which we always used to correspond with the direction in which he was going. Gradually he learned to accept direction.

The Collies seemed to crave learning anything connected with working the sheep. Grown dogs constantly watched the herder mounted on a horse. They could see almost a quarter-mile if conditions were right. Collies are natural drovers, moving sheep. Teaching them to pen was more difficult, but once they had the idea from field work, these steps became simple. The Collie does not move or crouch like the Border Collie, nor will it run over the backs of the sheep, preferring to outwait them, or to run around and see what is interfering up ahead. Collies have the advantage of being larger and more easily seen by the sheep than the smaller herding breeds.

When the pups had progressed to the stage where they understood the association between the signals and what was expected of them, they literally expressed their happiness and excitement in every motion.

Instinct

It is agreed that working ability in some breeds is an instinctive thing. Of course training and the stimulation of being near stock helps in training dogs, but there has to be the instinct to protect.

One time we were driving a group of sheep to shelter because of a blizzard reported to be moving in. It was already snowing hard. There were two of us on horseback and several dogs, working well. We were on our way to put the sheep in the comfort of a wooded area when I noticed 01' General stop. We called him, for we could see nothing, but he wouldn't budge. I worried about him the last few miles into shelter and after warming up, I discovered he had still not come in. It was terrible out there by then, and dark. I struggled back out in the pick-up and fought my way as close as I could to where we had left him.

With a searchlight I could see he was still there, nearly covered with snow. He made no sound, and didn't move, but seemed to be all right. I started poking around and found he was on the brink of a sandpit used for gravel by the highway department. It had filled with tumbleweeds and was covered by snow. Two sheep had fallen into the hole and were trapped in the debris, nearly hidden from sight by the snow. The Collie had waited for help to come for nearly an hour.

Another time a female Collie had been working with several men, driving ewes and lambs to summer pasture. Suddenly she bolted into the very orderly band of sheep, and though she heard every command, she would not leave the flock until she had worked her way twenty feet in. When the animals scattered, she was staring at a small bum lamb that was trying to keep up and hadn't been noticed by the men.

The Blizzard of 1949

The winter of 1949 will long be remembered as the year of the first hay lifts. That year thousands of animals were frozen in one of the worst blizzards in memory. For three days and nights there was a ninety-miles-an-hour wind, with blowing snow and temperatures that stayed at ten below zero. National magazines sent photographers who took pictures of cattle standing frozen along fences. They looked like statues and remained that way for several days, until they could be disposed of. I had lived in that country most of my life and seen storms of all kinds, but could not have imagined one more brutal. Wild animals froze everywhere: Cottontails and jackrabbits were found stiff behind clumps of grass and under bushes. The storm was a nightmare.

We had a little warning before the blizzard struck, and four of us on horseback started out to collect four thousand sheep. We had six Collies with us, our best drivers. We managed to gather all the sheep and were heading desperately toward a lane leading into several hundred acres of cottonwood groves that would furnish the best cover available in such a storm.

The sheep were going with the storm. We could barely make out dogs from sheep. By then the wind behind them was so furious and loud the dogs could not hear our shouted commands to them. Heads of dogs and sheep were covered with driven snow, which froze quickly from their breath until they appeared to have huge light globes over their heads. The ice protected their breathing, but prevented their attention to any outside influence. We were just minutes from the lane that turned to safety, but the sheep would not face the fury of the storm and were passing the turn. The Collies tore at their faces but could do nothing against the thousands of sheep pushing forward to the little protection they could find.

The Collies sensed our desperation, and barked continuously; we could see their mouths open, but could not hear because of the storm. At times they would drift away; when they got downwind they would stop immediately. With heads held nearly straight up they would scent their way back to the sheep. We had to turn away to save ourselves; there was no way the animals could be stopped. Four of the Collies followed us when we had to desert the sheep. The other two found their way back, when they could no longer find men or horses. They were taking terrible punishment and could scarcely breathe, but those Collies had no intention of quitting until we turned back. Even then they seemed confused and upset at leaving the sheep, and had to be coaxed away.

The sheep were eventually forced another mile into the corner of the pasture and covered with drifts that measured up to twenty feet. A few hundred had struggled to the top of the pile and were blown over the fence. We found them scattered over another mile. Many were just white lumps on the prairie. Their little hooves sticking up out of the snow were polished shiny black by the blowing snow and ice.

After the storm, men from neighboring ranches came by snowshoe and on horseback. Twenty or more worked around the clock for days with our own men, hauling sheep from under the huge drifts, putting them aboard hayracks to protect their steaming bodies until they were taken into the large barns and sheds.

The sheep had melted small holes in the snow with their breath. By probing with long poles we could locate them under deep drifts. The snow had protected them from freezing, but they couldn't get out or even move without help. Some were covered up for days and had eaten the wool from others before they were found. They shredded tough sagebrush stumps into fine strands. Most were still alive; the partially paralyzed sheep were put into burlap slings, suspended from the rafters. The men worked in crews, moving their legs until the sheep could eventually stand on their own.

The Collies helped find many sheep we could have missed. They would nuzzle the strange-looking mounds with feet sticking out at such impossible angles, and miraculously most of them would move. With the help of the Collies and our neighbors, we lost only about a hundred sheep out of four thousand!

Chapter 9

The Collie As a Herding Dog

by Lois Russell

In order to understand the truly unique qualities of the Collie, we must piece together the history and origins of this remarkable breed. Although there are no written records, no stud books or inventories with specific reference to the breed prior to the last half of the nineteenth century, we do know that the Collie in all its majesty did not spring forth from some breeder's carefully planned litter as a remarkable mutation, in the manner of the horse Justin Morgan—a complete and finished product.

Rather the Collie gradually emerged as a distillation of various breeds from many parts of Europe, western Asia and the Middle East. For centuries, there had been a steady migration of peoples sweeping into the British Isles from Europe and Scandinavia. Invading armies were followed by settlers and traders bringing with them their support systems, their livestock and their utility dogs. In due course, the great abbeys established in Britain also imported specialized strains of livestock and herding dogs from their original homelands.

Collie-type dogs with remarkably similar characteristics existed wherever mixed agriculture was practiced, in a broad band stretching from the Urals to the Pyrenees. Such dogs were the Owtcharka of southern Russia, possibly an antecedent of the white Collie, the Sarplaninac of Yugoslavia, the gentle giant Leonberger of Germany, the Pyrenean Sheepdog of France, to mention but a few.[1]

---

[1]*Several of the 19th century authors observed, when considering the origin of the Collie, that the canine that genetically most closely resembles the Collie is the Dingo. They then dismissed this as an impossibility owing to the global separation of the two races. However, Mrs. Iris Combe's research, noted below, Footnote 10, does make this a real probability. Phoenician traders sailed all around the world and could easily have acquired Dingoes whose descendants, in turn, eventually found their way through northern Africa to Europe and Britain during the heyday of the Roman Empire.*

It was, however, during the nineteenth century on the countless subsistence tenant farms in Britain, particularly in Scotland, Ireland and the northern counties of England, that the Collie we know as the "Scotch" Collie began to emerge as a distinct breed. This was undoubtedly in large part a by-product of the cattle droving trade.

By looking at the history of these dogs and the herding and farming practices of the time, we can develop a clear picture of how the dogs worked and the useful functions they performed. We can also see how the talents inherent in those working dogs are still evident in our modern Collie. Just as the physical appearance which served as a magnet for nineteenth century dog show devotees has endured and even been "improved" upon, so the character traits and basic instincts that made the farmers' kindly, adaptable, jack-of-all-trades Collies attractive to the drovers have survived undiminished in the Collies of today.

As cities grew, especially in the midlands of England, and primitive farming practices made it impossible to maintain large numbers of livestock on the impoverished little highland farms over the winter, all but a few breeding stock were sent with drovers to the distant industrialized urban centers where there was a ready demand for meat on the hoof. The black cattle from the Scottish highlands, although seldom weighing more than 700 pounds, were prized for the succulent beef they produced, especially after fattening on lush English pastures, and they brought the highest prices.

From the earliest times, every major community and county seat held livestock sales markets at least once or twice a year, and the licenses to hold these sales were a lucrative source of income for both the local administration and the crown. Cattle were the main livelihood of farm families serving as their most dependable cash crop, and the primary source of funds for paying their rent to their chiefs or landlords who, in turn, depended on this income to maintain themselves and to pay their tithes to the King.

Prior to the middle decades of the nineteenth century, throughout the highland farming areas a few sheep were kept for the fleece used in spinning fabric for clothes and blankets (plaids), but cattle were by far more important and more numerous. Meat was seldom included in the diet of farm families; only when an animal died of natural causes would it be eaten. Milk, cheese and oat cakes or porridge were the staples, supplemented occasionally by wild fowl and game. It was the same for the dogs.

Strict laws prohibiting anyone but nobles and royalty from hunting limited this source of food, but poaching, farmers stealing out to hunt under cover of darkness with a bow and arrow and a dog, was common. In fact, farmers often crossed their Collies with lurchers, a crossbred related to the Collie, or purebred Greyhounds to enhance their hunting ability. Some say that this is the source of the Collie's remarkably gentle mouth.

Typically, by the time winter held the land in its rigid grip, on each farm there would be one or two bred cows due to calve in early spring. Each would have a newly weaned calf at her side, and a yearling or a two-year-old that had just been bred. A comparatively wealthy farmer might also have a pair of older oxen to supplement the work done by the cows as draft and plowing animals.

During the frigid months, this little band of cattle shared the cramped one-room sod-and-stone thatched cottage with the farm family. Before turnips were introduced as a viable crop for fodder, their only food was what could be scrounged from the wheat and corn stubble left on the nearby cultivated fields, and by spring starvation among both people and animals was rampant. It was important that all excess cattle be removed from the farm before the bad weather began, and since this time of year also coincided with the annual collection of rents, there was an added incentive for the farmer to sell his stock to the drovers. For centuries drovers were the linchpin of the British economy and the primary provisioners for the great British armies and navies that were constantly being dispersed around the world.

The occupation of droving was a complex and chancy undertaking that originated during the Roman occupation and reached its apex in Britain during the 150 years between the beginning of the agricultural revolution and the culmination of the industrial revolution, from roughly 1730 to 1880. Drovers were independent contractors who either bought stock at the farms or, more often, took stock on consignment. The prerequisites for a drover's license, and every drover had to have one, were that he be a married man over thirty-five years of age and in good standing in his community.

Droving was a highly skilled trade that required an honest man of great experience caring for livestock, and with an intimate knowledge of the terrain over which he would be taking the valuable charges entrusted to him. Not only did he have to deliver the livestock in fat and healthy condition to the markets and negotiate a fair price for them, but he also had to serve as banker and often postman and advocate for his rural customers.

Enterprising men from Wales, Ireland and Scotland would travel throughout the country gathering up livestock from the farms, a few here, one or two there. They did not discriminate between cattle, sheep, donkeys, horses, hogs, geese or turkeys, and often had a motley assortment of species traveling with them. Once the individual consignments were gathered together, and the animals often numbered in the thousands, they were then sorted into manageable lots of 100 or so cattle and 200 to 300 sheep. Each group assigned a trusted assistant drover, usually a brother or son, and one or more herdsmen accompanied by a dog or two. One after another the herds would string out along the track and begin their long trek that might take several months. The Collies were invaluable in keeping the herds moving steadily along and the stragglers from becoming lost or intermingling with another group. Livestock that was not sold at the first fair was moved from fair to fair, gravitating ever closer to the various metropolitan centers where there was a constant demand for butcher's supplies and draft animals.

The old Roman roads were in sorry condition after fourteen centuries of neglect, and other existing roads were hardly more than rutted trails, dusty in the dry seasons and quagmires when wet. Traveling cross-country was difficult as the encroaching hedges and walls of enclosure increasingly limited access to stretches of open land. According to (Daniel) Defoe, writing in 1724, "the roads are packed(with livestock), over-used and ruined! The only way to make progress was to cross the fields, which is why pack animals were so popular. It took twelve hours to get from London to Oxford, a distance of sixty miles. Beyond Oxford the quality of the road deteriorated alarmingly. . . . The virtual impossibility of travel kept the regions of England distinct in every way: dialect, customs and lifestyle were different in places only fifty miles apart."[2] The drovers were among the few people who regularly traversed the entire countryside of Britain.

When Parliament ruled that all main roads in Britain should be widened to eight feet and "improved" to facilitate travel, toll gates were installed to raise funds for the "improvement" to be performed by the local squire. Although the tolls were collected, the improvements were glacially slow in forthcoming. The drovers considered this added expense unacceptable and opted to follow as much as possible unmarked routes through the highlands and over the mountains.

These enforced detours exposed them to the constant threat of raiders and inclement weather, so they needed dogs that were good watch dogs as well as hardy driving dogs with lots of endurance; dogs that could easily adjust to all sorts of unforeseen circumstances. The versatile farmers' Collies and their descendants served the drovers well.

There are a number of contemporary descriptions of the drovers and their Collies, men with their dogs beside them trudging along behind their herds mile after mile, for hundreds of miles. The more affluent drovers rode sturdy white ponies or in carts. The herdsmen traveled on foot. The dog's primary function was to push the stock forward regardless of the terrain. Obstacles such as rivers were met head on and forded. When a dangerous passageway was encountered, it was the dog's job to block the stock from falling off the edge of the road or into a rushing river. Often a dog moving the stock on a roadway, when it spotted an approaching vehicle, a stage coach or farm wagon, for instance, would on its own initiative squeeze the herd to the edge of the road or path to allow the traffic to pass safely. The dog deftly

---

[2]*James Burke,* The Day the Universe Changed *(New York: Little, Brown and Company, 1985).*

accomplished this maneuver by patrolling up and down the side of the herd in a fashion often seen in Europe, especially in Germany.[3]

At the start of a livestock drive, to assist in controlling the very tame but reluctant animals being taken to market, the drover would also purchase the farmer's Collie. It must have posed many problems for the drover to move three or four head of cattle away from the farm and family where they had been raised by hand and spent four, five, six, or more years laboring in the fields, always in close proximity to the farm family. Naturally, it helped considerably to have the dog with which the stock were familiar come along to serve as their guide and companion on this intimidating trip.

Most nights were spent at rural inns or friendly farms. No matter how bare the larder, the hospitable Scots always welcomed travelers and willingly shared their limited provisions with their guests. Most farmers on the droving routes kept a stance in a pasture adjacent to their cottages fenced with sod walls for the express purpose of containing the drovers' cattle overnight. There was usually a small grazing fee, but the drovers were grateful for the service. With their stock safely confined, the weary drovers would happily retire to the fireside with their dogs to enjoy a tankard of ale or whiskey and exchange tall tales and gossip. Droving also supported the countless inns and hostels scattered throughout the countryside, each separated by a day's march, about fifteen to twenty miles.

Occasionally nights were passed on the hilltops and then the dogs would be expected to guard the stock and keep it from straying. When traveling long distances through practically uninhabited country, the herds were allowed to disperse over quite a large area so that they would have an opportunity to graze as they moved along and the dogs were expected to patrol the perimeters of the herd. Along "improved" roads, enclosure walls were built twenty to thirty feet back from each side of the roadway so that the stock could graze on the verges as it traveled. On such roads, a dog usually either led the flock or herd or pushed the stock forward just by the power of its presence, trotting quietly along behind.

Much of the time progress was slow and serene, the primary objective being to avoid stressing the stock, which would cause it to lose condition and

---

[3]Pictorial Half-Hours *(1851) quoted by K. J. Bonsar,* The Drovers. *This tendency of some droving Collies to patrol the sides of a flock or herd to contain it in a certain area or on a certain line of forward motion was frequently observed by long-time CCA member and respected Judge Glen Twiford when he was managing extensive sheep and cattle herding operations in Wyoming. That this particular instinct is still evidenced in Collies is apparent by the fact that in about 1980 a Collie named Lassie won the French National Sheep Herding Trials on a European course designed to demonstrate the skills of the tending or patrolling dogs.*

market value. The style of herding required very little precise control of individual animals. It did require a steady momentum and a dog that could work quietly and patiently at a moderate pace for hours on end. A drover would not want a dog that was a determined "fetcher" constantly sprinting out in an attempt to head the stock; rather the drovers' dogs needed a variety of other talents and had to be extremely adaptable and tractable.

An occasional strong bark was helpful, however, both as a warning for intruders and as an extra incentive to move recalcitrant stock forward. Barking was also encouraged as the drove approached a farm where there was the danger that the farmer's stock might mingle with the drove and be nearly impossible to separate. At such times, both the drover's helpers and the dogs would move ahead of the herd. With loud shouts and much barking, they would alert the farmer to make sure his stock was secure before the drove arrived.

When the drove reached its ultimate destination, the livestock fair where the last of the herd was sold, or the grazier's pasture where the stock would spend a season being fattened for market, the dog's job was done and it was then sold along with the drover's pony, often to the grazier for his own use. Some dogs were sent home on their own while the drover returned by coach. K. J. Bonsar in *The Drovers*[4] relates that drover's dogs would usually stop at the same inns and farms on their homeward trip that they visited on the outbound march, and the following season the drover would pay the innkeeper for the food they consumed. One such drover's dog followed this routine for twelve years. Another made the incredible journey from the eastern extremity of Kent to Milford, the westernmost point of Wales, in one week. Remarkable dogs, those drovers' dogs.

Hugh Dalziel in *British Dogs,*[5] observed:

> There are many men of many minds, and it is equally certain there are many drovers of many kinds, and the dogs these men employ as helpers differ with the nature of the work and the part of the country the drovers ply their calling in.

> I have seen the drovers who, nearly fifty years ago, were wont to collect and take to Falkirk Tryst the no longer needed bulls from a wide dairy district, and these men and their dogs were of quite a different stamp to those whose milder work was to drive sheep to the great fairs—as widely different, indeed, from each other as both are from a Smithfield Market

---

[4]K. J. Bonsar, The Drovers *(London: MacMillan and Co., Ltd., 1970).*

[5]*Hugh Dalziel,* British Dogs *(London: L. Upcott Gill, 1889).*

drover of the present day; and the dogs employed by all differed as widely as their masters.

The drovers' Collies, most of whom for practical reasons were males, annually traveled hundreds of miles throughout the length and breadth of Britain. Free to breed every receptive bitch they encountered on the journey, they were able to exert an enormous influence far and wide in establishing the breed. It was not uncommon for one dog to cover over 200 bitches in a year. As time passed the dogs were sold with increasing frequency to dog show enthusiasts and breeders during the livestock sales at the end of the trip.

Once Queen Victoria became enamored of the breed, there was a surge of eager buyers for particularly handsome Collies of the traditional "Scotch" type at all the markets. The astute drovers were always alert to marketable animals, and in this fashion, it did not take long for the Collie to emerge as a distinct and recognizable breed with a remarkably consistent appearance and character.

As an aside, Iris Combe, the distinguished author, judge and authority on British herding breeds, especially Collies, commented in *Herding Dogs:*[6]

The study of Scottish dogs necessitated digging deep into social and rural history of the past. During the process it became even clearer to me that poets and painters have been largely responsible for romanticizing and popularizing the Scottish scene, and subsequent royal connections have made it fashionable. Journalists and dog breeders were among those who jumped on this bandwagon. Scottish terrier breeds began to oust the popular English terriers, and almost every variety of herding dog was soon claimed to be of Scottish origin. Researchers do not substantiate this claim. But today it might be difficult or even unpopular to try to convince the owners of those glamorous show Collies that their original ancestors came from the bogs of Ireland and not from the hills of Scotland.

As the agricultural revolution took hold in Britain, crop rotation and the introduction of new crops, particularly turnips and clover, made it possible for Irish, Welsh and Scottish farmers to winter over their livestock. Almost immediately, however, the impact of the Enclosure Acts, especially in England, began to take effect. Large segments of the population were forced off the land and into the cities to work in the burgeoning factories. The year-round

---

[6]*Iris Combe,* Herding Dogs, Their Origins and Development in Britain *(London: Faber and Faber, Ltd., 1987).*

demand for fresh meat was increasing at a phenomenal rate. The droving trade from the outlying regions expanded accordingly.

The scope of this man-made livestock migration is staggering and is described in detail in *The Drovers* by K. J. Bonsar.[7] From his extensive research in local record offices throughout England we learn that 20,000 Irish cattle were transported annually by barge across the narrow isthmus of the North Channel from Belfast to Portpatrick in Galloway on the southwest coast of Scotland. In that area they would join the tide of black Scottish highland cattle that had been fattened in Galloway and Dumfrieshire. Together they flooded into the markets such as Falkirk Tryst not far from Edinburgh. Purchased there by English graziers, the stock would then be delivered to their new owners by the drovers who would follow any one of a number of routes from Falkirk Tryst south into the various counties of England.

Simultaneously all sorts of livestock were moving eastward out of Wales in a river of living bodies. One Welsh drover alone in the late 1860s herded more than 2,000 head of cattle to the Northampton market in England. In 1862 the Metropolitan Cattle Market at Islington, outside of London, reported 304,741 bullocks, 1,498,500 sheep, 27,591 calves and 29,470 pigs. As K. J. Bonser noted, "Smithfield in London was the chief magnet toward which the drovers and the herds were drawn. . . . On one day alone—15 December 1862—the bullocks (sold at Smithfield) numbered 8,340."[8] We can only guess at the incredible number of men and dogs involved in this endless flow of beasts.

The second half of the nineteenth century marked the division of the Collie as a herding dog in two separate breeds, the Border Collie, originally called simply the "rounding" dog, and the Collie, commonly referred to in that period as the "Scotch" Collie. One of the most profound changes in Scotland and Ireland initiated by the Agricultural and Industrial Revolutions

---

[7]K. J. Bonsar, The Drovers *(London: MacMillan and Co., Ltd., 1970).*

[8]*The subject of the Smithfield Market in London is a fascinating glimpse into an entirely separate aspect of the droving scene and does not really pertain to our herding Collies, since few ever reached that destination. Smithfield had its own guild of drovers with their own specialized dogs. Bonsar did calculate that in 1852–54 "the weekly average of animals passing through the streets (of London) to market was 69,946 almost all concentrated on two days." The cattle were driven the whole of the night previous to the Friday market, and also during the Sunday night preceding the Monday market. Imagine going to bed in London on a Sunday night at that time, preparing for the work week ahead, and having to listen to the bellowing and bleating of 35,000 animals driven by shouting men and barking dogs through the narrow, echoing cobblestone streets. The same situation prevailed on the streets of New York City in the early 1900s.*

that began during the second half of the eighteenth century was the substitution of large scale sheep raising for generalized subsistence farming. In each county thousands of the tenant farmers that had rather densely populated most of Scotland and Ireland for centuries were evicted, and all vestiges of their dwellings destroyed during the Highland Clearances and the earlier Irish clearances.

The native farmers were replaced with a handful of solitary shepherds imported from England and the Border Counties, a few with their families, and each with several thousand sheep. It took almost a hundred years to complete this ruthless cleansing of the land of its indigenous people and their lifestyle. But the relatively few absentee landowners who claimed title to the entire land had few qualms and even less sentiment about replacing people with sheep, especially since sheep farming on a large scale was so much more lucrative than the rents paid by indentured tenant farmers.

In Scotland, nonresident landowners, often titled Englishmen and successful industrialists, acquired the historic holdings of the clan chiefs following the defeat of the Scots and the unification of Scotland and England. They converted their new lands into enormous "hirsels," vast ranges of Scottish land kept exclusively for sheep raising and eventually as hunting preserves. It was the wool from the sheep raised on those hirsels that supplied the ever expanding woolen mills in the British midlands, supported the extremely lucrative international trade in woolen goods and, coupled with the hefty revenues from the slave trade, gave Britain its wealth and power in the nineteenth century.

Ironically, less than fifty years after the last tenant farmers were shipped to North America and Australia in conditions strongly reminiscent of the African slave trade, the shepherds that replaced them were themselves displaced as the vast estates were converted to hunting preserves, playgrounds for the wealthy. Most of the shepherds emigrated with their dogs to Australia, New Zealand, western Canada and the western United States.

A single shepherd overseeing thousands of sheep scattered over a several-mile-square area needed a uniquely talented dog to share the work. Basically this was a dog that would run out ahead of the shepherd, sometimes as much as a mile or more ahead, and ferret out the widely scattered wild sheep. The dog would then gather the sheep and fetch them in a group to the shepherd. The term "rounding" derived from the circular pattern of the dog's outrun.

We are given the best description of the origins of the "rounding" dog by Iris Combe. Mrs. Combe's studies indicate that for a long period in some areas, livestock used to forage in the forests which covered much of Britain before they disappeared toward the end of the eighteenth century, succumbing to the insatiable need of a growing population to provide heat, steam and power.

Forest graziers do not need a dog that can drive or chase but one that can cast wide to locate a flock, or herd stray animals, then gather and hold them. And these are the precise qualities or instincts for which the modern "eye" dog like a Border Collie is famous.[9]

In her book, *The Smooth Collie*,[10] Mrs. Combe explains that the original dogs possessing the instinct to circle stock came to Britain during the Roman occupation. Whenever the Romans found it necessary to replenish their stock of sheep or goats, small flocks of those animals were generally imported from the north coast of Africa. The sheep were settled in the grasslands of southern England and the goats along the west coast of Wales. The flocks were accompanied by their herdsmen who brought with them a "gentle type of ancient herdsman's dog, popular with the Phoenicians," and the distinctive herding behavior of these dogs was their ability to circle the flock to gather it and keep it together. Once in Britain, these short coated, thin skinned dogs were crossed with assorted sturdier, rough coated breeds, both guarding and hunting breeds, some native and others imported by the Romans. Mrs. Combe continues, "It was at this stage that the British ("Scotch") Collie or general stock dog and the specialist sheepdog were each developed from a combination of root stocks."[11]

Other authorities attribute the wide ranging outrun, "rounding," and "eye" to the crossing of Collies with gun dogs (retrievers) during the nineteenth century. Instead of the "rounding" genes which are now concentrated in the Border Collie, it is much more likely that the majority of our Collies have a preponderance of the genes inherent in the less specialized farmer's and drover's dogs, especially the latter.

Edward Jones, the newspaper reporter, wrote in 1892 in his book, *Sheep-Dog Trials and the Sheep Dog*,[12] that there were few instances of "rounding" dogs working in Wales in the years between 1828 and 1873. About the later date, however, they began to be widely available and many were directly attributable to a white bitch that had jumped off a train headed south from Scotland and was caught in the area of Abergwessin, the mid-Wales district, in 1862. She is referred to as the Kenarth bitch and the strain from that bitch

---

[9]*Iris Combe,* Herding Dogs, Their Origins and Development in Britain *(London: Faber and Faber, Ltd., 1987).*

[10]*Iris Combe,* The Smooth Collie—A Family Dog *(Cambridgeshire: Iris Combe, 1992).*

[11]*Iris Combe,* Herding Dogs, Their Origins and Development in Britain *(London: Faber and Faber, Ltd., 1987).*

[12]*Edward Jones,* Sheep-Dog Trials and the Sheep Dog *(Brecon, Wales: Edwin Poole, 1892).*

"was kept more pure than any of the other ones, as the pups when grown up were 'kept up' to each other." Jones also wrote:

> The dog is a very prolific animal when circumstances favour its fecundity; and as the owners of the new breed would, doubtless, from interested motives, endeavor to rear as many young dogs as possible, with the view of supplying the demands of their neighbours,—the consequence was that the new strain soon supplanted the native breed, and thus laid the foundation for future sheep-dog trials. . . . It may be safely assumed that the ("rounding") Collies owe their development and perfection as sheep-dogs to the requirements of their duties and the influence of their surroundings, acting in the way of natural selection through an untold number of generations—the result of this process being an inherent instinct or capacity for working sheep. If their relative, the common cur[13] or chasing dog (the traditional "Scotch" Collie) has continued in his original and comparatively undeveloped condition, it is, doubtless, owing to the circumstance that the necessity for his improvement was not so urgent as in the case of (these) Collies.[14]

James Hogg, "the Ettrick Shepherd," the poet and author son of a shepherd, gave a revealing picture of the difference in the behavior of the shepherd's "rounding" dog and the farm Collie in *Blackwoods's Magazine*[15] in the early nineteenth century:

> It is a curious fact in the history of these animals that the most useless of the breed have often the greatest degree of sagacity in trifling and useless matters. An exceedingly good sheepdog attends to nothing else but that

---

[13]*"Cur" or "Curr" when applied to shepherds' dogs often meant a smooth coated Collie used for driving cattle, although Howitt, in the early 1800s used the word to describe what was surely a rough Collie herding sheep. It was also a common word for dogs in general.*

[14]*Edward Jones,* Sheep-Dog Trials and the Sheep Dog *(Brecon, Wales: Edwin Poole, 1892). This common "chasing" dog would have served livestock drovers quite adequately, and presumably was widely available at a cheap price as the popularity of the "rounding" dogs increased. The margin of profit of a drover was slim, indeed; so every effort was made to manage with minimum expense in the long-distance transport of livestock. It must be further assumed that then, as now, in any litter of "rounding" dogs, considering the mixed genes they carried, some dogs would be more proficient at "fetching" than others.*

[15]*Quoted by James Watson in* The Dog Book *(New York, Doubleday, Page & Co., 1905).*

particular branch of business to which he is bred. His whole capacity is exerted and exhausted on it, and he is of little value in miscellaneous matters, whereas a very different cur,[16] bred about the house and accustomed to assist in everything, will often put the noble breed to disgrace in the paltry services. If one calls out, for instance, that the cows are in the corn or the hens in the garden, the house collie needs no other hint, but runs and turns them out.

The shepherd's dog knows not what is astir, and if he is called out in a hurry for such work, all that he will do is to break to the hill and rear himself up on end to see if no sheep are running away. A bred sheepdog, if coming hungry from the hill and getting into the milk house, would most likely think of nothing else than filling his belly with cream. Not so his initiated brother; he is bred at home to far higher principles of honour. I have known such to lie night and day among from ten to twenty pails full of milk and never once break the cream of one of them with the tip of his tongue, nor would he suffer rat, cat or any other creature to touch it. The latter sort are far more acute at taking up what is said in a family.

Interesting that Hogg takes note at this early date of the difference in attitude between the intensity of the hill shepherd's dog—the Border Collie type—and the more relaxed but very versatile farm Collie who companionably shadowed his master as chores were done, ever ready to assist and respond to spoken or signaled directives. Farmers could ill afford to keep dogs as pets in that period, so their dogs of necessity provided a multitude of useful services, from herding the livestock from one grazing to another or chasing them out of the crops on the unfenced cultivated land, to baby sitting the little children, or frightening away intruders, even to flushing a deer or retrieving a bird or two during an illicit nighttime hunt. Collies were even used to run the treadmills that pumped water and ground grain.

Although such dogs did spend a certain amount of time, as they still do, just lying around the house snoozing, they readily adapted to the routine of the farmstead and once familiar with that routine performed their customary functions efficiently and often without supervision.

It should be noted that livestock of all species, including poultry and fowl, also learn the farm routine which is, after all, based on their needs, and they will cooperate in executing that routine. Often they will anticipate what they are expected to do at a certain time and will be waiting at the gate, for instance, when it is time to return to the barn at the end of the day. When the gate is opened, they will calmly file out, head for the barn and go to their respective stalls or milking stanchions without any guidance.

---

[16]Hogg was here referring to the "Scotch" Collie.

Dogs herding such well-trained stock would naturally be scorned by a hill shepherd, and Hogg no doubt picked up the unfortunate word "useless" to describe the farmer's dog from his father. It is rather incongruous for him to describe a "useless" dog performing such useful services, and, of course, the above quotation does not begin to mention the myriad other helpful tasks that the ever loyal farmers' dogs performed.

The next piece in the puzzle is sheepdog trials, since that is where the most talented and best trained sheepdogs actually demonstrated on a miniaturized scale the skills they employed in their day-to-day work. There were two very different forms of sheepdog trials reflecting the two separate groups of herding Collies, one an outrun course for "rounding" dogs and the other a driving course for the all-purpose farmers' and drovers' dogs. The first sheep herding trials were held in Bala, North Wales, in 1873, and this sport of shepherds eventually spread through England, Scotland and even Ireland during the succeeding twenty years. Edward Jones described in detail the early trials.

Sheepdog Field Trials are of very recent origin. That such should be the case is somewhat surprising considering the extent to which the practice of testing the superiority of almost every kind of skillful or athletic performance, whether human or animal, prevails by the ordeal of competitive contests, and how rapidly they spread from place to place immediately after being started . . .

Shepherds as a class, are almost entirely removed out of the influence of rivalry, owing to the isolation which characterizes their daily avocations. But probably the best explanation as regards Wales is the fact that the introduction of the present improved strain of sheepdogs is of recent date—Collies or "rounding dogs" being first introduced into the country about 60 years ago (1830). Certainly they were "few and far between" within the recollection of the present generation—the prevailing type of sheepdog being one that would merely chase sheep and catch or take hold of them if required to do so. . . . The services of such a race of dogs were of much value, although they fell far short of the services rendered by the improved strain of shepherd's dogs, which has now-a-days almost supplanted them. The progenitors of the improved breed were, undoubtedly, obtained from Scotland—some by purchase, others by the immigration of Scotchmen accompanied by their native dogs.[17]

Jones elsewhere described the various types of Collies prevalent in Wales at that time and noted that there was a popular strain of blue merle dogs,

---

[17]*Edward Jones*, Sheep-Dog Trials and the Sheep Dog, *1892.*

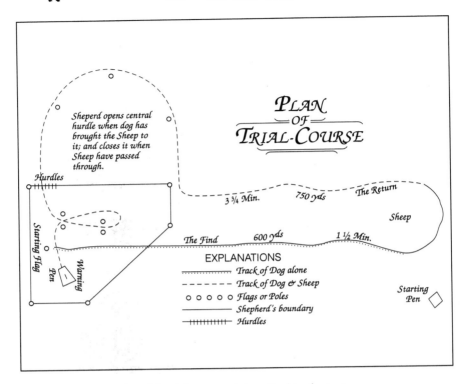

Diagram of a typical Welsh trial course as described in the text.

also called harlequins, that differed from other Collies only in the color of their coat. It is unclear whether or not this was the strain referred to by others as "Welsh heelers," and whether or not they might have a link to the Australian Blue Heelers, now known as Australian Cattle Dogs.

Above is a diagram of the typical course used at Bala and other Welsh trials where the major test was an outrun to sheep preferably out of sight of the dog, and the fetching of those sheep to the handler.

The fact that the "rounding" dog was still in the developmental stage as late as the 1870s is obvious from the very "indifferent" work attributed to the competitors in Jones' description of the actual course runs in the early years of the Welsh trials. He also points out that there was a difference in the type of work required of dogs in the Welsh trials from the work required of dogs in trials offered in the north countries (counties) of England.

Trials in those counties of England began to be offered shortly after the initial event at Bala and before there were any recognized trials in Scotland. Obviously, the breeds of sheep common to the English counties bore little resemblance to the wild, fleet-footed sheep of Wales. Jones speaks rather quizzically about the heavy, placid, slow moving sheep common to the

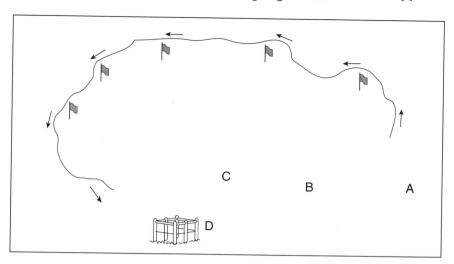

Diagram of a typical Northern counties trial course (c. 1878) as described in the text.

English pasture lands as though a "rounding" dog would not know what to do with them.

The relaxed and slow paced working style of the farm and droving Collies that were by that time firmly established in the northwest and midland English pastoral regions were ideally suited to the nature of the local stock and clearly reflected the contrast in the agricultural practices in the two areas. Collies in England, both Rough and Smooth coated, were also employed as often for moving cattle as for sheep, and were, no doubt, of the "original and comparatively undeveloped" working type. This fact can be deduced from the requirements of the sheep herding trials held in that northwest and midland area of England where the progenitors of our Collies lived.

In 1878 the North-Western Counties Sheepdog Trials Association inaugurated the very popular and successful series of trials in the counties of Cumberland, Westmorland and Lancashire in England. The trials continued for several decades and were still well supported at the turn of the century. When comparing the course offered in Wales with the English course, it becomes quite apparent that whereas in Wales "gathering" or fetching the sheep from a distance was the primary test, in the English counties "driving" or sending the sheep off to a distance was the main task the dogs had to perform. In general, on the English course both stock and dog were expected to move at a steady, sedate pace of about three to four miles an hour as compared to the nine miles an hour or faster expected on the Welsh courses.

Above is a diagram of a trial course typical of the Northern English counties and Yorkshire.[18]

---

[18]*Ibid.*

"The course is indicated by a succession of flags placed at intervals, on the far side of which the dogs drive the sheep, the time occupied and the manner in which the work is done being placed to the credit or otherwise of the competitors.

"The sheep are liberated near A, the shepherd standing at B sends his dog to the sheep, which are to be driven in the direction indicated by the arrows on the far side of the flags to D, a pen of hurdles into which the sheep have to be driven. The judges and officials stand at C, a position from which they can observe all the work."[19] The shepherd was permitted to signal his dog with voice and hand gestures and to assist the dog in penning the sheep. Jones mentions that the dogs generally worked about 15 yards behind the flock, wearing (moving) back and forth behind them to keep them grouped. The fact that sheepdog trials in England were exclusively of the driving type further implies that the skills of the dogs competing did not include a strong "rounding" tendency. Nor did large herds of domesticated breeds of sheep with strong flocking tendencies grazing in enclosed pastures need that talent to any appreciable extent, certainly not a long wide-ranging outrun.

It is worth noting that the course offered for the International Collie Trials held at the Philadelphia Centennial in September, 1880, probably one of the first sheepdog trials held in this country, almost duplicates the course used by the North-Western Counties Sheepdog Association in England. The course was in the form of a horseshoe about sixty yards wide and seven hundred yards from one end to the other. There was a pen at each end. The track that the sheep were to follow was sixty feet wide, marked on one side by a four-foot-high fence with a single rail placed on top of the posts.

The dog was to take a group of five sheep out of pen No. 1, drive them around the track, through a line of flags, and pen them in pen No. 2. Prior to the start of each run, the shepherd was permitted to walk the course with his dog. Once the run began and the sheep were on the course, the shepherd was permitted to precede or follow the sheep, as he chose, but was not permitted to assist the dog except by signal or voice. An interesting fillip was added at the end of the regulation competition when each shepherd was given the opportunity of exhibiting the particular talents of his dog by performing a demonstration of his own kind of work with a large flock of sheep. He was also encouraged to show the training of his dog for other practical purposes as a farm or house dog. At no time during this competition was there any test of "rounding" skill.[20]

---

[19]Ibid.

[20]Ralph Cooper, Catalogue of "Scotch Collies" (Reading, Ohio, 1881).

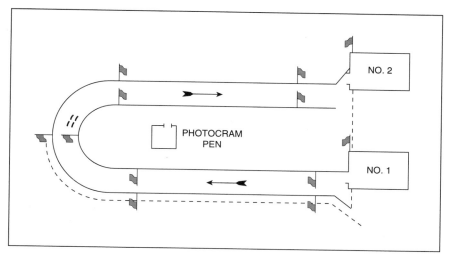

Diagram of the International course used at the 1880 Philadelphia Centennial.

The Collies that competed in Philadelphia were closely related to those of the north and midland counties of England since the majority of them were importations from those areas. As has been observed earlier, they were only a generation or two, if that, removed from the all-purpose farm dogs acquired by the drovers and resold to midland farmers and livestock graziers.

Victims of the inevitable march of progress, by the 1890s Collies were rapidly losing their place in the agricultural scheme in Britain. The Highland Clearances had ended the kind of farming that produced the Collie. Although droving flourished until near the end of the nineteenth century, it was only a matter of time before the steam engine—and the railroads it made possible—would put the drovers out of business. The turn of the century was the knell of a long and distinguished career as an all-purpose herding dog for the versatile Collie. Had it not been for the dog show Fancy, the Collie as we know it would probably have become extinct.

We do know that most modern Collies in this country are derived primarily from a handful of dogs bred during a twenty year period in England, Ireland, Scotland and perhaps Wales. The period extended from 1867, the year the first significant show Collie, Cockie, was whelped, to the mid-1880s, the period when Marcus and others were imported into the United States and the newly formed AKC began registering Collies.

At this time, both in Great Britain and here, the Collie Fancy was a closely knit fraternity with several prolific authors. They carefully chronicled individual dogs they personally knew, the early show winners from whom the breed as we now know it stemmed. Among the foundation dogs were Cockie, Mec, Shamrock, Trefoil, Carlyle, Charlemagne, Rutland and Marcus.

James Watson, an English Collie breeder who moved to America, where he became a popular breed judge, was instrumental in importing a number of influential Collies. Writing in *The Dog Book*,[21] Watson noted in 1905 that the first volume of the English stud book, published in 1874, listed seventy-eight "sheepdogs and Scotch Collies." Only two of the Collies were owned in London, the rest belonged to landowners and farmers in the midland counties of Lancashire, Warwickshire, Yorkshire and Nottinghamshire, the English pasturelands where drovers brought their stock to be fattened.

"Fifteen of the dogs listed had pedigrees, only three extending beyond sire and dam." Watson also mentions that the two outstanding dogs of the day were Champions Cockie and Mec, and that Cockie was the dog which introduced the red sable color to the show breed, the predominant color then being solid black with tan markings or the tricolor with which we are all familiar.

When explaining the origins of the early show Collies Rawdon B. Lee[22] stated in 1890, "As a fact, the best of these early-day sheepdogs were picked up by their exhibitors in the cattle markets of our country and larger towns, whither the farmers and dealers (drovers) had brought them with their sheep and other stock."

Mr. W. White, a Nottinghamshire livestock farmer and the original owner of Cockie, from whom, as Rawdon Lee asserts, "are descended almost all the best Collies of the present day," never fully disclosed how or where he acquired Cockie. Rawdon Lee was quite convinced, however, that Mr. White had picked up Cockie at a livestock market in the area of Nottingham in England.

Nottingham is well over 250 miles from the sheep producing counties of Scotland. It is extremely unlikely that any shepherd would have left his flock untended for several weeks and traveled to a midland market in England when there was an unlimited supply of drovers available, constantly passing through the highlands for the express purpose of transporting livestock to the distant sales centers. It is even more unlikely that a highland shepherd would part with his precious "rounding" dog, what was then still a comparatively rare and coveted type of sheepdog. It was especially unlikely that that shepherd would part with his treasured dog to a cattle farmer who had the obvious intention of exhibiting the dog at dog shows. Dog shows and the Kennel Club were no more popular with shepherds in the nineteenth century than they are today. Instead, it would appear that Cockie must have

---

[21]*James Watson, The Dog Book, 1905.*

[22]*Rawdon B. Lee, A History and Description of The Collie or Sheep Dog (London: Horace Cox, 1890).*

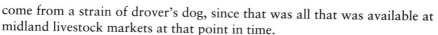

come from a strain of drover's dog, since that was all that was available at midland livestock markets at that point in time.

All available evidence indicates that the great majority of our foundation Collies were farmers' and drovers' dogs, but there was a small proportion with some "rounding" blood.

In addition to Cockie, Mr. Henry Lacy's Mec, born in 1870, was another foundation dog without a pedigree. He was purchased at a small show held at Bedford Leigh in Lancashire, a market site well south of the Scottish border. Almost certainly Mec was of a similar working background as Cockie, since both were acquired at drovers' markets. Although there is no record proving that either of these dogs were actively involved in droving, they were surely descended from the typical droving, "chasing" dogs acquired from drovers at local livestock markets and fairs. Long before the dog show Fancy began buying Collies at those sales, the midland farmers would purchase drovers' dogs and then breed them to their bitches, also descended from drovers' and all-purpose farmers' dogs. They were the type of dog found universally by the late 1800s on most midland farms working a wide variety of stock and competing on the driving courses at the local sheepdog trials.

Mr. S. E. Shirley, a founder of the English Kennel Club, introduced to the show scene in 1873 a three-year-old showily-marked tricolored dog named Shamrock, and it is from Shamrock that the beginning of the recorded pedigree lines can be traced. This dog originated in Lough Fea, northern Ireland, where Mr. Shirley maintained his farms. Raised by one of Mr. Shirley's shepherds, Shamrock was a "rounding" sheepdog and returned to his herding duties after completing his show career. From the same kennel came Trefoil, whelped in 1873, sire of Charlemagne. Charlemagne's dam was Maud, a daughter of Cockie. Rawdon Lee stated:

> No doubt, this continuity of type handed down from the Trefoil and Shamrock strains points to their purity in the first instance, and one may almost wonder what our present Collies would have been like had the above strains, and their distinguished ancestor, old Cockie, never had an existence.[23]

It is interesting to note, however, that Mr. Shirley also raised gun dogs at Lough Fea, and even more intriguing to learn that Ormskirk Charlie, by Christopher of the Trefoil line, won the Llangollen trial in Wales in 1893. This would have been on an outrun course for "rounding" dogs. James Watson described Charlie's work.

---

[23]*Ibid.*

No dog could display a better exhibition of work when on the lowland, but he very often had to give way to smaller dogs when the run out was up a mountain, his extra size and weight proving a disadvantage.[24]

However, Rawdon Lee stated:

Ormskirk Charlie, bred by Mr. Richard Thornton of Winmarleigh, Lancashire, is by Christopher from Prim of Winmarleigh. The dam of Charlie was a good working bitch, and her pedigree goes back to the Trefoil blood on one side. Her owner considered Prim of Nateby, her granddam, as all-round one of the best working bitches in Lancashire, being equally good with sheep and cattle. With the latter her intelligence was such that, when sent to bring in the cows to milk, she always separated the young from the old stock without assistance. Evidently Charlie has inherited some of her cleverness.[25]

Without detracting from the good Prim's reputation, it may be assumed that the cows, heavy with milk, were glad to be permitted to depart the pasture for the milking parlor, while the heifers were equally glad to be allowed to continue grazing undisturbed; so the cows' cooperation must have assisted the dog greatly in separating the two groups.

In the late 1870s Mr. W. W. Thompson purchased an almost all-black dog named Marcus in the Lothian area of southeastern Scotland, probably at a show at the Falkirk Tryst or similar market. Again, it was unlikely that the dog was purchased from an isolated shepherd especially when his flocks were expanding at a rapid rate. Although this is speculative, it was more likely that a grazier or drover was the merchant of this dog, or if it had, indeed, been released by a shepherd, that the dog's working ability did not include an adequate "rounding" technique to make it a useful dog for the shepherd. Marcus was eventually imported in America where he had a substantial impact on the breed, and won at a number of shows in 1882 and 1883.

Another dog of uncertain ancestry was Carlyle, although Rawdon Lee does assign him a pedigree of sorts. Charles H. Wheeler wrote in *Kennel News* and quoted by James Watson, that Carlyle was "bred from an old Scotch strain of working Collies, (who) came from Denbigh, in North Wales and was first exhibited by Mr. Skidmore by the name of Garryowen." Wheeler referred to him as "very good in type of head, placement of eye and Collie character; was likewise good in coat and ears. In colour he was black-and-tan, but, being

---

[24]*James Watson*, The Dog Book, *1905.*

[25]*Rawdon Lee*, A History and Description of The Collie or Sheepdog, *1890.*

heavily marked with tan similar to a bloodhound, was often called sable colour (mahogany sable?).” Another source claims that Carlyle’s eyes were extremely light in color and implies that he might have been a sable merle, since he may possibly have produced some double-dilute litters, but this cannot be confirmed. Here, however, is another possible infusion of “rounding” genes.

> Old Bess, black-tan-and-white, was a true collie in type, very intelligent, and a clever worker with sheep. From the union of her with Duncan (a grandson of Old Cockie) the issue was Lorna Doon, Nesta[26] Floss, Varna, Bonnie Laddie, Druce, and Malcolm I, and thus the Duncan-Bess quality strain was founded.

> Following Charlemagne, the next sensational dog to be produced was Rutland, a black-and-tan, bred by the Rev. Hans F. Hamilton . . . Being by Wolf ex Madge I, Rutland was a combination of the blood of Old[27] Mec, Trefoil, Old Cockie and Marcus.

There were many more early stars, of course, especially after the late 1880s, but, one way or another, they trace back to the eight listed above. Considering the above pedigree of Rutland as an example, it appears that it was made up of approximately three parts drovers’ dogs and one part “rounding” dog. Based on our observations of Collies’ performance during introductions to livestock and early herding training, this proportion still appears to prevail among Collies being bred today.

When Collies are first exposed to livestock we must recognize that in most cases we are probably looking at the instinctive behavior of the original generic farmer’s herding dog, not the more sophisticated and specialized reflex reaction of the “improved rounding” dog, the Scottish hill shepherd’s dog, or the quintessential trials dog.

The Collie today has had little done to enhance its original herding skills; simple skills that sufficed for small farmers with a few head of assorted livestock that led an ordered daily existence in close proximity to each other and to the humans who owned, cared for and worked with them. Those were the same herding skills specifically sought out by drovers who selected from farmers’ dogs those individuals that appeared to have the additional strength and endurance to travel many hundreds of miles over rough terrain in all sorts of weather. What both farmers and drovers needed were dogs capable of

---

[26]*James Watson imported Nesta and she produced at least one litter before meeting with an untimely accident. Many of the Duncan-Bess strain were imported into this country.*

[27]*The term “old” was used to signify that a dog had produced winning offspring.*

keeping stock flowing sedately toward their destination, patient enough to permit the stock to snatch an occasional mouthful of grass, and astute enough to use their own initiative to bend the flock or herd away from danger along the way.

The conformation of the Collie, quite similar to the early European "tending" dogs,[28] clearly shows the role the breed was designed to play. The Collie is built to provide strong, steady forward movement with little need for great speed or rapid shifts of direction. The nimble and speedy Border Collie, on the other hand, with its exaggerated hindquarters and crouching forehand closely resembles the great African cats, the fastest and most agile animals on earth over relatively short distances. This is precisely the conformation needed by dogs who must control individual wild sheep in steep, rocky hill country, as well as manage several hundred such animals being hastily removed from their native habitat at shearing time.

Considering the genetic make-up and conformation of the Collie, it should not be surprising if the majority of today's dogs do not show much instinct for a fast, far-ranging outrun or for fetching. Most of today's dogs are direct descendants of extremely competent farm and droving dogs. The miracle is that the instinct to herd livestock in any fashion survives apparently undimmed by time. Of course, with training, Collies should be able to execute adequately, if casually, the functions performed so quickly and adroitly by the amazingly talented modern version of the Scottish hill shepherds' "rounding" dogs. Very rarely, however, will the outrun of a Collie be of the quality of that of a Border Collie, and often a Collie with excellent stock sense will have no concept of an outrun at all. Nor will the average Collie necessarily exhibit a strong desire to keep stock grouped closely around the shepherd or handler. Instead, it will usually prefer to work between the handler and the stock, or beside the stock, pushing the stock away from the handler. These are tendencies that may be confusing to a handler more familiar with working Border Collies.

The early imported show Collies were concentrated in kennels in the East, and eventually, as the breed grew in popularity, successive generations and later imports spread to other areas of the country. The purpose of the imports was to win in the showring and breeding programs were secondary. With the exception of the dogs imported to run in the Philadelphia Centennial trial, little consideration was given to working ability. Contemporary authors, however, never failed to mention the herding feats of the dogs they discussed, if any were known. Fortunately, subsequent generations have served to carry on the genes apparently unimpaired. James Watson sent several of

---

[28]In a personal conversation, Edeltraud Laurin, author, well known judge and past president of the Belgian Tervuren Club, described the "old fashioned" German Shepherd she knew well as a child in Germany, and which can occasionally be seen working sheep in that country today. She said, "It looked exactly like a rough Collie."

his show winners to the Chicago area where they became invaluable workers in cattle operations. One well-known winner was, in fact, loaned to a cattleman who found her so valuable that he refused to return her for the next show season. Watson never specified whether the bitch worked in the stock yards or on a farm, but he hastened to explain that she learned her complicated job in three days and subsequently trained all the young dogs that followed her.

How typical of the Collie to see the need and fill it. This trait of almost immediately and permanently imprinting on first experiences is another facet of Collie character that makes it important to ensure that when a Collie is first exposed to livestock that the dog be given ample opportunity to express its natural instinct without being permitted to develop bad habits. Instinct testing the ever gentle Collie can be touchy business. As an example, a dog that is first allowed to chase stock out of control will probably need such firm corrections to cure that bad habit that the dog may be completely discouraged from any further attempt at herding.

Although the emphasis among East Coast fanciers of the breed has always been on showing, further west, especially in Wyoming and the mountain states, several important stud dogs such as the sons of Ch. ToKalon's Blue Banner, CD, were selected for their working ability as well as their ability to win in the breed ring. Over a period of thirty years Glen Twiford's Wind-Call Kennels produced a significant number of accomplished stock dogs that were also breed champions. The style of herding practiced on the Twiford ranches closely resembled droving or "tending" with flocks of two or three thousand sheep constantly being moved from one grazing area to another by a mounted shepherd accompanied by two Collies.[29]

---

[29]*Some people who have observed Collies working on both the east and west coasts feel that there is a marked difference in the style of work shown in the two regions. This may be due to the influence of particular dogs and their individual genetic makeup. It is entirely possible that ranchers in the west chose those Collies that demonstrated greater "rounding" skills than the average; so there may be a greater proportion of Collies showing the desire to fetch in one area than is normally the case other places. Certainly, even today, some pedigrees do produce a high percentage of "rounding" or fetching dogs, some even showing a proper outrun. Fortunately for the breed a leading representative of such a line went Best-of-Breed at a recent National Specialty show.*

Another interesting occurrence took place recently on the west coast. A registered bitch imported from England was bred to a littermate of the above mentioned dog. A three-year-old son from that breeding was observed "working" a lone horse in a pasture. The fascinating thing about that seemingly trivial incident was the fact that the dog was working exactly as a Border Collie does. It was "eyeing" the horse, darting back and forth and in between crouching low in the grass, then creeping up in the classic stalking manner. The dog also showed the same determined intensity of the Border Collie by continuing at his game for hours on end, day after day. It would be fascinating to study the pedigree of that imported bitch.

The American Kennel Club herding program offers the Fancy an important opportunity to preserve the rich heritage of the breed and insure that future generations of Collies continue to be the unique animals we know and love. Given a favorable opportunity to ignite their latent instinct most Collies will approach working stock with unqualified joy. Whether "rounding" dog, "droving" dog, or "patrolling" dog, they all certainly "perform the useful functions for which they were originally bred."[30] Whatever their working style, they all carry on their distinguished heritage and are a credit to the breed.

THE SMITHFIELD MARKET IN LONDON—A POSTSCRIPT

As an example of how comparatively rural Britain remained as late as 1873, when the population of England was almost 20,000,000 people, Sir Arthur Bryant described the outskirts of London in his *English Saga,* Collins (1940):

> In the new Bayswater Road one could watch haymakers in the open field to the north: A little farther on, where the gravel Oxford turnpike fell into Notting Dale, the pig-keepers who supplied the London hotels squatted in rustic confusion . . . How rustic London still was could be seen from its summer greenery. The West-end was full of trees and green squares and courts. The fields were half-a-mile away from Buckingham Palace and Grosvenor Square, and snipe were occasionally shot in the Pimlico marshes . . . Any Monday morning herds of cattle were driven by drovers . . . through the narrow streets to Smithfield: Pedestrians were sometimes gored by the poor beasts.

Smithfield was the chief livestock market for London and was open on Fridays and Mondays. It had its own guild of drovers who picked up the livestock brought by the Welsh and Scottish drovers to Barnet or Islington north of the city, or to pastures on the outskirts of the city itself. At Barnet the livestock were given an opportunity to rest and be refreshed after their journey that often began 300 or more miles away. It is ironic that the stock that were handled so solicitously on their long trek so as to be delivered fat and unscathed were promptly treated to such rough and abusive handling as was practiced by the Smithfield drovers. The Smithfield drovers had their own race of herding dogs that closely resembled smooth Collies with stumpy or no tails. A relative of the Australian Shepherd Dogs perhaps?

---

[30]General Regulations for Herding Tests & Herding Trials *(New York: The American Kennel Club, 1991).*

Bryant continued, "A considerable number of men and boys are employed as drovers, whose business is to attend the great cattle market, which is held for the sale of bulls, cows, oxen, sheep, calves and pigs in Smithfield every Monday and Friday throughout the year. The cattle, sheep, etc., after resting at Islington and its neighbourhood on Thursday, are driven to Smithfield by these people, the whole of that night previous to the Friday's market, and also during the Sunday night preceding the Monday's market. They are also engaged the whole time of the two market days in driving the cattle, sheep, etc. purchased by the butchers to the different parts of the metropolis and adjacent parts."

A Terhune family group includes (left to right) Bruce, Bobby Wolf, the Master and the Mistress (holding Tippy the Persian Cat). The stone in front of the bottom step is initialed E. P. T. for Terhune's father, Reverend Edward Payson Terhune, builder of Sunnybank. *Courtesy of the Terhune Sunnybank Memorial Fund Museum Collection*

Chapter 10

The Heroic Collie
in Fact and Fiction

It is traditional that a stock dog is the protector of smaller and weaker creatures from whatever threatens. So ingrained is this trait that the Collie should be willing to forfeit its own life to safeguard those in its care. This protective side of the Collie's nature has been the subject of stories, books, movies and television dramas. It has also been demonstrated in real life dramas over and over again.

Albert Payson Terhune, the famous journalist, immortalized his life style and his dogs in his "Sunnybank" novels, and the exciting adventures of "Lassie" are part of growing up in America.

But there are other Collies that have saved people and animals from burning buildings, runaway vehicles, dangerous animals and hazardous extremes of weather. In this chapter you'll get to meet some of them. Their courage and loyalty will amaze and hearten you, and give you an added sense of pride in being associated with a breed that is in every way the friend of man.

FAMOUS COLLIES IN FICTION

by LaVerne Walker

Introduction

Albert Payson Terhune's stories about his Sunnybank Collies did a great deal to promote the breed in the 1920s and 1930s. In 1940 Eric Knight wrote the universally-loved classic, *Lassie Come Home,* a book that inspired eight motion pictures and a long-running television series. The wisdom, loyalty and intelligence these dogs displayed inspired many people to acquire

This monument was dedicated to Albert Payson Terhune on his 100th birthday, December 21, 1972 at Sunnybank. A bronze plaque on the front of the monument bears a likeness to Terhune, created by sculptor Michael DeNike. The sundial, with its base of Pompton granite was a family gift to Terhune's parents, the first owners of Sunnybank, on their Golden Anniversary in 1906.
Marilyn Horowitz

Collies of their own. As a result, the breed rose to a level of popularity that has continued to the present day. In large part this loyalty is due to the Collies these authors brought so vividly and unforgettably to life.

Albert Payson Terhune

The Terhunes always had Collies on their Sunnybank estate in Pompton Lakes, New Jersey. The Collies were, in fact, an important part of life at Sunnybank. Albert Payson Terhune had been a successful journalist for many years before he could get one of his dog stories published. It happened like this:

> A frequent visitor to Sunnybank was Ray Long, editor of Redbook magazine. Lad, the venerable house dog, had always treated Long with studied aloofness, despite all overtures from the famous editor. Finally one day the old dog greeted the guest by laying his head on Long's knee. Ray Long was delighted with the Collie's final acceptance and suggested to Terhune that he write a story about Lad. Terhune, who had been suggesting dog stories to editors for ten years and getting rejection slips for his trouble, replied heatedly that no one would publish them. Long promised to print the story if Terhune would write it.

In January, 1915 Albert Payson Terhune's first dog story, "His Mate" was published in *Redbook* magazine. In it Terhune described Lad, his mate, Lady, the Mistress and Master and their home, which he dubbed the Place. He wrote of the law which every Collie learned from puppyhood and the consequences of breaking it. The story brought instant response from readers and Terhune had a ready market for his dog stories from then on.

After Lad's death Terhune assembled the stories about him into a book, as a memorial to the dog and because his dog stories had sold so well. No publisher was interested, but Terhune persisted in his search. As a last resort he approached John Macrae, president of E. P. Dutton, a Scotsman who was very proud of his heritage. Terhune felt that Macrae might publish a book about the breed which shared the same national origins as the publisher. Terhune's long shot paid off; reluctantly Mr. Macrae agreed to publish the book.

Lad: A Dog was published in April, 1919, in a limited edition which sold for $2.00. A few weeks later Terhune received a letter from Macrae which began: "*Lad* is on the rampage. He can't be stopped." By 1922 the book had gone through nineteen printings; in fifteen years it sold 250,000 copies. By 1975 it was in its eighty-second printing!

Terhune's writing has the rare ability to bring his dogs to life. He promoted Collies in a way no private breeder could. The Collies in his stories saved lives, guarded property and performed heroic deeds. They worshipped their Master and were always drawn to protect the young and defenseless. Many, both children and adults, who read his stories were moved to own a Collie with the wisdom and loyalty of Lad, and Collie popularity rose as a result.

Terhune continued to write books about his Sunnybank Collies and other dogs. Twenty-three more dog books followed *Lad: A Dog*, eagerly awaited by his growing number of fans.

Irving Litvag, in *The Master of Sunnybank*, comments about Terhune's writing:

What would have seemed outright nonsense and pulp quality fantasy in the hands of another writer was transformed by Terhune's skill into a series of stories that captivated his readers. Terhune never claimed that the real Lad had all, or even several of these adventures. But he did insist always, despite the skepticism of many people in the dog world, that he only described canine feats of heroism, intelligence or physical prowess that had actually been performed by a dog somewhere and recorded in newspapers or history books.

Despite Terhune's reputation as a journalist, it was his dog stories that made him a celebrity. Letters arrived from all over the country, visitors poured through the gates of Sunnybank and Terhune was in demand for his knowledge of canines. He had one of the first dog programs on radio; it aired weekly from New York City from 1934 to 1936. During the broadcasts, he gave advice on all phases of dog care interwoven with fascinating stories. At the same time his syndicated columns were appearing in hundreds of newspapers all over the country.

Despite his fame, Terhune was not really interested in dog shows, although he was approved by the American Kennel Club to judge Collies. He was content to enjoy his Collies' companionship at Sunnybank. In response to criticism he entered two homebreds in local shows and they did well. Criticized again, he entered two eleven-month-old litter brothers, Sunnybank Sigurdson and Sunnybank Explorer in the prestigious Westminster Kennel Club show. They came home with several medals and blue ribbons, a Reserve Winners rosette and over $150 in cash. For a very short time the Terhunes seriously campaigned their Collies. Only showing within a 100-mile radius and using Robert Friend, his kennel manager, or himself as handlers, Terhune took four males to their championships. In 1922 he finished Ch. Sunnybank Sigurd, then his two sons Ch. Sunnybank Sigurdson in 1923 and Ch. Sunnybank Explorer in 1928, and Explorer's son, Ch. Sunnybank Thane, who finished the same year as his sire. When Terhune had finished three generations of champions he felt he had proven his point and retired his dogs from the showring.

Albert Payson Terhune died in 1942 and his wife lived on at Sunnybank with a nurse-companion until her death in 1964. The remaining nine-and-a-half acres of the estate were then sold by her attorney. When a realtor announced that Sunnybank was to be subdivided into a housing development, local residents and Collie lovers, headed by Claire Leishman, began a campaign to save Sunnybank. They were successful; in April, 1967, Wayne Township bought the Sunnybank land and on October 15, 1967, it was officially opened to the public as a park. Fallen into disrepair, the house had to be razed, but the Terhune Sunnybank Memorial Fund has financed restoration projects at the Park and is collecting Terhune books, photographs and memorabilia for the museum building which the Parks Department has promised to build. Sunnybank was for years the site of the Collie Club of Northern New Jersey's outdoor match show and a Sunnybank Memorial Festival is held every fall. Sunnybank is safe at last.

Eric Knight

In 1940 another literary influence on the Collie breed appeared. Eric Knight, a British author, wrote *Lassie Come Home*, a beautiful book about the devotion of a Collie and her influence on the lives of those she loved. Unfortunately Mr. Knight was a casualty of World War II and this was his only dog book.

Metro-Goldwyn-Mayer purchased the movie rights to *Lassie Come Home* and two young actors, Elizabeth Taylor and Roddy McDowell, were cast in the key roles. Then auditions began for Lassie.

Rudd Weatherwax, an established dog trainer, was working on another film in the MGM lot at the time. He had a dog he wanted to be considered for the film. Unfortunately his Collie, Pal, was a male.

Rudd Weatherwax and Lassie

In this scene from the feature film, *Challenge to Lassie,* Lassie is granted the approval of Scotland's highest court. *Metro-Goldwyn-Mayer*

Pal had come into Mr. Weatherwax's possession by a strange set of circumstances. He had come to his kennel as an incorrigible, barking puppy to be trained. When it came time for his owner to pick him up, he decided to settle a $70.00 boarding/training bill instead by leaving the puppy with Rudd Weatherwax, who readily agreed.

It was late summer before shooting for the picture finally began. By this time the female chosen for the part had completely shed her beautiful coat and looked thin and gaunt on camera. More screen tests were hastily scheduled and Pal got his chance to try for the part.

A major scene called for the dog to swim a fast-moving river. Pal was taken out in a boat to the middle of the river, put over the side and told to swim for shore. When he got there, instead of shaking himself as a dog normally would, he took a few faltering steps with his head down and collapsed on his side as if he had swum the entire river. The director told Weatherwax that Pal went into the river, but Lassie came out.

Pal's career had begun. From then on the part of Lassie would always be played by a male. Six more feature films were made with Pal and many famous actors and actresses. The last was *The Painted Hills,* released in 1951. A seventh Lassie film was made in the late 1970s, *The Magic of Lassie,* starring Jimmy Stewart.

In 1954 another chapter in Collie history began with shooting of the first episode of the *Lassie* television series. Pal was retired by this time and four generations of his descendants carried on in his place. Up to 1974 the Lassie series spanned two decades with 589 original episodes. Throughout, Lassie has never failed to maintain the image two generations of Americans learned to expect of this remarkable dog.

With reruns, then a new Lassie series, and finally a new movie Lassie, the saga continues and a new generation of Lassie fans has found the heroine of Knight's story to be everything a Collie should be. Bob Weatherwax, Rudd's son, has continued to control the Lassie empire and image.

Several additional generations of Lassie descendants have portrayed the dog Eric Knight first wrote about, based on his own beloved Collie of fifty years ago. In 1994 three daughters of Eric Knight were present when the Collie Club of America Quarter Century Group inducted their father into its Collie Hall of Fame.

VALOR: A WAY OF LIFE

by Jo Campbell

Introduction

The stories of Albert Payson Terhune and the *Lassie* television series and feature movies have sustained the impetus given the Collie by the interest of Queen Victoria and President Calvin Coolidge in our breed.

These books and films have presented the Collie to the public with dignity and love.

Collie breeders have learned to acknowledge this effort with appreciation. Breeders try to ensure that Collie puppies going to new homes will preserve and perpetuate the Lassie image of courage, wisdom and devotion. Without the real-life image the Lassie films and Terhune stories could not survive as they do, release after release, edition upon edition.

Was the image that Terhune and the script writers presented of Sunnybank Lad and of Lassie real? Are Collies capable of the exceptional and often psychic feats portrayed in Technicolor and in print? In impressive measure the breed continues to live up to its image through recorded deeds of exceptional valor.

The award recipients and others described in this chapter show that Collies have made conspicuous marks in the annals of heroism. Alone of all the animals humans have domesticated, dogs care; Collies more than most. They have rescued members of their human families from enraged animals and rescued livestock from burning buildings. They have found lost children and have protected their lost or stricken owners from the elements with the warmth of their bodies. There is no end to the variety of perils Collies have faced, nor of the ingenuity they have used to help their human companions in numerous emergencies.

Ken-L-Ration Awards

Countless stories of gallant rescues have been told and then lost to memory. Since 1954, when a Collie named Tang won the first Ken-L-Ration Gold Medal as America's Dog Hero of the Year, the Quaker Oats Company has performed a valuable service by recognizing canine heroism.

TANG

Tang was one of these Collies whose herding instinct adapted perfectly from lambs to children. Four times, the award announcement declared, he had leaped in front of cars to push a tot to the curb, seconds before tragedy could strike.

Tang's heroism is owed largely to fate and a persuasive veterinarian. Air Force Captain and Mrs. Maurice Dyer of Denison, Texas had lost a beloved Collie and could not bring themselves to adopt another. A veterinarian talked them into taking a look at Tang. Just emerging from puppyhood, the sable dog had been badly mistreated and was distrustful of people, especially children. Considering this unpromising background, the Dyers were surprised when they saw something in his eyes that reminded them of their lost Collie. Albeit and with misgivings, they took him home, where love worked its wonders. Within six months Tang had developed his full Collie potential.

On one occasion Tang planted himself squarely in front of a parked delivery truck and refused to budge, barking loudly all the while. When the puzzled driver alighted to see what had caused the strange behavior of the normally friendly dog, he found that a two-year-old girl had clambered into the back of his truck. From this perch she would most certainly have fallen

Tang, here with a young friend, won the first *Hero of Heroes* award in 1954.

Blaze, with little Dawn Hecox, received the Ken-L-Ration award for heroism in 1954.

when he started his vehicle. The moment she was removed Tang stopped barking and returned calmly to the sidewalk.

The Dyers credited Tang with having saved no fewer than five children from death or severe injury.

BLAZE

Blaze, named for his handsome face marking, was the second nationally-acclaimed Collie in the Ken-L-Ration awards, receiving the Hero of Heroes plaque in 1957. Dawn, daughter of Mr. and Mrs. Duane Hecox of Timewell, Illinois, owes her life to her Collie playmate. The two-and-a-half-year-old child was attracted by some baby pigs in a fenced pen next to her yard, and crawled through the fence for a closer look. The sow felt her litter was threatened. Charging at top speed, she knocked Dawn to the ground and was severely mauling the youngster when Blaze came on the scene.

Despite a long-held fear of the formidable sow, Blaze cleared the fence in a bound and attacked so savagely that the sow gave ground. Dawn, shocked and bleeding from serious injuries, had time to crawl back through the fence to safety.

Wounds from the sow's tusks put the little girl on the critical list for two days, and it took many weeks of care before she recovered. The official record does not reveal whether Blaze sustained injuries, but it would be surprising if he did not. A hog is a dangerous foe for man or dog and only devotion to Dawn made Blaze take the risk.

Duke, with young Penny Grantz, is shown preparing to leave for the 1961 award ceremonies honoring his heroism.

DUKE

Fire, an element so dreaded by most creatures that only man brings it to life intentionally, was responsible for the near-tragedy that won the 1961 gold medal for Duke, a rollicking Collie from Niles, Ohio.

Buddy, 1964 Dog Hero of the Year, with his owner Matthew Crinkley whose dairy goats and livelihood he helped save from a devastating fire.

Hero, the brave Collie who lived up to his name by saving his young friend Shawn Jolley from the attack of a berserk mare, was the 1966 Dog Hero of the Year.

On a blustery March afternoon, ten-year-old Penny Grantz went into her backyard to burn some papers. The wind made her skirt billow into the stream of glowing embers rising from the flames. Panic-stricken at the sight of her flaming skirt, the youngster raced toward the house, twenty-five yards away.

Duke seized Penny's blazing skirt in his teeth. The Collie tore and pawed the garment off her to the ground, burning his tender mouth in the process.

We do not know whether previous experience had taught the Collie about fire, or if he simply did battle in the best way he knew—with snapping fangs and grappling paws as he would against any foe which hurt his little mistress. Experts say dogs could not reason it out; Collie owners have come to accept such acts of devotion without question.

BUDDY

Matthew Crinkley and his family, of Budd Lake, New Jersey, count their luck in terms of their livestock saved from fire by Buddy, 1964 winner of the heroism award. For this unusual exploit the twenty-month-old sable also received the title of Businessman's Best Friend from an association of his master's colleagues.

An early morning fire had been roaring for some time in the maternity barn of their dairy goat farm before Buddy's frantic barks in the yard were heard by his waking owners. They rushed to the window just in time to see the barn crash into flaming ruin.

The Crinkleys were astonished and elated to see Buddy marching back and forth like a reviewing general, watching over the entire flock of seventy milking goats he had herded out of the barn. The Collie had received severe burns on his paws and smoke damage to his delicate nasal passages in the process while rescuing the stubborn animals.

Buddy's warning barks gave the Crinkleys time to wet down the smoking roof of a second barn which housed their thirty remaining goats. Counting the kids born later to the rescued mothers, the Crinkleys calculated that their Collie had saved three hundred goats. This not only saved the owners' livelihood, but also preserved a vital service to area people who needed goats' milk for illnesses ranging from allergies and digestive disorders to ulcers.

How does a dog's owner repay such a debt? Unlike a human, the dog expects no repayment.

HERO

Collie lovers claim that their favorites have both beauty and brains. Hero, a blue merle from Priest River, Idaho, was the first show dog to prove it, capturing the title of America's Dog Hero of 1966. Quaker Oats' press writers described Hero's exploits as "an exhibition of courage, stamina and intelligence that has never been exceeded in the history of the award."

Owned by Mr. and Mrs. George Jolley, Hero was a good ranch companion as well as a promising show dog. Peril seemed nowhere near as Mrs. Jolley, with her three-year-old son, Shawn, worked in the barn loft pitching hay down to the horses coming in from the pasture. The first inkling Mrs. Jolley had that her son was not beside her was when he screamed from the barn floor below. She looked down to see the youngster running toward the end of the barn with a mare in pursuit.

Shawn tried to slide under a tractor at the end of the barn but his clothing caught on a projecting piece of the equipment and he was pinned, at the mercy of the unaccountably raging animal.

His frightened mother shouted for Hero.

The mare was rearing to trample Shawn when a blue-and-white bolt whizzed into view. Transformed from his usual good-natured self, Hero was a blaze of fury. Before the lethal hooves could descend, the Collie's teeth were fastened onto the horse's tender nose and his eighty pounds deflected the horse's charge—and her attention.

The enraged mare swung her head furiously from side to side, whipping Hero back and forth. Finally, the dog's grip gave way with a rending of tender flesh. Hero landed violently against the tractor wheel, sinking into a stunned heap. Spurred by the mare's return attack on Shawn, however, Hero leaped up to distract her again.

Now she gave her full attention to the Collie adversary, and Mrs. Jolley was able to put Shawn safely atop the hay. She joined the battle, parrying the striking hooves with a pitchfork. After a few more blows at Hero the mare suddenly raced out the stable door with Hero in close pursuit. Only when she had disappeared into the distance did the Collie sink to the ground, blood pouring from his nose and mouth.

Mrs. Jolley rushed him to a veterinarian in Spokane, forty-five miles away. The doctor found that Hero had suffered crushed forefeet, four broken ribs and five teeth either broken or knocked out.

Only six weeks after this the indomitable Hero scored a major show win. However, the Jolleys did not continue on to finish Hero's championship; it became too much of a strain. The showing stopped each time while they had to explain to an enthralled judge how their Collie had lost his teeth. They did not need anyone else to tell them that their dog was a champion. He had already proved that to them.

It is interesting to note that Hero, Harlequin Hero O'Shane, was sired by Ch. LuNette's Blue Print and that his dam was Ch. Kitsap's Shadow O'Shane, who produced five champions. Hero had two champion littermates, and both parents were BIS winners.

Dove tracked, and thereby saved, little Martha Mitchell when the child was lost in deep woods. Martha is shown admiring the medal Dove received in recognition.

DOVE

Blackrobe Snow White Dove, CD, was honored with a Hero Award in 1967. The December, 1968 Collie Club of America *Bulletin* tells the story:

> Dove can take medals or leave 'em, but her little mistress, Martha Mitchell, feels differently. In August, 1967, during Frank Mitchell's summer stint as a naturalist on Cape Cod, two-year-old Martha became separated from the family. Her absence was noticed within thirty minutes, and the search began in deepening twilight. Mitchell broke out his search mechanism—Dove.
>
> "We went down to where we had seen Martha last and gave Dove a stocking," Frank explained. "She picked up the scent and I had to trot to keep up with her.
>
> "It took Dove ten minutes through mosquito-ridden brush. And there was Martha," Frank Mitchell said at the time.
>
> "It isn't that Dove has done something outstanding; she's just done what she's been trained to do when she was needed!"
>
> Inheriting his dam's intelligence, Dove's son Blackrobe Nez Perce Joseph was the Highest Scoring Dog In Trial at the 1971 Collie Club of America Specialty show.

MICHELLE

Michelle won recognition in 1972 as a militant stock worker, taking second place in national honors. Her story was told in the *National Enquirer* and reprinted in the Collie Club of America *Bulletin* in October, 1973.

Michelle saved her owner Lester Woods from the attack of an enraged cow in 1972. She was cited for her bravery by Ken-L-Ration and took second in national honors for her great act of courage.

Lester Woods has come close to the ways of Nature in working his farm in the rich plains of Everton, Missouri, the story ran. But last year the sixty-year-old farmer got a deeper, more meaningful understanding of unselfish loyalty and devotion from a dog he had been forced to cripple for life. This is his story:

"I was alone and helpless and knew that frantic, crazy cow was going to crush me to death. But I'm still around today because my loving and faithful dog saved my life—the very dog who became a cripple because of what I once did."

Mr. Woods' story harked back to five years before when the romping Michelle had jammed her paw in a power mower driven by the family's oldest son. There was only one thing for him to do, Mr. Woods decided. He amputated a small part of the Collie's left front paw with his pocket knife. The accident left Michelle with a limp but dimmed not at all her devotion to her master.

He was glad the Collie forgave him her pain, Mr. Woods said, "because I really needed her help.

"I was crossing the pasture one afternoon when I saw a newborn calf that looked like it had twisted its head under its mother. I went over to see if I could help. Well, that cow must have thought I was going to hurt her calf. She jumped up and charged me and hurled me at least fifteen feet.

"Then she jumped on top of me. I was helpless under one thousand pounds of crazed and angry cow. There wasn't anything I could do but yell.

"But then Michelle came to my rescue. She tore into that cow like a fury and gave me my one chance to escape sure death. The cow turned on

Michelle and I crawled into a ditch where the cow couldn't get at me, and passed out.

"When my wife found me, she said Michelle was licking my hand and wouldn't leave until I was taken to the hospital. That cow gave me a fractured collarbone and a sprained back.

"Well, our dog was a real hero after that. She won a silver medal and a $500 award in national competition.

"You know, it seems that most people—even farmers like me—never really appreciate the love and loyalty of a dog until they go through an ordeal like me. Now I believe that Michelle was put on this earth just to watch over me. And that suits me just fine."

Albert Payson Terhune asked in various ways, "What did we do to deserve Collies like these?" The owners of Michelle, Hero and the others know they were blessed, whatever the reason.

The Collie Club of America Hero Award

The Collie Club of America launched its own award for heroism in 1962, presenting an engraved certificate to Bruce, owned by Dorothy McGuire of Maywood, New Jersey. Collie judge and journalist Arnold Woolf picked up the story of Bruce from *Collie Clamor*, published by the Collie Club of Northern New Jersey, and told it in his Rockland County (New York) *Journal-News* column. Woolf also officiated for the Collie Club of America in presentation ceremonies.

Clamor had titled the story "Bruce Turns in Fire Alarm" and as Woolf retold the account:

Mrs. McGuire was busy doing household chores, having already taken the youngsters to school since there was a bad thunderstorm. The sky had become a very odd shade of yellow-orange.

Suddenly there was a lightning flash and a half-minute later Bruce, downstairs on the first floor, began barking frantically. Mrs. McGuire rushed downstairs to see what was causing the commotion and found the window curtains burning. She was able to put out the fire with several buckets of water.

Mrs. McGuire commented "I would not have known that the fire had started had it not been for Bruce's alarming bark. We owe our home to Bruce. We owe him our love, too, but he always had our love and always will."

LADY AND SCUDDER

The Pittsburgh *Press* in November, 1965, gave front page space to the story of Lady and Scudder, two Collies who kept five-year-old Lisa Nearhood warm through thirteen cold hours until 300 volunteer searchers found the lost child. The temperature plunged to the twenties and the Collies served

Bruce with his owner, Dorothy McGuire and CCA representative Arnold Woolf at the 1962 presentation of the Collie Club of America award for heroism.

not only as insulation, but also as guides for the child. The area was full of gullies, culverts and dense, wooded growth, which could have swallowed the youngster had she stumbled into their depths. It was obvious to police and fire fighters that the dogs had guided her wandering steps away from these perils.

At last the search party heard a small voice call, "Here I am." They took Lisa home, where she told her distraught parents, "My doggies kept me warm." Her father promised that the two dogs "will have royal treatment from now on."

D DAWG

D Dawg (Ch. Alteza Emblem) similarly protected his master, Don Perkins, on a near-zero-degree night in the Texas panhandle. The story was told in the Amarillo newspapers and subsequently in *Collie Cues*.

Knocked out by a fall after a nighttime kennel inspection tour, Perkins regained consciousness at the urging of D Dawg. Finding that his legs were not functioning and he could not arouse his wife who was asleep in the house at the time, Perkins tried to drag himself through the 5-degree chill to the back door. He remembers deciding at one point that it was too far and he would just sleep a bit.

D Dawg (Ch. Alteza Emblem) saved his owner Don Perkins from almost certain death after Perkins had been knocked unconscious during an accident in near-zero-degree temperature at his home in the Texas panhandle.

D Dawg refused to let his master doze off. "Every time I tried to stop crawling, he'd come over and lie on my face for awhile." Perkins said. "And then he'd start whining and barking. He wasn't about to let me go to sleep. I can't even guess how long it took me to reach the house, but it seemed like forever."

Finally close enough to lob a board through a window, Perkins aroused his wife. The ambulance was quick; doctors told Perkins only one of his toes had suffered frost bite, and his feet would be extremely sensitive to cold. When they realized how long he had been in the cold, they said it was a miracle he was not dead.

Perkins said D Dawg had always been his favorite Collie. He was by Ch. Celestial's Chico of Laridale and is one of eight champions out of Ch. Alteza The Silver Lining.

PRINCESS

The Collie Club of America *Bulletin* reprinted another *National Enquirer* story about one fire-alarm Collie who did not know when to quit.

Early on a January morning in 1974, Princess detected smoke coming from the ceiling of her home with Joseph and Catherine Wehrenberg in

Mahopac, New York. She began to bark furiously, running from door to door of the bedrooms where the family slept.

When the parents and their nine children awoke, the smoke was stifling. The youngsters, ranging in age from one to twenty, were led by their parents out of the blazing house to safety.

"If that dog hadn't barked," Wehrenberg later told police, "the ceiling would have fallen on my whole family. It would have been a funeral pyre for eleven people."

Wehrenberg found Princess under a bed when he walked through the fire-ravaged house after the blaze was out. She had died of suffocation. "It looks like she'd gone back in the house to make sure the kids were all out," he said, crying unashamedly at the sight of the still form. Wrapped in a blanket, Princess was buried in the rocky ground behind what was left of the house.

GENTLEMAN COLE

One of the greatest ambassadors for Collies died as this book was being completed. Ch. King's Valley Select, "Gentleman Cole," a registered service dog for the disabled owned by Jean Levitt, was an outstanding example of a versatile Collie. He had fifteen working titles including Conformation, Stock and Draft Work, Obedience, and was the first dog to attain the American Working Collie Association Versatility champion title, in September, 1993. Bred by Leslie and Eva Rappaport in Oregon, and sired by Ch. Tartanside Protocol out of King's Valley Royal Fanfare, he came to Jean to become her "left arm and best friend." He worked to promote the activities of Therapy Dogs International and the Delta Society in numerous ways. He carried a backpack or pulled a cart or travois in displays and demonstrations, modeled, took an active part in many public relations initiatives for service dogs, and was a beloved ambassador for Collies everywhere.

Professional Heroes

While there were not many Rough Collies in the armed forces during World War II due to the breed's long coat and the care it required, there were some and they are worth remembering here.

The story, *Valiant Comrades*, by Ruth Adams Knight, was based on the experiences of one such Collie. The war film, *Son of Lassie*, was chiefly fiction. *This Week Magazine* told of another: Valiant, welcomed home to Brooklyn, New York by his master in April, 1945. Like other returning veterans, this army sentinel dog showed the effects of his wartime training as the best-behaved dog in his famous hometown.

Rescue Dogs of Switzerland

The rescue dogs of Switzerland are described in Ada Bishop's *All About the Collie*, with particular emphasis on the exploits of a Smooth Collie, International Champion Peterblue Harvey. Owned by Miss M. Meyer in Switzerland, Harvey holds a gold medal for his rescue work.

Rescue dogs are trained to search for lost or injured people, covering large areas of mountainous country. Mrs. Bishop tells us:

> They do not work specifically on a scent, but on a random basis in finding lost and injured persons. These rescue dogs wear a small jacket on which is printed a Red Cross, which obviates the danger of the dogs being shot or molested. Around the neck the dogs wear a collar to which is fastened a leather, cigar-shaped pendant about six inches long known as a *temoin*.
>
> When the dog reaches the lost or injured person, he circles around and grasps the pendant firmly in his jaws. The pendant in the dog's mouth is an indication that a lost person has been found. The temoin must not be dropped until an order is given, but must be carried off from the accident area to the handler.
>
> The handler then attaches a lead to the dog which leads him to the lost or injured person.
>
> Training for this work is quite rigorous and includes obedience training, guarding, swimming, jumping over obstacles and so on. A point of interest concerning these dogs is that in Switzerland, the dog license fee is very high. For dogs engaged in this rescue work, however, a 50 percent concession is given. They are, however, liable to be called upon at any time by the authorities if they are required for work.
>
> Harvey holds the rank Class III Rescue Dog, the highest grade to be granted.

Marijuana Dog

Dave Guild, a member of the Honolulu, Hawaii, Police Department and Collie Club of Hawaii, trained his Candy (Lady Cynthia of Signa, CDX) to detect drugs. She has done some astonishing work for the Islands' customs people.

The fascinating story of how the Guilds trained Candy was told by Janet Holbrook in *Collie Cues*.

Dave found her to be well above average in intelligence. Yet, as is often true with an intelligent child, sometimes exceptional training methods are in order. Candy's first introduction to traditional obedience methods was a disaster. She reacted stoically to the sharp jerks on her collar and the drill-sergeant commands. In fact, Candy became an obedience school drop-out. But a new instructor, Mary Castillo, adopted special methods to suit her dolphin-like disposition. "Collies have two things in common with dolphins,"

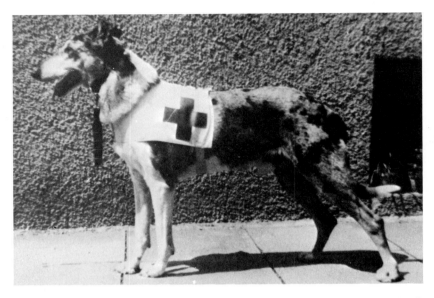

International Ch. Peterblue Harvey, one of the famed rescue dogs of Switzerland, was used to find lost or avalanche-trapped travelers. Here he stands girded for action, the *temoin* (described in the text) hanging from his collar. Harvey held the rank of a Class III Rescue Dog, the highest grade a dog could be granted.

Harvey holds the temoin in his mouth, showing how a rescue dog signals the handler that a lost or exhausted hiker has been found in the alpine snows. Harvey's owner, Miss M. Meyer of St. Sulpice, described him as "a really wonderful companion, always happy to work and help when asked."

Janet Holbrook explained in the article, "a high degree of intelligence and outstandingly gentle natures. Neither . . . responds to force."

A police official saw Dave practicing scent discrimination exercises with Candy. He was intrigued and wondered, "Could she smell out marijuana that way?" They experimented and found that Candy could pick out the substance from other odorous packets containing spices, tea and coffee.

At the customs office, Candy's pinpointing ability was most valuable. Surrounded by hundreds of packages, it was necessary to be very accurate since any suspect package had to be turned inside out and linings ripped out to locate the cache. Candy never made a mistake.

She makes her greatest contribution sniffing out incoming bundles with large source quantities arriving, helping the agents to track down suppliers. Dave explained, "Control at the source is of the greatest importance."

The rescue tradition has been maintained by the Collie family for generations, from Scotland to the Hawaiian Islands. Candy is performing in the greatest tradition of her ancestors. Just as Collies once rescued lambs on the Scottish moors, Candy may, in the last analysis, be performing just as important a rescue of the people she loves from perils at least as deadly as the jaws of predatory wild creatures.

Collies and the Forces of Nature

Janet "Jidge" Holbrook of Buffington Collies has had some fascinating experiences involving the breed's special affinity with the awesome forces of nature. Several accounts were printed in *Collie Cues*.

EARTHQUAKE SYNDROME

The Holbrooks had moved to the West San Fernando Valley of California in 1954, when Jidge observed what she later termed pre-earthquake behavior in her Collie, Bucky. He would leap to his feet from a sound sleep and stand rigidly, listening, as though he were attempting to place some sound. Ten minutes later Jidge would feel an earth tremor.

Their other Collies later exhibited similar behavior. In minor tremors the dogs showed extreme agitation from fifteen minutes to two hours before a quake. They paced up and down, panting a great deal, listening to sounds beyond the range of human hearing.

A week before the big quake of February 9, 1971, Duffy, the Holbrooks' house dog at the time, was hard at work, pacing up and down, "scanning" the air with his nose, panting and listening. Soon all four Collies were shaking their heads and scratching at their ears. They panted so much that they drank almost four times their normal water supply.

While the Holbrooks could not find any 'quake research at that time which took animal predictive behavior into account, later research has investigated such activity in the United States and in Japan. Collies and Collie-people are ahead, as usual.

TORNADO ALERT

Earthquakes are not the only natural phenomena which signal ahead to alert Collies, Mrs. Holbrook recalled:

> One summer morning a friend's daughter, Jean Headlee, decided to go on a picnic with friends, calling the family's Collie, Lady, to join them. Lady had been pacing nervously, getting in their way as they loaded the picnic gear. When the group was ready to leave, Lady crawled under the car and would not come out to any amount of coaxing or commands. She was finally pulled out, but the moment she was released, she scooted back under the car, blocking the departure.
>
> Jean decided that Lady did not want them to leave. Puzzled, but respecting the dog's behavior in spite of a clear sky, she turned on the radio seeking a weather report. Every station was broadcasting tornado warnings. The Headlees barely got everything battened down and the family, including Lady, into the basement before the tornado struck!

Communication: The Vital Link

Many of the heroic deeds described in this chapter depend on the Collie's ability to communicate with people, and on receptivity to that communication by both species.

Celebrated dog behaviorist Dr. Michael Fox attributed the "Lassie Come Home" phenomenon to this kind of communication on a very high level. While the homing dog is in the minds of his worried family, Fox theorizes, the dog receives the "beam" and makes steady progress toward them. When his people are distracted or give up, the lost one becomes disoriented or pauses along the route, in Dr. Fox's opinion. This makes sense to many dog people, whether or not they are students of extrasensory perception in any other form.

Test your own "canine communications quotient," while you are working, playing or just living with your Collies. Observe what is going on; you will find that you take subtle communications for granted.

How many times have you done something because your dog "told" you it needed doing? You extracted a bone fragment from a back tooth, untangled the collar buckle from long hair. How many water dishes have you refilled or doors have you opened because your dog "told" you there was a need? How many times have you made an unplanned trip to the veterinarian because your dog said she needed help? These homey matters are only a step from the "Lassie Come Home" syndrome or urgent communing of which heroics are made.

Patrick Lawson in *More Than Courage* speculated on the actions of animals which seem to demonstrate heroism and human attachment. This collection of dog and horse stories published by Whitman in 1960, concluded with a chapter called, "The Answer."

Lawson ponders whether an animal's heroic actions stem from instinct plus training, or intelligent reasoning. Has instinct ever been fully defined, he asks. Are we sure we know what intelligence really is? Where does one end and the other begin? He says, "Trainers of dogs and horses say that one must have the same patience with these animals as with a six-year-old child, but does this indicate a lack of intelligence or that the dog and horse cannot speak our language and we cannot converse in theirs?"

Despite efforts to understand the animals, we can only say with certainty, according to Lawson, that dogs and others are more intuitive than we. They understand what we feel far better than what we say. Animals respond eagerly to those who approach them with sympathy and kindness. Such treatment and understanding can even restore a dog from total disillusionment, like the hero, Tang.

Lawson predicts: "Treat a dog as though it were capable of intelligent reasoning and that encouragement may mark the beginning of a new means of communication, not between animal and human, but between friend and friend."

The Collie may feel that the human family belongs to him, not the other way around. Therefore, attacks on his family by other creatures are definitely, as Terhune liked to express it, "not on the free list." We are grateful.

Best of Breed 1925—Ch. Treffynon Blue Sol (1921), by Poplar Pugilist ex Eltham Park Blue Blossom.

Best of Breed 1995—Ch. Gambit's Freeze Frame (1989), by Ch. Gambit's Chill Factor ex Gambit's Arts 'n Krafts, bred and owned by Linda Hash Robbins and Barbara Hash O'Keefe. He was also Best of Opposite Sex in 1993 and cowinner of the Bannerblu Bowl for the leading blue merle that year.

Chapter 11

The Collie Club of America—
Its History and Purpose

by Mrs. E. T. (Ada) Shirley

The recorded history of the Collie as a show dog in America begins with the 1877 Westminster Kennel Club fixture. By the following year, 1878, Collies were benched at nearly all shows held in the United States. Most shows at that time were held in the New York area, with a few in New Jersey, Pennsylvania and Connecticut and some even as far west as Illinois.

The first Collie registered in America was a "black, white and tan imported male called 'Brack,'" a son of Carlyle, whelped in 1880. The first Collie bitch registered in America was "'Dora,' black and tan, American-bred bitch," bred by Martin Apgar. These dogs were listed in the American Kennel Register in 1883; owner of both was Martin Dennis. Both Apgar and Dennis were active in the early Collie Club of America. The American Kennel Club was established in 1884 and became the registering organization for all purebred dogs in the United States. Many of its founders were Collie breeders, who formed the Collie Club of America in New York City on August 26, 1886, with fifty-eight charter members. It was apparent from the outset that there would be a close association between the parent club for the breed and the national governing body for the entire American dog Fancy.

Mr. Jenkins Van Schaick became the first President of the CCA and continued to serve in that office until his death in 1889. Mr. Thomas H. Terry was appointed as the delegate to the American Kennel Club and served as its vice president.

With adoption of a constitution and by-laws, it was established that the club would be called the Collie Club of America and the object was for the improvement and encouragement of the breed. A Standard was also drawn up, based mainly on that of the English Collie Club. Changes have been made

Best of Breed 1927, 1929—
Ch. Southport Blue Knight
(1925), by Knight O' Blue
Mist ex Lindean Lysbeth.

Best of Breed 1930, 1931,
1932—Ch. Lucason of Ashtead
O' Bellhaven (1928), a Best in
Show winner by Lucas of Ashtead
ex Jean of Ashtead.

at intervals through the years to keep pace with the development of the breed in America.

As the first Collie club to become a member of the American Kennel Club, CCA was designated as the breed's parent club. For many years, annual meetings and shows were held in the New York area, usually at the time of the Westminster Kennel Club show.

In 1889, there were 124 Collies entered at Westminster, and ten Collies were listed by the American Kennel Club as having completed their championships. The first CCA Sweepstakes and Specialty were held in conjunction

Best of Breed 1933—Ch. Nymph of Arken (1929), by Ch. Alstead Adjutant ex Ch. Halbury Jean.

Best of Breed 1934—Alstead Audrey, by Ch. El Troubador of Arken ex Tazewell Tropical.

Best of Breed 1935, 1936, 1939—Ch. Honeybrook Big Parade (1934), by Ch. Future of Arken ex Honeybrook Helen.

with the New Jersey Kennel Club all-breed show in 1887. A number of the club's founders offered special trophies for various classes at the Specialty shows, but these were retired by members who won them three times consecutively. Later trophies were offered in memory of some of these early members; three are still awarded as perpetual trophies at the CCA annual Specialty. The Hunter Trophy for Best American-bred is given in memory of William C. Hunter, secretary of the Collie Club of America for several years. The Morgan Cup for Best of Breed is offered in memory of J. P. Morgan, who served the club as president, vice president and director until he retired from showing dogs in 1908. The Shotwell Trophy is awarded to the Best Brace in memory of J. D. Shotwell, secretary-treasurer of the club for many years.

The then-operative point system for becoming a champion was based on the total number of dogs entered in a show. A dog became a champion after being awarded ten points in Winners classes. In 1893, the Collie Club of America was asked by the American Kennel Club to approve Open and Puppy classes for Collies at all shows.

Around the turn of the century, there were two important additions to Collie circles. Several ladies became active as breeders and exhibitors and Mrs. C. M. Lunt and Miss Minnie Bullocke joined the CCA. Mrs. Lunt was the first woman to be elected president of the club (1918–21). Ten other women have since held the office. The second addition to the Collie scene was the introduction of the Smooth Variety at dog shows. In 1908 the CCA voted that Smooths should compete on equal terms with Roughs. The annual Specialty shows continued to grow in entries as well as quality.

In 1912 a new constitution and by-laws were drawn up for the express purpose of expanding the Collie Club of America to include all parts of the United States and Canada. This was the forerunner of efforts to extend the Club's activities away from the East Coast.

One of the first CCA publications was a thirty-two page booklet entitled, *The Collie Standard Simplified*. It was compiled by several leading authorities on the breed in both America and England. Written so that the novice could understand it and sold for twenty-five cents a copy, it was illustrated with pictures of many well-known Collies up to about 1920.

In 1922, the *CCA Bulletin* came into existence, edited by Miss Genevieve Torrey, secretary of the club at the time. Called *Just Collies*, it was published monthly.

In 1932 the present system of awarding championship points was introduced by AKC, based on the actual number of dogs of each sex in each breed at the show present to determine the number of points awarded. AKC also set up the litter registration system in which each litter was registered by the owner of the bitch soon after whelping.

The Collie Club of America supported many sheepherding trials during the 1930s. Over 100 trials were held in the United States, with British as well

Best of Breed 1937—Ch. Arthea Knight Errant (1934), by Ch. Cock Robin of Arken ex Tazewell Katherine.

Best of Breed 1938—Ch. Bellhaven Black Lucason (1931), a multiple Best in Show winner by Ch. Lucason of Ashtead O'Bellhaven ex Viola of Ashtead O'Bellhaven.

Best of Breed 1940—Ch. Black Douglas of Alstead (1939), by Ch. Mamaron Medal ex Old Farm Satin of Anthracite.

Best of Breed 1941, 1942, 1944—Ch. Beulah's Golden Sultan (1938), by Ch. Beulah's Golden Favor of St. Adrian ex Beulah's Nightshade. *Brown*

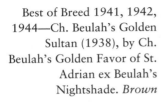

Best of Breed 1943—Ch. Braegate Model of Bellhaven (1938), twice a Best in Show winner, by Eden Electrician ex Braegate Lass. *Tauskey*

Best of Breed 1946—Ch. Laund Liberation of Bellhaven (1942), a Best in Show winner by Golden Rufus ex Pat of Mammystown.

Best of Breed 1947—
Ch. Wooley's Lane Electra
(1944), by Lodestone Live
Oak ex Wooley's Lane
Golden Lass. *Tauskey*

Best of Breed 1948—Ch.
Wooley's Lane Leal, a litter
sister to Ch. Wooley's Lane
Electra. *Tauskey*

Best of Breed 1949, 1950, 1951, 1952—
Ch. Hazeljane's Bright Future (1947), by
Ch. Hertzville Headlight II ex Ch. Black
Fortune of Caledon. Bright Future won five
Bests in Show and was the only four-time
CCA Specialty winner in history.
Lippincott

Best of Breed 1953—Ch. Gaylord's Mr. Scalawag (1950), by Poplar By Storm ex Ch. Gaylord's Gay Glory.

Best of Breed 1954—Ch. Emeral's My Son O'Duke (1951), by Ch. The Duke of Silver Ho, CD ex Roseacre's Princess Pat. *Frasie Studio*

Best of Breed 1955, 1957—Ch. Parader's Bold Venture (1950), a multiple Best in Show winner by Ch. Parader's Golden Image ex Parader's Cinderella.

as American entries competing in them. Classes for both single dogs and dogs working in pairs were offered and quite a few well-known Collie kennels participated.

Efforts to build up the membership resulted in publication of a leaflet in 1935 entitled, *Why You Should Join the Collie Club of America*. It was sent to every Collie exhibitor in the United States, and the membership did begin to grow.

In 1940 a real disaster struck the Collie Club of America. Fire in the residence of the secretary completely destroyed all club records, as well as some of the perpetual trophies. For the next few years, concerted efforts were made to reconstruct the records. Yearbooks, magazine articles, show catalogs and other sources of information were used to reestablish the secretary's books. Also in 1940 separate point ratings were granted for Smooth Collies.

During World War II, the Collie Club of America supported Dogs for Defense, one of whose founders was Mrs. William H. Long, Jr. War Savings Stamps were given as prizes at Collie Club of America Specialty shows, and all members who were serving in the Armed Forces were considered to have paid their dues for the duration. The constitution was altered to allow the executive committee to vote by mail. Any state having ten or more members was eligible to elect its own district director for the executive committee.

Best of Breed 1956— Ch. Jorie's Mr. G (1954), by Jorie's Vagabond Prince ex Jorie's Tiffanja.

CCA membership grew rapidly and by 1947 there were over 1,000 members and thirty-six local clubs, twenty-four of which had the necessary ten parent club members to make them eligible for the CCA trophy for their local Specialty show. In 1948 zone rotation for annual meetings and Specialty shows was established, and the constitution required the annual meeting to be held between February 1 and May 1 of each year.

In 1956 the executive committee established a committee to work on an *Illustrated Standard for Collies*. It was completed and published in the 1959 *Year Book*, with artwork by Mrs. Lorraine A. Still. This work has since been published in book form and used for education of judges and other projects. (The *Illustrated Standard* is reproduced in chapter 4 of this book.)

Collie forums and conferences have been encouraged by the parent club, and several national symposiums have been held. The club has encouraged study of hereditary eye defects, both progressive retinal atrophy and the Collie eye syndrome, at various universities. The education committee also encourages local eye clinics and publication of articles on health and breeding problems.

Best of Breed 1958, 1959—Ch. Cherrivale Darn Minute (1956), a winner of three Bests in Show by Ch. Gaylord's Mr. Scalawag ex Cherrivale Clockwise.

The *Year Book,* first published in 1934, has come out regularly and has grown from a modest volume to over 300 pages in each edition, chronicling the breed's and the club's year. In addition, members receive the bimonthly *Bulletin.*

Annual Specialty shows are held in rotation around the country with obedience having been added to conformation judging in the two Varieties in 1965. Junior showmanship is also featured, and herding was added in 1988 and is a regular feature, together with judges' and breeders' seminars.

The club has a large library of films, slides and tapes including the Specialty shows since 1962 as well as educational programs. It has also published a number of educational pamphlets and booklets. In 1963 the late Bernard Wentworth Emmons completed his work, *The History of the Collie Club of America*, brought up to 1965 and published by the club in 1972. In 1979 the club brought out the first volume of *American Collie Champions: 1884–1961*, and in 1980 *American Collie Champions 1961– 1976* was published. A third volume was issued for the club's centennial celebration in 1986, and a fourth is in preparation as this book is being written.

An annual calendar printed by the club features top winners of the previous year. Numerous other breed clubs use or emulate the materials made available by the Collie Club of America.

Today the Collie Club of America has about 2,500 members, and there are over eighty local Specialty clubs in operation. These are the people and clubs who foster and direct the breed through the American Kennel Club. The Collie Club of America has had its ups and downs, but the original purpose of improving and promoting the breed has never been lost. Throughout the 110 years of the club's history, the membership has supported that purpose wholeheartedly with the love and devotion given by dedicated people. This is the Collie Club of America.

REFERENCES

American Kennel Club Complete Dog Book. 1995.

Collie Club of America Bulletin. (bimonthly).

Collie Club of America show catalogs 1948–95.

Collie Club of America Year Books, 1934–94.

Emmons, Bernard W. *History of the Collie Club of America 1886–1965.*

Best of Breed 1960—Ch. Country Lane M'Liss 1954), by Ch. Kinmont Sheyne ex Ch. Wharton's Country Gal. She is pictured here with owner Mrs. R. F. Hillman. *Ludwig*

Best of Breed 1961—Ch. Merry-Hill's Bruce O'Happy Home, CD (1958), by Flair of Arland ex Arrowhill Molleen of Erin's Own. Pictured here in his Specialty win under judge Robert G. Wills with his breeder Mrs. Paul R. Godden handling. *Ludwig*

Best of Breed 1962, 1963—Ch. Stoneykirk Reflection (1958), by Sterling Shawn ex Stoneykirk's Wendy. Nine times a Best in Show winner, he is shown here with handler William J. Trainor and judge Dale McMackin. *Brown*

Best of Breed 1964, 1966—Ch. The Clown Prince of Floravale, CD (1960), a Best in Show winner by Ch. Cul-Mor's Conspiratour ex Floravale Whistle Bait.

Best of Breed 1965—Ch. Wind-Call's Night Hunter (1962), by Wind-Call's Wanderer ex Ch. Wind-Call's Silver Sapphire.

Best of Breed 1967—Ch. Jadene's Breeze Along (1961), a Best in Show winner by Ch. GinGeor Bellbrooke's Choice ex Ch. Gregshire's Little Honeycomb. *Shafer*

Best of Breed 1968—Ch. Noranda Daily Double (1962), a three-time Best in Show winner by Ch. Royal Rock Gamblin' Man ex Ch. Noranda Discretion.

Best of Breed 1969—Ch. Robel's Jason (1962), by Ch. Merrie Oaks Chip O'Dinger ex Merrie Oaks Sweet Love. *Ludwig*

Best of Breed 1970—Ch. Black Hawk of Kasan (1966), by Ch. High Man of Arrowhill (Rough) ex Ch. Kasan's Fine And Fancy, a Best in Show winner was the only Smooth to date to win Best of Breed at the CCA Specialty. *Shafer*

Best of Breed 1971—Ch. Baymar's Coming Attraction (1967), by Ch. Two Jay's Hanover Enterprise ex Two Jay's Molly Bee.

Best of Breed 1972—Ch. Wickmere Chimney Sweep (1969), a double Best In Show winner by Ch. Wickmere War Dance ex Watts Branch Coventry Lady. *Ashbey*

Best of Breed 1973, 1974, 1978—Ch. Tartanside the Gladiator (1969), also the winner of two Bests In Show by Ch. Hi Vu The Invader ex Tartanside Tiara. *Graham*

Best of Breed 1975—Ch. Lee Aire's Flambeau Monobo (1973), by Ch. Ransom's Regency ex Ch. Lee Aire's Live Wire.

Best of Breed 1976—Ch. GinGeor's Indelibly Blue (1970), by Ch. GinGeor's Indelible Choice ex Ch. Carla's Blue Ruin. *Ashbey*

Best of Breed 1977—Ch. Tamarack Asterisk (1974), by Ch. Two Jay's Hanover Enterprise ex Ch. Tamarack Jack-Pot.

Best of Breed 1979—Ch. Rio Bravo Achilles (1975), by Ch. Shoreham Three D's Grenadier ex Car-Isma's Patsy of Woodacre. *Bergman*

Best of Breed 1980—Ch. Azalea Hill's Top Man, CD (1974), by Ch. Tartanside the Gladiator ex Ch. Azalea Hill's Marianne. *Graham*

Best of Breed 1981—Ch. Carnwath's Evergreen (1977) by Ch. Ravette's The Silver Meteor ex Baliclare's Che Wink. He is shown here in his victory under judge Dr. Richard F. Greathouse, handled by Steve Barger, being awarded the J. Pierpont Morgan Trophy. *Larry Reynolds*

COLLIE CLUB OF AMERICA ANNUAL SPECIALTY BEST OF BREED WINNERS

1925 Treffynon Blue Sol*

1926 *There was no CCA Specialty held this year.*

1927 Ch. Southport Blue Knight

1928 *There was no CCA Specialty held this year.*

1929 Ch. Southport Blue Knight

1930 Ch. Lucason Ashtead O'Bellhaven

1931 Ch. Lucason Ashtead O'Bellhaven

1932 Ch. Lucason Ashtead O'Bellhaven

1933 Nymph of Arken*

1934 Alstead Audrey*

1935 Ch. Honeybrook Big Parade

1936 Ch. Honeybrook Big Parade

1937 Ch. Arthea Knight Errant

1938 Ch. Bellhaven Black Lucason

1939 Ch. Honeybrook Big Parade

1940 Black Douglas of Alstead

1941 Ch. Beulah's Golden Sultan

1942 Ch. Beulah's Golden Sultan

1943 Ch. Braegate Model of Bellhaven

1944 Ch. Beulah's Golden Sultan

1945 *There was no CCA Specialty held this year.*

1946 Laund Liberation of Bellhaven*

1947 Wooley's Lane Electra*

1948 Wooley's Lane Leal*

1949 Ch. Hazeljane's Bright Future

1950 Ch. Hazeljane's Bright Future

Best of Breed from the classes, finished later

1951 Ch. Hazeljane's Bright Future

1952 Ch. Hazeljane's Bright Future

1953 Ch. Gaylord's Mister Scalawag

1954 Ch. Emeral's My Son O'Duke

1955 Ch. Parader's Bold Venture

1956 Ch. Jorie's Mr. G

1957 Ch. Parader's Bold Venture

1958 Ch. Cherrivale Darn Minute

1959 Ch. Cherrivale Darn Minute

1960 Ch. Country Lane M'Liss

1961 Ch. Merry Hill's Bruce O'Happy Home, CD

1962 Ch. Stoneykirk Reflection

1963 Ch. Stoneykirk Reflection

1964 Ch. The Clown Prince of Floravale, CD

1965 Ch. Wind-Call's Night Hunter

1966 Ch. The Clown Prince of Floravale, CD

1967 Ch. Jadene's Breeze Along

1968 Ch. Noranda Daily Double

1969 Ch. Robel's Jason

1970 Ch. Black Hawk of Kasan (Smooth)

1971 Ch. Baymar's Coming Attraction

1972 Ch. Wickmere Chimney Sweep

1973 Ch. Tartanside the Gladiator

1974 Ch. Tartanside the Gladiator

1975 Ch. Lee Aire's Flambeau Monobo

1976 Ch. GinGeor's Indelibly Blue

1977 Ch. Tamarack Asterisk

1978 Ch. Tartanside the Gladiator

1979 Ch. Rio Bravo Achilles

1980 Ch Azalea Hills Top Man, CD

1981 Ch. Carnwath's Evergreen

1982 Ch. Starr's Blue Jeans

1983 Ch. Tel Star's Cosmic Capers

1984 Ch. City View's Advantage

1985 Ch. Tartanside Apparently

1986 Ch. Starr's Blue Jeans

1987 Ch. Cinderella's One For the Road

1988 Ch. Candray Constellation

1989 Ch. Jil Cris Liberty Legend

1990 Ch. Marnus Gold Medalist

1991 Ch. Aurealis Silverscreen

1992 Ch. Sealore's Grand Applause

1993 Ch. Pebblebrook Intrigue

1994 Ch. Thornacres Simply Grand

1995 Ch. Gambit's Freeze Frame

Best of Breed 1982 and at the 1986 CCA Centennial Specialty and Best of Opposite Sex 1984—Ch. Starr's Blue Jeans (1979), by Ch. Karavel Sudden Wyndfall ex Hi Vu Silver Mystery. Breeder Pamela Durazzano, owners Louis and Pam Durazzano. *Krook*

Best of Breed 1983—Ch. Tel Star's Cosmic
Capers (1978), by Ch. Tel Star's Super Sonic
ex Ch. Tel Star's Celestial Glory. Bred by
Kenneth and Jo Ann Fox, owned by Jo Fox.
Pam Eddy

Breed 1984—Ch. City View's Advantage, by Ch. Tamarack Eclipse ex Ch. City View Silver Charm. Bred and
owned by Betty Bowser.

Best of Breed 1985—Am. & Can. Ch. Tartanside Apparently (1981), by Ch. Tartanside Heir Apparent ex Ch. Tartanside Fairwind Fantasy. His younger brother was Winners Dog at the same Specialty. Bred and owned by John G. Buddie. *David Ashbey*

Best of Breed 1987—Ch. Cinderella's One For the Road, by Ch Cinderella's Hit the Road ex Kadon Sophisticated Lady. Bred by Kathy Hunt-Murad, and owned by Terrie McCullough Parker and Ellie McCullough.

Best of Breed 1988—Ch. Candray Constellation (1984), by Ch. Candray Hi Vu Tradition ex Candray Marigold. Bred and owned by Janice Wanamaker.

Best of Breed 1989—Ch. Jil-Cris Liberty Legend (1979), by Ch. Hanover's Flaming Legend—Jil-Cris Velvet Touch. He made this impressive win from the Veterans Class. Bred and owned by Joe Koehler. *Cindy Alvarado*

Ch. Marnus Gold Medalist (1988), by Ch. Twin Oaks Joker's Wild ex Marnus Twin Oaks Impulse. Bred and owned by Marcia K. Keller.

Best of Breed 1992—Ch. Sealore's Grand Applause (1987), by Ch. Applause Parader Persuasion ex Starr's Dark Crystal. He also won the Stud Dog Class at the same Specialty. Bred by Daniel Cardoza and Pamela Durazzano and owned by Judith and Annette Stringer and Steve Haslett. *Timberleaf*

Best of Breed 1993—Ch.Pebblebrook Intrigue (1987), by Ch. Westwend Hogan's Hero ex Ch. Pebblebrook's Sweet 'Nuff. Bred and owned in Canada by Dieter and Marion Liebsch.

Best of Breed 1994—Ch. Thornacres Simply Grand (1989), by Ch. Clouddawn's Grandeur Promise ex Thornaces Simply Devilish. Bred by Mary Ann Keefer and Dan Pierce, owned by Virginia Reed-Mehr. In this handsome photo he poses proudly with the J. Pierpont Morgan Perpetual Trophy and the Ralph Morrison Memorial Challenge Trophy. *Steve Gristick*

Appendix

Organizations

American Kennel Club, 51 Madison Avenue, New York, NY 10010. Send for free copy of *Rules Applying to Registration and Dog Shows, Obedience Regulations* and information about subscription to *AKC Gazette* and *Events Calendar.*

AWCA (American Working Collie Association). Gail Jay, Secretary, 2100 Fiero Avenue, Schenectady, NY 12303.

Collie Club of America, Mrs. Robert Futh, Treasurer, 47 Kielwasser Road, Washington Depot, CT 06794-1119.

Dog Writers' Association of America. The Secretary's position changes from time to time. For the name of the current Secretary, consult the AKC or the Publisher.

Educational material available from Mrs. Louann Young, 20823 Apache Trails, Crosby, TX 77532 (reasonable charge for each item).

Care of Your Puppy

Collie Breeder's Manual

CCA Year Books (published annually, many back issues available)

Your Collie's Ears

Your Collie's Eyes

Grooming—Your Collie from Kennel to Showring

Illustrations of the Collie, His Character and Conformation

Terhune Sunnybank Memorial Fund. Mrs. Claire Leishman, 290 Oakwood Ave., Paramus, NJ 07652.

Magazines

AKC Gazette, 51 Madison Ave., New York, NY 10010.

Collie Expressions, P.O. Box 149, Manassas, VA 22110.

Collie Review, 3771 Longview Valley Road, Sherman Oaks, CA 91423.

Dog World, 300 W. Adams St., Chicago, IL 60606.